FORGIVENESS

Other Books by Gary Inrig

Hearts of Iron, Feet of Clay
The Parables
Pure Desire
True North
Whole Marriages in a Broken World

FORGIVENESS

Discover the Power
and Reality of Authentic
Christian Forgiveness

GARY INRIG

Discovery House®
from Our Daily Bread Ministries

Forgiveness
© 2005 by Gary Inrig
All rights reserved.

Discovery House is affiliated with Our Daily Bread Ministries,
Grand Rapids, Michigan.

Requests for permission to quote from this book should be directed to: Permissions Department, Discovery House, P.O. Box 3566,
Grand Rapids, MI 49501, or contact us by e-mail at
permissionsdept@dhp.org

Interior design by Sherri L. Hoffman

Library of Congress Cataloging-in-Publication Data
Inrig, Gary.
Forgiveness: discover the power and reality of authentic Christian
    forgiveness / by Gary Inrig.
        p. cm
    Includes bibliographical references (p.   )
    ISBN: 1-57293-140-X
1. Forgiveness of sin. I. Title
    BT795.I57 2005
    234'.5—dc22   200402954

Printed in the United States of America
Tenth printing in 2016

With gratitude to those with whom I have served as elders over the years at Bethany Chapel, Reinhardt Bible Church, and Trinity Church, bands of brothers who have

shared the load,

shown great grace,

and served our wonderful Lord.

CONTENTS

INTRODUCTION

*O*n September 11, 2001, life in the United States changed forever. Our early morning routine was interrupted by a phone call from our son in North Carolina, who said, rather insistently, "Turn on your television. A plane's flown into the World Trade Center in New York City." While I was trying to process that, he said, "Oh, no! There's another one!" As the television flickered on, I was stunned at what I saw and immediately recognized that this was no accident, but a deliberate attack. That was the beginning of a day filled with almost every negative emotion human beings can experience—fear, anger, grief, confusion, sadness, and the list goes on. The thought that people could hate others enough to commandeer commercial airliners, filled with innocent travelers, and fly them into the symbols of the nation's commercial strength (the World Trade Center towers) and its military strength (the Pentagon) in a deliberate attempt to kill innocent people was almost more than the mind could absorb. The feelings of horror aroused as we watched those massive towers crumble—taking with them the lives of trapped workers and courageous rescuers—will linger for a lifetime.

The events of that day were the work of skilled, determined, and evil terrorists, willing to carry out atrocities on ordinary people in pursuit of their depraved goals. We were learning firsthand what much of the world already knew—that some people are willing, and even delighted, to inflict incredible suffering on others in an attempt to further their cause. We cannot, and must not, underestimate the depths of evil to which such people will sink. So now we accept as routine security measures that which previously would have seemed to be totally unnecessary.

On the Friday following the September 11 attacks, when the atrocity was still raw and smoke continued to billow from the ruins, our small city held a prayer service in a large outdoor amphitheater at the center of town. Various pastors led in prayer, asking the Lord to minister His grace into the fear, pain, anger, grief, and anxiety we were all feeling. We prayed for heartbroken families; for courageous rescuers, digging relentlessly through the debris for remains of their fallen comrades; for the president and our leaders charged with making momentous decisions; and for ourselves, that we would respond appropriately. Most of the prayers were heartfelt but relatively predictable, until one pastor prayed, briefly but urgently: "Lord, you have commanded us to love even our enemies. So we forgive those terrorists who have perpetrated this act against us. We forgive Osama bin Laden."

I had been quietly murmuring my "amen" to the various prayers, but this one shut my mouth. I could not, or would not, say "amen." I almost blurted out, "No." But was my instinctive response either right or righteous? Was his prayer what I should have been praying? Did my Lord's teaching on forgiveness mean that I was to pray for the forgiveness of terrorists who had not only planned and carried out such an attack, but who were, at that very moment, almost certainly rejoicing in their success and plotting more such acts? Are Christians always to forgive all offenders immediately when they are wronged? Could we or should we forgive Osama bin Laden while searchers were still combing through the rubble at Ground Zero, hoping to discover survivors or even some bodily remains of the thousands of victims? Should people in California, most of whom were only remotely attached to the events, forgive Al Qaeda for what they had done to other people and families? After all, we weren't the ones sitting by our phones desperately hoping we would hear from or of a missing loved one. We weren't the ones standing on the streets of downtown New York, with photos of our missing loved ones, anxiously seeking any morsel of information about their location or fate.

That moment crystallized questions that had been running through my mind for a long time about the nature of authentic Christian forgiveness. Too much of what I heard well-intentioned people say seemed trite, superficial, and simplistic. Sometimes they crossed a line into the realm of the foolish and harmful. This becomes apparent when the media barrages us with another story of a disgruntled employee or a disturbed student who has run amuck with an automatic weapon, gunning down coworkers or fellow students. As an almost automatic response, some people will quickly talk about the need to forgive the perpetrator. A few years ago a fourteen-year-old freshman named Michael Carneal shot and killed three of his fellow students engaged in a before-school prayer meeting in West Paducah, Kentucky. Within two days, before Michael had shown any remorse, other members of the prayer group erected a sign saying, "We forgive you, Michael." I deeply admire their desire to honor the Lord Jesus by their response. But is that the right way? Are true Christ-followers always to forgive instantly? Were they the right ones to declare forgiveness? One writer, observing such responses from his deeply held Jewish tradition, a perspective that insists on the necessity of repentance before forgiveness, wrote an article protesting automatic and immediate forgiveness. It was provocatively titled "The Sin of Forgiveness."[1] Did he have a point? Is it possible for some kinds of forgiveness actually to be sinful?

However, our most important questions about forgiveness don't arise from lead stories on the evening news. They usually emerge out of the rough and tumble of daily life, the mundane interactions of ordinary events. We get mad at a close friend and begin to hold a grudge. A spouse disappoints or betrays us and shows no sign of remorse. An employer breaks a promise or takes advantage of us. Sometimes the level of offense rises to a higher order. Parents or caregivers abuse or mistreat us, emotionally, physically, or financially.

A spouse abandons us for another person. A "friend" slanders us or abuses our friendship. The scenarios are endless. But two things are clear. First, we all will need to forgive or to be forgiven, because we all both sin and are sinned against. Second, we will struggle with forgiveness, because it always begins with pain. After all, I need to forgive only people who have hurt me in some significant way. I certainly don't need to forgive someone for some good thing he has done or for some joy he caused me. It is because forgiveness is birthed in pain, pain that can sometimes be intense, that forgiveness can be one of the hardest things we are ever called to do.

Forgiveness of sins through the grace of God and the finished work of the Lord Jesus lies at the heart of the gospel.

It is impossible to exaggerate the importance of the subject of forgiveness to the Christian faith. Forgiveness of sins through the grace of God and the finished work of the Lord Jesus lies at the heart of the gospel. The wonder of God's forgiveness in Christ should grip the heart of every Christ-follower. We have been forgiven at an enormous cost, the death of the Lord Jesus Christ on the cross. Christians are forgiven people, who have been brought into the family of God through the grace and mercy of our forgiving God. The place to begin a true understanding of forgiveness, then, is with a careful consideration of God's glorious forgiveness. In our first few chapters, we will probe its basis, its conditions, and its responsibilities. We need to know why we can receive God's forgiveness, how we can receive it, and how we are to continue to live in it. God's Word gives us the answers, so we will turn our attention to several important passages that unravel various aspects of God's forgiveness in Christ.

If the Bible makes it clear that Christians are forgiven people, it also makes it clear that we are to be forgiving people. Being forgiven is wonderful; being forgiving probes to the core of our being. Therefore we need a clear picture of what true forgiveness looks like and some good answers to some very difficult questions about it. If I forgive someone, does that require me to rebuild our marriage or our friendship? Do I just forgive, even though she won't admit she did anything wrong? How long do I wait—until I feel able or willing to forgive? How do I evaluate if his words represent genuine repentance or cheap regret or personal manipulation? Does forgiveness mean that I somehow forget all that has happened? Does my tormentor just get off scot-free, when he's put me through so much? I want to forgive. But how do I do it? What does it look like? Again, we will turn to God's Word for insight, clarification, and direction.

These are all important and relevant questions. However, a study of forgiveness cannot be simply an intellectual exercise. It inevitably forces us to face people and situations we might prefer to ignore. And that is something we cannot and must not avoid. A failure to forgive or to seek forgiveness can well be described as a kind of spiritual anorexia.[2] The tragedy of anorexia is that a person somehow becomes convinced that food, the very thing that is God's provision for health, is something dangerous, to be avoided. Even as her body wastes away, she clings to the notion that eating is bad for her. It is a delusion that kills, slowly but surely. In the same way, we can refuse to forgive or to seek forgiveness because we are convinced that this is a way to punish someone else or to protect ourselves. But it is a delusion that kills. It murders marriages, families, friendships, and churches. It poisons one's soul, and it can even kill. Researchers have discovered direct links between forgiveness and physical and emotional health.

Researchers have discovered direct links between forgiveness and physical and emotional health.

Chronic anger and stress, the almost inevitable consequences of an inability or unwillingness to forgive, are both toxic. They elevate blood pressure, as well as reduce both immune system functioning and stress hormone levels. One fascinating study indicates that forgiving others was associated with better self-reported mental and physical health among those over age forty-five. As one researcher observed, "The benefits of forgiveness seem to increase with age."[3] Edward Hallowell puts it vividly:

> You should learn to forgive for exactly the same reason you should quit smoking, work to lower your cholesterol, go on a diet to lose weight or take up exercise to control your blood pressure. Forgiving improves your life by improving your physical and emotional health and by increasing your chances of living longer. If that isn't reason enough to forgive, consider that living in anger and resentment can be as bad for you as smoking cigarettes or having high blood pressure or an elevated level of cholesterol. In other words, high blood pressure and resentment can kill you. . . . Scientific studies show that angry, resentful people have heart attacks more frequently than those who forgive more naturally. People who harbor anger and resentment are more likely to erupt and lose control, and they are more prone toward violence. They are more likely to self-medicate with alcohol or other drugs, and they are less able to make positive human relationships that last.[4]

I don't want to be misunderstood. The best reason for forgiving is not that we will live longer or feel better. It is not even that this may well be the means by which God brings substantial healing in our relationships. The best reason for forgiving or for seeking forgiveness is that, in this way, we will glorify God and reveal His character to those around us. That is the goal of all Christian living, and when we walk in obedience to Him, our desire to honor Him results in our being in the place where He can most readily bless us. So, as we walk the road of forgiveness, we are imitating Him, and in doing so, honoring Him.

Chapter 1

WIPING THE SLATE CLEAN

We were sitting at a table with four other couples, all strangers to my wife, Elizabeth, and me, making getting-to-know-you conversation. As we talked about how long we had been married, one woman's intensity surprised me as she revealed, "My mother said our marriage would never last. She said he was no good for me, and she didn't talk to me for forty years after we married. That was forty-seven years ago. Guess she was wrong." The wound may have been old, but the pain was obviously fresh!

Following her outburst, the man sitting next to her said, more quietly but with deep feeling, "That's nothing. My mother liked another girl I had gone with and wanted me to marry her. But I loved 'Joan.' We got married, but my mother never used her right name. She called my wife by the other woman's name for twenty years."

On the grand scale of human misdeeds, I admit these don't rank very high. They were petty cruelties, but they had wounded both couples to the soul. Such things don't usually make headlines, although they may, if they explode into violence. We live in a world of great evils, so that terrorists fly planes into buildings, explode bombs on crowded commuter trains, carry out suicide attacks in crowded public places, and take the lives of hundreds of school children. Political leaders in various countries prey on the prejudices of their followers, setting them like a pack of wild dogs on others in vicious acts of genocide. Executives in positions of great trust and responsibility feather their own nests and vote themselves huge salaries and benefits, even as they manipulate the financial statements of their corporations and destroy the life savings of hard-working employees and stockholders. Religious leaders use positions of trust to prey sexually on vulnerable children and adults. Industries, in an unrestrained rush for profits, deny their civic responsibility and choose to pollute our environments, both physical and moral.

Those sins affect us, often directly. But more often, we have to deal with smaller and more personal sins. Even these can yield a bitter harvest. I almost never stand before an audience to speak without reminding myself that many of these listeners have been the recipients of behavior that can only be described as evil. Too many women have experienced the horror of rape or sexual abuse; too many children are being raised in broken homes because of irresponsible and self-indulgent parents; too many churches have been split apart, because people pursued self-serving agendas, whatever the cost to others. My heart aches when the local media tell of another young child whose life has been snuffed out because gang members engaged in a mindless act of rage or revenge. We regularly hear stories of employers or managers who abuse their positions, treating others unfairly and using them to maximize their own power. Ask almost anyone the name of someone who has done him wrong, and you will not need to wait long to get an answer! And many of those hurts are not merely imagined. All of us have been sinned against, sometimes in terrible ways.

Ask almost anyone the name of someone who has done him wrong, and you will not need to wait long to get an answer!

But honesty forces us to admit that we have sometimes inflicted the pain. We have all sinned, against God and against other people. I don't find that easy to admit or even recognize, but it is undeniably true. We can try to deny our sins; to redefine them as something else; to rationalize them, shifting the blame to others; to repress them, drowning the accusing voice of conscience in busyness, distractions, or even chemicals. I would not deny that many of us carry around false guilt, the harassing voice of an overly sensitive conscience. Nevertheless, all honest people are aware that they do not live up to their own best standards, never mind God's. In our more honest moments, we know that we have wronged others, usually those closest and most precious to us. Some of those offenses, whether done deliberately or unintentionally, are far from trivial in their effect. In fact, a person unable or unwilling to admit personal guilt is a very dangerous person. As Mark Twain said, "Man is the only animal that blushes—or needs to."

Is Sin Outdated?

Voices in our modern world tell us that the idea of sin is hopelessly outdated and judgmental. Sin implies the existence of moral absolutes that make actions right or wrong. Even after the atrocities of September 11, many ponder whether anything can be labeled as evil. All moral judgments, they tell us, are acts of tradition, preference, moral arrogance, or power. But this response is not only foolish, it is also enormously destructive. Neil Plantinga says it well:

> Slippage in our consciousness of sin, like most fashionable follies, may be pleasant, but it is also devastating. Self-deception about our sin is a narcotic, a tranquilizing and disorienting suppression of our spiritual central nervous system. What's devastating about it is that when we lack an ear for wrong notes in our lives, we cannot play right ones or even recognize them in the performances of others.[1]

Fortunately, the realities of modern life are pressing on us a more realistic appraisal of human nature. G. K. Chesterton said that original sin is the only doctrine one can confirm by reading the front page of the daily newspaper. Five months before September 11, *Newsweek* carried a cover article titled "The Roots of Evil." What do social scientists, philosophers, and theologians say?

The traits of temperament and character from which evil springs are as common as flies on carrion. "The capacity for evil is a human universal," says psychiatrist Robert I. Simon, director of the program in Psychiatry and Law at Georgetown University School of Medicine. "There is a continuum of evil, of course, ranging from 'trivial evils' like cutting someone off in traffic, to greater evils like acts of prejudice, to massive evils like those perpetrated by serial sexual killers. But within us all are the roots of evil."[2]

This insight is nothing new. It's as old as Adam and Eve who grieved the loss of one son by the hand of another. The Bible takes sin seriously, confronting us with the fact that we are all both sinners and people who have been sinned against. Romans 3:23 says it succinctly: "All have sinned and fall short of the glory of God."

Is Forgiveness Real?

But Scripture also takes forgiveness seriously. Martin Luther wrestled deeply with his own sinfulness, and when he experienced God's grace, his life changed forever. As he wrote, "Where there is the forgiveness of sins, there is life and blessedness." From beginning to end the Bible speaks of the forgiveness of God. Our God is a forgiving God. In fact, one of the most important theological statements in the Bible is God's self-description to Moses in Exodus 34:6–7: "The Lord, the Lord, the compassionate and gracious God, slow to anger, abounding in love and faithfulness, maintaining love to thousands, and forgiving wickedness, rebellion and sin. Yet He does not leave the guilty unpunished; He punishes the children and their children for the sin of the fathers to the third and fourth generation." The rabbis called this passage "the thirteen attributes," because it gives such a full description of the character of God. In fact, this Scripture is so fundamental to a proper understanding of God that it is quoted or alluded to thirteen more times in the Old Testament.[3]

It is the John 3:16 of the Old Testament, the verse everyone knew by heart. The psalmist declared:

If you, O Lord, kept a record of sins,
  O Lord, who could stand?
But with you there is forgiveness;
  therefore you are feared (130:3–4).

Micah ended his book with the joyful declaration:

Who is a God like you
  who pardons sin and forgives the transgression
  of the remnant of his inheritance? (7:18).

Isaiah 55:6–7 gives us the wonderful promise:

Seek the Lord while he may be found;
  call on him while he is near.
Let the wicked forsake his way
  and the evil man his thoughts.
Let him turn to the Lord, and he will have mercy on him,
  and to our God, for he will freely pardon.

Most translations render the last phrase, "he will abundantly pardon." As Charles Spurgeon eloquently commented,

> That is to say, he will really pardon. The forgiveness is valid; it is valid on earth in the court of conscience, and above in the court of heaven. The pardoned sinner is truly pardoned, and no one shall ever condemn him. His sin is not merely supposed to be gone; it is gone. It is not put a little way off from him, but "as far as the east is from the west, so far hath he removed our transgression from us."[4]

One of the special promises of the New Testament is "he is faithful and just and will forgive us our sins and purify us from all unrighteousness" (1 John 1:9). Our God is a forgiving God. It is a central truth of His character and one of His greatest gifts to His people. He desires His people not only to delight in the freedom of their personal forgiveness through faith in the Lord Jesus, but also to become forgiving people who imitate Him.

John Bunyan's classic *Pilgrim's Progress* has been standard fare for Christians down through the centuries, although it has largely dropped off the radar screen of modern Christians. Bunyan's story is presented as a dream, which begins with a traveler dressed in rags, with a book in his hand (representing the gospel) and a burden on his back, a vivid symbol of the guilt and shame he carries. He has heard God's news, with its promise of a heavenly city, and he sets out as a pilgrim for that city. His name is Christian, and he makes his hard journey until he comes in sight of the cross. Then, in a beautiful passage, Bunyan describes the great moment of divine forgiveness:

> Up this way therefore did burdened Christian run, but not without great difficulty, because of the load on his back. He ran thus till he came at a place somewhat ascending, and upon that place stood a cross and a little below, in the bottom, a sepulchre. So I saw in my dream that just as Christian came up to the cross, his burden loosed from off his shoulders, and fell from off his back, and began to tumble; and so continued to do, till it came to the mouth of the sepulchre, where it fell in, and I saw it no more.
>
> Then was Christian glad and lightsome, and said, with a merry heart, "He hath given me rest by his sorrow and life by his death." Then he stood still awhile to look and wonder; for it was very surprising to him that the sight of the cross should thus ease him of his burden. . . .
>
> Then Christian gave three leaps for joy, and went on singing,
>
> "Thus far did I come laden with my sin,
> Nor could aught ease the grief that I was in,

Till I came hither. What a place is this! . . .
Blest cross! blest sepulchre! blest rather be
The Man that there was put to death for me."[5]

Forgiveness is all about the grace
of God. In God's Word we could look *Forgiveness is all about*
many places to see God's forgiveness. But *the grace of God.*
I want to direct our attention to two passages. First, we will travel off the beaten path to a striking picture found in the Old Testament book of Zechariah. Then, in the next chapter, we will spend time where Bunyan's Christian did, at the cross of the Lord Jesus.

Zechariah's Vision

About six hundred years before the birth of the Lord Jesus, any objective observer would have concluded that the nation of Judah had ceased to exist. Its capital city, Jerusalem, had been destroyed by the invading armies of the great empire of Babylon. Its inhabitants had been either carried away captive to Babylon (modern Iraq) or had fled for refuge wherever they could find it. Judah had been cremated; its national ashes scattered on the winds. No nation could hope to survive such treatment! Even more significant, this condition was due to the hand God turned in judgment against His own people because of their long history of covenant betrayal, rebellion, and failure.

But God had not abandoned either His people or His promises. Even as the devastation was taking place, He inspired His prophet Jeremiah to write to those already in exile, " 'When seventy years are completed for Babylon, I will come to you and fulfill my gracious promise to bring you back to this place. For I know the plans I have for you,' declares the Lord, 'plans to prosper you and not to harm you, plans to give you hope and a future' " (Jeremiah 29:10–11).

The Lord acted just as He said He would. In 538 B.C., the power of Babylon was broken, and the new empire of Persia emerged as the great world power. An edict of the Persian emperor reversed the Babylonian policy of exile, and the Jews were permitted to return to their homeland. Many of the Jewish people had made peace with their new location and lifestyle and had little or no interest in the total upheaval that a return to Judah would involve. Common sense said that it would be a huge undertaking to attempt to regain a foothold in their embattled homeland. The new occupants would certainly not welcome them with open arms! As a result, only forty thousand were willing to take the risk of return, under the political leadership of a governor named Zerubbabel and the religious leadership of a high priest named Joshua.

Upon their return, they found themselves as a tiny minority, surrounded by hostile enemies who had no interest in surrendering their newly acquired lands without a fight. Those enemies were not only determined to retain their land, but they also possessed superior resources and manpower. Humanly speaking, Judah's cause seemed hopeless.

But Judah's God was the living God, who delivers His people when they turn in faith to Him. One of the Lord's ways of calling them to faith was to send His prophet Zechariah, to whom the Lord gave a series of visions containing God's promises to and purposes for His people. The following passage is one of those visions, specifically directed to the nation of Judah at that particular time in history. But it also speaks powerfully to us as a marvelous dramatic portrayal of how God deals with broken, failing people who come to Him in faith.

> Then he showed me Joshua the high priest standing before the angel of the Lord, and Satan standing at his right side to accuse him. The Lord said to Satan, "The Lord rebuke you, Satan! The Lord, who has chosen Jerusalem, rebuke you! Is not this man a burning stick snatched from the fire?"
>
> Now Joshua was dressed in filthy clothes as he stood before the angel. The angel said to those who were standing before him, "Take off his filthy clothes."

Then he said to Joshua, "See, I have taken away your sin, and I will put rich garments on you."

Then I said, "Put a clean turban on his head." So they put a clean turban on his head and clothed him, while the angel of the Lord stood by.

The angel of the Lord gave this charge to Joshua: "This is what the Lord Almighty says: 'If you will walk in my ways and keep my requirements, then you will govern my house and have charge of my courts, and I will give you a place among these standing here.

"'Listen, O high priest Joshua and your associates seated before you, who are men symbolic of things to come: I am going to bring my servant, the Branch. See, the stone I have set in front of Joshua! There are seven eyes on that one stone, and I will engrave an inscription on it,' says the Lord Almighty, 'and I will remove the sin of this land in a single day.

"'In that day each of you will invite his neighbor to sit under his vine and fig tree,' declares the Lord Almighty" (Zechariah 3:1–10).

We Stand Before a Holy God in Our Sin and Failure

Our passage presents a vision, not an actual historical event. Joshua the high priest (not Joshua, the great successor to Moses, who lived about eight hundred years earlier) is standing in the heavenly courtroom. He is there personally, but, as the nation's high priest, he is also the representative of his people. He stands in God's presence in a totally unacceptable condition, wearing "filthy clothes." This is not meant to be a fashion statement! In Old Testament worship great attention was paid to the sacred garments of the high priest. In the course of his duties, he was usually arrayed in splendid official robes "to give him dignity and honor" (Exodus 28:2). When he appeared in the Holy of Holies on the Day of Atonement, he would wear "a sacred linen tunic" (Leviticus 16:4), a garment of simple purity. But it was unthinkable for him to appear before God in filthy clothes. So when he stands in such clothing before a holy God, we are intended to understand the defiled condition of God's people. They have a long history of sin, rebellion, and apostasy and can make no claim on God's special favor on the basis of their merit or national righteousness. They are a blemished nation, with their shame on open display.

At Joshua's right hand there is another figure: "Satan, standing at his right side to accuse him" (v. 1). We are not given many portrayals of Satan in the Old Testament. In fact, the major description of his work is found in Job 1–2, a passage that has interesting parallels to this one in Zechariah. In the book of Job, Satan is the one who delights to attack and criticize God's people. When God challenged him with the godly character and personal piety of Job, Satan countered that the only reason anyone would serve God was out of self-interest. God had been good to Job; that was the only reason he or anyone else would serve Him. Were he to lose his blessings, Job would lose his faith! The Lord responded to Satan's challenge by giving Satan permission to attack Job. Satan lost no time. He unleashed a series of attacks on Job's health, wealth, and family, attempting to drive a wedge between Job and his Lord.

In the book of Zechariah, the situation is somewhat different. Satan had no need to point out Joshua's shortcomings. He is obviously unfit for the presence of God. Satan is there only as the prosecuting attorney, to make sure that Joshua's sins and shortcomings are properly pointed out and punished. He is acting as he always does, as "the accuser of our brothers" (Revelation 12:10), the one who wants us to wallow in our sins and failures, so we will feel disqualified from fellowship with God.

The third person involved in this encounter is described both as "the angel of the Lord" and "the Lord." We find this exchange of terms several times in the Old Testament: A person first described as "the angel of the Lord" is later addressed as "the Lord" Himself. The best explanation is that on these occasions the Lord Jesus took temporary visible form, prior to His incarnation.[6] Joshua, in his filthy garments, is standing before God Himself. The obvious question?

What will a holy, righteous God do with a person whose sins and shortcomings are so blatantly obvious?

We return to Joshua—in an appalling condition. If anything, the translation "filthy garments" understates the reality. The Hebrew word describes filth such as dung, urine, and vomit. His garments were utterly unsuitable for the presence of other people, never mind the holy God of the universe! He looked awful and smelled even worse. What this filth represents is made clear when the angel says, "Take off his filthy clothes" and then declares to Joshua, "See, I have taken away your sins" (v. 5). The filth represents the disgusting reality of his sins, as well as the sins of his people.

We have a hard time recognizing how our sinfulness appears before the Lord. We take sin for granted, because we not only find it all around us, we constantly deal with it within ourselves. Definitions of sin can sound clinical: "Sin is any act—any thought, desire, emotion, word, or deed—or its particular absence that displeases God and deserves blame."[7] But the Bible is full of metaphors that tell us what sin is like. Neal Plantinga notes:

> Sin is the missing of the mark, a wandering from the path, a straying from the fold. Sin is a hard heart and a stiff neck. Sin is blindness and deafness. It is both the overstepping of a line and the failure to reach it—both transgression and shortcoming. Sin is a beast crouching at the door. In sin people attack or evade or neglect their divine calling. These and other images suggest deviance: even when it is familiar, sin is never normal. Sin is disruption of created harmony and resistance to divine restoration of that harmony. Above all, sin disrupts and resists the vital human relation to God and it does all this disrupting and resisting in a number of intertwined ways.[8]

At times we get a glimpse of how deeply defiled we are. It was the experience of Isaiah, who in the presence of a holy God, could only declare, "Woe to me!" (6:5), or more precisely, "I am ruined!" It is the declaration of a holy God that

All of us have become like one who is unclean,
    and all our righteous acts are like filthy rags (Isaiah 64:6).

It is the universal condition: However we may appear to one another, we stand guilty before a holy God. As Aleksandr Solzhenitsyn memorably discovered in a prison camp in the Russian gulag, "If only there were evil people somewhere committing evil deeds and it were necessary only to separate them from the rest of us. But the line dividing good and evil cuts through the heart of every human being. And who is willing to destroy a piece of his own heart?"[9] But for Solzhenitsyn that discovery was not a source of despair. Rather, it was the beginning of hope and salvation, as he began to look outside of himself to the grace of God as his only refuge.

Joshua's condition, like that of all of us, was not only appalling, but also precarious. To be covered with filth in the presence of God was to be in danger of final rejection. But he is totally silent, with nothing to say in his own defense. This is not the silence of denial but of admission, the recognition that I cannot deny what is plain to everyone, nor can I excuse or explain it. He is speechless, because there is nothing he can say in his own defense. How could he claim to be fit as long as he was wearing clothes like this? His guilt was self-evident. Paul tells us that this will be our universal experience before the heavenly throne: "so that every mouth may be silenced and all the world held accountable to God" (Romans 3:19). The first step in forgiveness is ownership, the silent acknowledgment that what God says about us is true. Martin Luther noted, "The unwillingness of the sinner to be regarded as a sinner is the final form of sin."

For years baseball fans have found themselves involved in the same argument, especially around the time for the announcement of the results of balloting for the National Baseball Hall of Fame: Should Pete Rose be inducted? No one doubts that, on the basis of his performance on the field, he should be. The man known as Charley Hustle holds the record for most hits in a career and has a career record clearly worthy of enshrinement. But despite all his achievements, Rose had a significant gambling problem; all the evidence indicates that he gambled on baseball games, perhaps even some in which his own team was involved. This was in direct violation of an emphatic rule of baseball, in place since the infamous Black Sox scandal of 1919. Gambling is viewed as a major threat to the integrity of the game. Rose desperately wants to be in the Hall of Fame, but for thirteen years he could not bring himself to admit that he had done what the evidence clearly revealed he had. In fact, he emphatically insisted on his innocence before three different baseball commissioners. So there came an impasse. Until he would own his actions, major-league baseball found it impossible to forgive him.

Then early in 2004 Rose published a book in which he admitted that he had, in fact, bet on baseball. He even acknowledged placing bets with bookies up to five times a week while managing the Cincinnati Reds. That confession drew an intriguing response. His timing seemed intended to draw attention away from that year's Hall of Fame nominees and direct it toward himself and increase his book sales. Many who did read it were far from convinced that he was telling the whole truth when he denied that he had bet on games in which his own team was involved. Most of all, his confession seemed to lack a deep sense of remorse. As he said, "I'm sure that I'm supposed to act all sorry or sad or guilty now that I've accepted that I've done something wrong. But you see, I'm just not built that way. . . . So, let's leave it like this: I'm sorry it happened, and I'm sorry for all the people, fans and family that it hurt. Let's move on."[10]

The effect of Rose's "confession" was fascinating. Even some of his previously ardent supporters began to jump off the bandwagon. It seemed to most that he just didn't "get it," missing the difference between admission and confession. An offender doesn't have the option to say, "Let's move on!" He doesn't hold the upper hand in the situation! Pete Rose desperately wants to be recognized for his achievements. But what he wants even more is induction on his own terms, and that isn't going to happen.

In the spiritual realm, acceptance into God's presence doesn't happen on our terms either. God cannot ignore our filthy garments. And neither will Satan! He is there in God's presence to make completely clear what kind of unworthy person is standing before Him. And so we are presented with the great dilemma. How can a holy God remain true to His own character and, at the same time, forgive the sins of a sinner? He clearly states His standards in Scripture. "I will not acquit the guilty" (Exodus 23:7). "He does not leave the guilty unpunished" (Exodus 34:7).

> *The Lord is slow to anger and great in power;*
> *the Lord will not leave the guilty unpunished (Nahum 1:3).*

What then is Joshua's future, if he can't deny his sin, if Satan won't ignore it, and God can't overlook it? That isn't just his problem; it's the problem of every one of us.

From a Gracious God We Receive Forgiveness

The amazing thing is that the one who speaks for Joshua is not Joshua but the angel of the Lord, the Lord Jesus Himself. Joshua stands before God as a believer, as one who is not trusting in himself, but in God. Joshua represents God's people, with its capital of Jerusalem, and the Lord "has chosen Jerusalem" (v. 2). This choice was certainly not based on merit; Jerusalem had abdicated any claim upon God. God's election is always on the basis of grace, and it is made evident by our faith. Joshua is "a burning stick snatched from the fire" (v. 2). Sticks don't crawl out of fires; they lie there hopeless, awaiting their inevitable destruction. But someone else may risk the flames to snatch out a burning stick. And that is the picture of God's dealing with Joshua and the central truth of all forgiveness. God

Himself entered the fire to remove by His power someone doomed to destruction.

This passage does not directly indicate how this divine deliverance would come about. Not until the New Testament, at the cross, do we begin to comprehend what was involved. Everything in the gospel centers on the cross. As Miroslav Volf notes, "Indisputably, the self-giving love manifested in the cross and demanded by it lies at the core of the Christian faith."[11] God Himself entered the fire to save us. God the Son took on human nature and entered time and space. He came, as He Himself said, "to seek and to save what was lost" (Luke 19:9). That involved not only living among us, but also going to the cross to take our sins and our guilt. We will ponder that more deeply in the next chapter. But even here in the book of Zechariah, five hundred years before the Lord Jesus would come, there are pointers to that great event. When Zechariah tells us that God says, "I will remove the sin of this land in a single day" (v. 9), and later when he quotes the Lord as saying of the nation of Judah, "They will look on me, the one whom they have pierced" (12:10), he is prophesying, in remarkable detail, the work of the Lord Jesus on our behalf. "On that day a fountain will be opened to the house of David and the inhabitants of Jerusalem to cleanse them from sin and impurity" (13:1). In both the Old and New Testaments, there is no final forgiveness apart from the work of the Lord Jesus Christ on the cross.

Having defended Joshua to Satan, the Lord issues an order: "Take off his filthy clothes" (v. 4). Joshua cannot be in God's presence as he is. The Lord does not ignore our sins or minimize them. He orders their removal. So Joshua stands naked before his God: "See, I have taken away your sins" (v. 4). This is a wonderful picture of the divine act of forgiveness. Our sins are stripped away—removed and banished. It is God's work to remove them, since only He can.

One of the great themes of the Bible is to see what God does with the sins of His people when He forgives us. Remember that this is always and only because the Lord Jesus bore them on Himself, on the cross. We need to rejoice in God's promise. I'll never forget one of the first new believers' classes I taught, when I simply read the passages that describe what God does with the sins of those He forgives. I sensed amazement and gratitude at the wonder of what God has done. A lot of excited conversation followed. God, in grace, sets us wonderfully and fully free!

Consider these Old Testament statements about what God does with our sins:

He drowns them: Micah 7:19
You will again have compassion on us;
 you will tread our sins underfoot
 and hurl all our iniquities into the depths of the sea.

He erases them: Isaiah 43:25
I, even I, am he who blots out [wipes away]
 your transgressions, for my own sake,
 and remembers your sins no more.

He dissolves them: Isaiah 44:22
I have swept away your offenses like a cloud,
 your sins like the morning mist.

He puts them behind his back: Isaiah 38:17
You have put all my sins behind your back.

He forgets them: Jeremiah 31:34
For I will forgive their wickedness
 and will remember their sins no more.

He covers them: Psalm 32:1
Blessed is he
 whose transgressions are forgiven,
 whose sins are covered.

He does not record them: Psalm 32:2
Blessed is the man
    whose sin the Lord does not count against him.

He totally removes them: Psalm 103:12
As far as the east is from the west,
    so far has he removed our transgressions from us.

Wonderful as these statements are, in the New Testament we reach the high point of understanding forgiveness.

He forgives them: Ephesians 1:7
In him we have redemption through his blood, the forgiveness of sins, in accordance with the riches of God's grace.
Colossians 1:13–14
. . . the Son . . . in whom we have redemption, the forgiveness of sins.

He wipes them out and erases them: Acts 3:19
Repent, then, and turn to God, so that your sins may be wiped out, that times of refreshing may come from the Lord.

He takes them on Himself: 1 Peter 2:24
He himself bore our sins in his body on the tree, so that we might die to sins and live for righteousness; by his wounds you have been healed.

He does not charge them to our account: 2 Corinthians 5:19
God was reconciling the world to himself in Christ, not counting men's sins against them.

He charges them to Christ's account: 2 Corinthians 5:21
God made him who had no sin to be sin for us, so that in him we might become the righteousness of God.

He nails them to the cross: Colossians 2:13–14
When you were dead in your sins and in the uncircumcision of your sinful nature, God made you alive with Christ. He forgave us all our sins,

having canceled the written code, with its regulations, that was against us and that stood opposed to us; he took it away, nailing it to the cross.

He purges us from them: Hebrews 1:3
After [the Son] had provided purification for sins, he sat down at the right hand of the Majesty in heaven.

He does away with and puts away sins: Hebrews 9:26
But now he has appeared once for all at the end of the ages to do away with sin by the sacrifice of himself.
1 John 3:5
You know that he appeared so that he might take away our sins.

He cleanses and purifies us from them: 1 John 1:7
The blood of Jesus, his Son, purifies us from all sin.

He sets us free from them: Revelation 1:5–6
To him who loves us and has freed us from our sins by his blood, and has made us to be a kingdom and priests to serve his God and Father—to him be glory for ever and ever! Amen.

From a Gracious God We Receive Righteousness

But the forgiveness of sins is only the beginning of what the Lord does for His people. Let's pick up Zechariah's vision: Joshua stands naked before a holy God. Having said, "I have taken away your sin," he also says, "I will put rich garments on you" (v. 4). The Lord then gives orders to His attending angels: "Put a clean turban on his head." They not only put on the turban, but "they clothed him" (v. 5) in the rich garments God had promised. He stands now before a holy God in garments provided by God Himself. Such garments were worn only on special occasions, and a turban was a symbol of office and ministry.

Forgiveness of sins is only the beginning of what the Lord does for His people.

Again we are pointed to the Lord Jesus. Christians are forgiven, but they are much more than forgiven. We are declared righteous by God Himself, and He does not merely declare us righteous; He imputes the righteousness of Christ to us. We have become the righteousness of God (2 Corinthians 5:21), a righteousness that is not ours, but which comes through faith in the Lord Jesus (Philippians 3:9).

When I was a child in Sunday school, we were taught definitions of Bible words. *Justified,* I was told, means that in God's eyes I am "just as if I had never sinned." That was very helpful, because I still remember it, and it describes one important aspect of justification. To be justified is to be forgiven, but it is much more than that. It is to be declared righteous, to have been dressed by God in the righteousness of His Son, the Lord Jesus Christ. God does not see us as people in excrement-covered garments, or even as people washed and naked before Him.

Nor does He see us as only partially covered. A friend recalls hearing a preacher compare the righteousness that God gives us to a hospital gown. Well, whatever the virtues of such gowns, they provide a very inadequate covering! You had better keep your back to the wall! The preacher went on to describe how we need to provide the rest of the covering by our own righteousness. My friend immediately realized the hopelessness of that. He didn't need a partial covering, but a complete one. And that is what he found when he came to Jesus. By God's grace, through faith in His Son, we are declared righteous and clothed fully, freely, and luxuriantly in the perfect righteousness of Christ, with His merit transferred to our account. This is the gift of the cross.

During the presidency of Andrew Jackson, a postal clerk named George Wilson robbed a train and, in the process, killed a guard. He was captured, convicted of murder, and sentenced to hang. But there were doubts about some issues related to the case, and President Jackson intervened, offering a pardon. But because Wilson hated

Jackson, he refused the pardon. The nation was young, and no one had ever refused a pardon. The Supreme Court was asked to decide whether someone could do such a thing. Chief Justice John Marshall handed down the decision: "A pardon is a parchment whose only value must be determined by the receiver of the pardon. It has no value apart from that which the receiver gives to it." Because George Wilson had refused the pardon, whatever his reason, he would suffer the full penalty for his crime by being hanged.

What foolishness! If we turn our backs on the forgiveness freely offered by our crucified Savior, we do the same thing. Our God is a forgiving God, and we can live in the freedom of full, final, and finished forgiveness. But we must receive the gift He offers through faith in His Son. When we do, we are able to start over again, knowing that we are clean, inside and out, in the presence of a holy God. The striking paradox is that, when we choose neither to hide our sin nor to deny our sin, but to own it before the holy God, we are set free by His grace in Christ.

Chapter 2

A COSTLY FORGIVENESS

The initial months of 2004 witnessed an amazing cultural phenomenon. Tens of millions of people filed into movie theaters, first in North America and then around the world, to witness a graphic portrayal of the last twelve hours of the life of Jesus, including His death on the cross. *The Passion of the Christ* hit theaters amidst a storm of controversy. Even before the movie was completed, some critics attacked Mel Gibson for contributing to anti-Semitism, claiming that his movie contained the kinds of stereotypes that vicious people had too often used to incite great acts of evil against the Jews. For example, James Carroll, a former Catholic priest who writes an opinion column for the *Boston Globe*, directed a stream of venom against both Gibson and the movie, which he called "obscene." He continued,

> It will incite contempt for Jews. It is a blasphemous insult to the memory of Jesus Christ. It is an icon of religious violence. . . . The subject of this film . . . is the sick love of physical abuse. . . . It [contains] the most brutal film episode I have ever seen, approaching the pornographic. . . . It is a lie. It is sick. Jews have every reason to be offended by "The Passion of the Christ." Even more so, so do Christians.[1]

Mr. Carroll's reaction is more than a little bit "over the top," as my English friends would say. But I respect his concern that the movie would cause some to answer the question, "Who killed Jesus?" with the simplistic answer, "the Jews, of course," thereby justifying anti-Semitism. Christ-followers cannot tolerate any prejudicial treatment of the very people from whom our Savior came. Thankfully, there is virtually no evidence that such fears have come to fruition.

The question raised so often in connection with the movie—"Who killed Jesus?"—must finally be answered with the response, "I did." But the movie also raised another question: Is that the way it really happened? There were secondary embellishments and artistic decisions, but, in the main, the movie contained a faithful reflection of the gospel accounts. That, in turn, leads to the most important question of all: Why? Why did Jesus die? If He did have to die, why a death like this? Why is His death so important? Those are questions that anyone reflecting on the cross must face. As one college student said after seeing the movie, "My death is no more important than my birth or every day in between. Why should it be any different with Jesus? If all that mattered was His death, why did He spend three years teaching and preaching?" And even more important, if God was in this, why would He do it like this? Another student declared, "It doesn't make any sense to me that God would need to be satisfied by sending His Son to be killed. That's a vengeful God and not a God I want to worship."[2]

The cross stands at the very heart of the gospel. The Lord Jesus defined His life in terms of the cross: "The Son of Man did not come to be served, but to serve, and to give his life as a ransom in the place of many" (Matthew 20:28). The New Testament puts its central message in the most simple of terms: "Christ died for our sins according to the Scriptures" (1 Corinthians 15:3). Most Christ-followers who view Mel Gibson's movie will never again think of the cross in quite the same way. The sheer brutality of what Jesus endured has been etched on our minds. But the danger is that we are so gripped by the horror of the cross that we miss the meaning of what happened there. Why did His death matter so much? Why focus on it and ignore His teachings?

The danger is that we are so gripped by the horror of the cross that we miss the meaning of what happened there.

What part did God have in all this? The "how" of Jesus' death produces horror; the "why" produces wonder and worship. We have received a costly forgiveness.

Seven hundred years before Jesus endured the cross, God gave one of His prophets, a man named Isaiah, a remarkable vision of what would happen to the one whom God would send as His suffering Servant. Isaiah 53 is one of the richest passages in the Old Testament, one that has always captured the imagination of God's people. Almost every verse of the chapter is quoted or referred to in the New Testament. More important, the Lord Jesus quoted words from this prophecy as He prepared His disciples for what would happen when they left the upper room and for the sufferings that lay before Him: "It is written, 'And he was numbered with the transgressors' [quoting Isaiah 53:12]; and I tell you that this must be fulfilled in me. Yes, what is written about me is reaching its fulfillment" (Luke 22:37).

Isaiah described what happened to Jesus in vivid detail. Imagine that we were to discover a document written before Christopher Columbus had even set sail for the new world. Suppose this document were to describe the city of New York and the horrific events of September 11 in remarkable detail. We would be right to consider that a book like no other, one sent from God. So it is with Isaiah 53. At the same time, this amazing prophecy makes it clear that His was a death unlike any other, the fulfillment of God's eternal purpose.

The entirety of Isaiah 53 richly deserves careful study. One scholar describes it as "the jewel in the crown of Isaiah's theology, the focal point of his vision."[3] However, although I encourage you to read the entire passage (actually Isaiah 52:13–53:12), we are going to focus especially on verses 1–6 and what Isaiah foretold of the wonderful cross.

> *Who has believed our message*
> *and to whom has the arm of the Lord been revealed?*
> *He grew up before him like a tender shoot,*
> *and like a root out of dry ground.*

He had no beauty or majesty to attract us to him,
  nothing in his appearance that we should desire him.
He was despised and rejected by men,
  a man of sorrows, and familiar with suffering.
Like one from whom men hide their faces
  he was despised, and we esteemed him not.
Surely he took up our infirmities
  and carried our sorrows,
yet we considered him stricken by God,
  smitten by him, and afflicted.
But he was pierced for our transgressions,
  he was crushed for our iniquities;
the punishment that brought us peace was upon him,
  and by his wounds we are healed.
We all, like sheep, have gone astray,
  each of us has turned to his own way;
and the Lord has laid on him
  the iniquity of us all.

The life Jesus lived was remarkable in every way. His teachings, His miracles, His influence on others, His lifestyle all sparkle with a unique brilliance. However, the central meaning of the Lord is not found in the living of His life but in the giving of it. The entire experience of crucifixion was brutal beyond description. Yet the instrument of that dreadful death became the symbol of the gospel. Isaiah 53 never specifically mentions the cross, but it depicts what our Lord endured there. Leon Morris captures the biblical centrality of the cross:

> The New Testament makes the cross central. The Gospels are basically books about the cross. They make the cross the climax to which all else leads up. . . . If it were the fact of the death and not its significance, they would have devoted more space to the details, to the physical agony and the like. In point

of fact they treat the physical sufferings of Christ with great reserve. They are not concerned with agony for agony's sake. . . . They are concerned with God's provision for our salvation. . . . Everywhere [in the New Testament] Christ is central, and everywhere it is the cross of Christ on which attention is focused in particular. That is the one indispensable thing. Without the death of Christ there could have been no salvation. With that death the salvation of God becomes a glorious reality.[4]

The Suffering Servant: A Horror That Caused Scandal

Centuries after Isaiah wrote, a man sat reading Isaiah's description of the suffering Servant of the Lord (52:13–53:12). The man was puzzled by the identity of this mysterious figure. When a complete stranger approached him and asked, "Do you understand what you are reading?" his response expressed his perplexity. "Tell me, please, who is the prophet speaking about, himself or someone else?" (Acts 8:34). He instinctively recognized that the description didn't fit Isaiah the prophet, nor did it fit any other figure he could recognize from Israel's past. And the Servant didn't function as a personification of the nation of Israel itself, since the passage indicates "for the transgression of my people he was stricken" (53:8). He immediately recognized the truth when his companion, an early Christian leader named Philip, "began with that very passage of Scripture and told him the good news about Jesus" (Acts 8:35).

Isaiah writes this passage in the voice of a group of people who are now believers, but they once were among those who "esteemed him not" (v. 3). They describe their initial and then their later evaluation of this "servant" of the Lord (52:13). When they first encountered Him, they had heard a report that this was a special individual, perhaps even the Messiah. But what they saw did not square with what they had heard. "Who has believed our message?" (v. 1) probably carries the sense, "Who believed the message we had heard about

Him?" How could this pathetic individual be the anointed One? The second question uses the expression "the arm of the Lord" to refer to God's saving power in action. But "to whom was the arm of the Lord revealed" in this suffering, despised individual? As we shall see, the speakers quickly have reason to evaluate Jesus very differently, but they give three reasons for their former confusion.

The first was that *His origins were obscure*:

He grew up before him like a tender shoot,
and like a root out of dry ground (v. 2).

Jesus didn't come from the ranks of the privileged, powerful, or prosperous. He was the peasant son of peasant parents, who came to manhood in the cultural backwater of Nazareth. He eked out a living in a very small town and spent most of His life in obscurity. His birth and His background made no impression on the society in which He lived. Who would expect the Lord's Deliverer to emerge out of such conditions?

Second, *His appearance was unimpressive*. He had "no beauty or majesty to attract us to Him" (v. 2). This is not to say that He was physically unattractive, but rather that He was not of such commanding physical presence as to make Him immediately stand out. Nor did He surround Himself with the outward trappings of power and success that most cultures ascribe to a person of importance. He seemed utterly ordinary. No one in the ancient world paid any attention to an obscure itinerant preacher in a tiny, unimportant country. His own countrymen wanted and expected a charismatic leader, the Messiah, whose persona commanded respect, whose bearing embodied success, and whose giftedness magnetized His followers. Instead they found themselves with a peasant laborer, a carpenter, not a king.

But most of all, *His death was disgusting*. Throughout Isaiah 53, we are made aware that this is a person enduring gruesome and disfiguring suffering and a violent death. What we have already been told in 52:14 is graphic:

Many . . . were appalled at him—
  his appearance was so disfigured beyond that of any man and his
form marred beyond human likeness [perhaps better: marred from
that of a man].

Isaiah forces us to ask what has happened. How and why did
He suffer in this way? The Old Testament may leave us in doubt, but
the fulfillment of Isaiah's prophecy in the events of Jesus' crucifixion
makes it clear that these words are not an exaggeration.

Crucifixion did not exist as a method of execution when Isaiah
wrote, but by the first century, the Romans had perfected it as an
instrument of state terror, primarily intended to keep slaves and captive
nations under control. Martin Hengel, whose work on crucifixion is
the definitive scholarly work on the subject, makes these observations:

> For the men of the ancient world, Greek, Roman, barbarians
> and Jews, the cross was not just a matter of indifference, just
> any kind of death. It was an utterly offensive affair, 'obscene'
> in the original sense of the word. . . . [In the Roman Empire]
> crucifixion was a punishment in which the caprice and sadism
> of the executioners were given full rein. . . . The Roman
> world was largely unanimous that crucifixion was a horrific,
> disgusting business. . . . Death on the cross was the penalty
> for slaves as everyone knew; as such, it symbolized extreme
> humiliation, shame and torture.[5]

When *The Passion of the Christ* was released, there was a chorus of
indignation from many critics who felt the film was far too violent. It
certainly isn't pleasant to watch the prolonged scourging of Jesus and
the sheer agony of crucifixion. It is appropriate to debate whether
such raw violence should be portrayed in a movie. But, whatever the
merits of Gibson's portrayal, it is important to recognize that the
movie does not exaggerate the violence Jesus endured. Alex Metherell, who combines a medical degree with a doctorate in engineering,
has studied at great length the biomedical and engineering aspects

of crucifixion. Two of his conclusions deserve our attention: "The engineering load analysis, when added to the physiological information, will make it obvious why the Roman form of crucifixion is the most horrible, cruel, painful and humiliating form of execution ever devised." And "neither the flogging nor the crucifixion as shown [in the movie] was as bad or as violent as the actual event."[6] There can be no doubt that the physical effects of crucifixion were enormous, not only for the Lord Jesus, but also for anyone who was crucified.

However, as brutal as Jesus' death was, the majority of those who witnessed His sufferings felt contempt rather than compassion.

He was despised and rejected by men,
a man of sorrows, and familiar with suffering (v. 3).

The word *despised* suggests that they held Him in contempt, and *rejected* means that they dismissed Him as having no value or significance. They scorned Him as an incessant sufferer not a compelling leader. He was "like one from whom men hide their faces," a person to be turned from in disgust, so "we esteemed him not," we evaluated Him as a human zero (v. 3). The gospel accounts tell us that those who witnessed Jesus on the cross hurled "insults at him" (Mark 15:29, 32), "mocked him" (Mark 15:31), and "sneered at him" (Luke 23:35). What could such a person possibly do for anyone else? The only reasonable conclusion was that He was suffering for some terrible sins of His own against God. Why else would God permit this?

The cross has always been a big problem. In the ancient Roman world, it was considered ludicrous that Christians worshiped a criminal and His cross. An early enemy of the faith, a man named Celsus, poured out his contempt: "What drunken old woman telling stories to lull a small child to sleep would not be ashamed of muttering such preposterous things?" From the very first, Christ crucified was "a stumbling block to Jews and foolishness to Gentiles" (1 Corinthians 1:23).

The modern world may say nice things about "Jesus," usually a Jesus transformed into a rather harmless moral and spiritual teacher proclaiming a generic kind of spirituality that calls for no repentance. However, the cross confronts us with something very different: the depths of our sinfulness, the reality of God's nonnegotiable holiness, the demands of His righteousness, and our urgent need of deliverance. But if we refuse to own our sin, the cross will only arouse revulsion. The notorious John Shelby Spong, who continued to serve as an Episcopal bishop while he denied nearly all of the basic truths of the Christian faith, declared that the cross as a sacrifice for sins was "an image that has to go," since "I would choose to loathe rather than to worship a God who required the sacrifice of his son."[7]

For my part, I will stay with the apostle Paul: "May I never boast except in the cross of our Lord Jesus Christ" (Galatians 6:14). The cross, which at first seems to be a place of great horror, on closer observation turns out to be a place of wonder and great beauty. Intense as the physical sufferings endured by the Lord Jesus, those must not be the center of our attention. It could be argued that others have died physical deaths that were equally or perhaps even more excruciating. But the meaning of the cross is not so much how He died but why. Something beyond the physical occurred at Calvary, and that is where Isaiah 53 takes us, as the speakers declare how they came to see Jesus and His cross in an entirely different light. The truth of the resurrection puts the cross in an entirely different light. The empty tomb makes it clear He was a Person like no other who died a death like no other, because it brought an outcome like no other. Easter turns the cross from a horror to a wonder, which brings us to verses 4–6 of Isaiah 53.

God's Suffering Servant: A Wonder That Brings Forgiveness

Looked at one way, the cross is man's atrocity. Looked at in a more important way, the cross is God's solution to man's deepest needs. And so, beginning in verse 4, the people who once viewed

Jesus as the deserving, despised sufferer, declare that they came to understand His death in a very different way.

First, the people confess that *God's Servant bore our brokenness:* His death was a sacrifice.

> *Surely he took up our infirmities*
> *and carried our sorrows.*

Although the words *infirmities* and *sorrows* usually refer to physical problems and illnesses, here they represent our inner brokenness, our spiritual sickness before a holy God. Jesus died on the cross, not because something was wrong with Him, but because everything was wrong with us. In fact, the words *infirmities* and *sorrows* in verse 4 are the same Hebrew words translated as *sorrows* and *suffering* in verse 3. The very things that made us turn away from Him belonged to us! The sicknesses were ours, not His, but He took them on Himself, and carried them away. The critical word is *our.* It was about us, not Him! It may have appeared that He was getting what he deserved, that He was

> *stricken by God,*
> *smitten by him, and afflicted*

because of His own failings. Such was not the case. He was bearing the brokenness of others. This is said repeatedly throughout the chapter.

Second, the people confess that *God's Servant took our place:* His death was substitutionary. The terms Isaiah uses describe a violent death: He was "pierced," a word that is nearly always used in contexts involving fatal wounds, and "crushed," pulverized, broken. But now they are more specific: It was for our transgressions and our iniquities, our legal guilt before a holy God. Jesus was not suffering under the hand of God for the wrongs He had done but for the sins of others. "The punishment that brought us peace was upon him, and by his wounds we are healed." These words bring us to the very center of the meaning of the cross. When Jesus died, He did so not merely as a martyr, as an example, or as a revelation of the loving heart of God. He did not merely die before His people or with His people but for them. His death was a payment for the guilt of others.

An article in *Time* magazine attempted to describe the various ways Christians have understood the cross of Christ. A few weeks later, the "Letters" column contained reader responses to the question asked by the article: "Why did Jesus have to die?" The letters covered the landscape: "Jesus attempted to show us that death is not the end." "Jesus came to show us God the Father." "[Jesus died] to show us how life works and to empower us to live fully now and forever." "Jesus stood up to the injustices of the world and was crushed in the process."[8] These statements fall tragically short of what Isaiah knew: "He was pierced for our transgressions."

My father-in-law, as a teenager, jumped ship in an Atlantic port, to make his way across the United States and up to Winnipeg. He was driven by a hunger to find his father, who had abandoned his family in Wales and failed to return as promised. When he found him, he was heartbroken to discover that his father was involved with another woman. He couldn't tolerate his father's behavior, and that meant he was now alone in a strange city. He didn't speak much English, but a Welsh family welcomed him and took him to places where he began to hear the gospel of the Lord Jesus Christ. One bitterly cold winter night, he got on a streetcar to ride home from a meeting in Elim Chapel. Because of his limited language, he had understood only part of the message. But he did remember this: The preacher had quoted Isaiah 53:5 and told his audience to put their own names in at the appropriate places. So he began to recite to himself the words of the *King James Version*: "He was wounded for Leslie's transgressions, He was bruised for Leslie's iniquities." Even as Leslie said those words, the Holy Spirit opened his eyes to see the glory of Christ, and he realized instantly that Jesus had taken his place. "It was like the blinders fell off; I realized that He had died for me." And He had. My father-in-law never got over that moment and lived from that day with the complete certainty that he was a forgiven man. He had a Substitute who had taken his place!

The third declaration is that *God's Servant paid God's price*: His death is a saving death. Those who stand at the foot of the cross, seeing the death of Jesus in a new light, also see themselves in a new light:

> *We all, like sheep, have gone astray,*
> *each of us has turned to his own way (v. 6).*

Every believer in Christ is a person who has seen and owned God's verdict that "all have sinned and fall short of the glory of God" (Romans 3:23). The basic story line of the Bible is that we were created not only by God but also for God. Yet we, in Adam, turned our backs on God and chose to go our own way and to do our own thing. The basic human problem is sin, a "going our own way" in independence of and rebellion against God. We must be clear that sin is not merely a violation of an abstract or arbitrary moral law. It is an offense against God Himself. He is not merely the righteous Judge; He is the one against whom we have sinned. But the wonder of the gospel is that our gracious God did not abandon us to the consequences of our choices. In love, He pursued us, finally sending His own Son to live among us and, at the cross, "the Lord laid on him the iniquity of us all." As John Oswalt observes, "This is not a matter of a raging tyrant who demands violence on someone to satisfy his fury. It is a God who wants a whole relationship with his people, but is prevented from having it until incomplete

Sin is not merely a violation of an abstract or arbitrary moral law. It is an offense against God Himself.

justice is satisfied. In the Servant he has found a way to gratify his love and satisfy his justice."[9]

God's justice meant that He could not give our sins a pass. He must deal with them. God's grace meant that He Himself would become the solution, when the Son of God became man so that He could take our sins upon Himself as a full and atoning payment for sin, or, as Isaiah puts it, as a guilt offering. By means of the cross, the triune God both expressed His gracious love toward undeserving sinners and satisfied the demands of His holy nature. Isaiah 53 goes on to tell us that this was God's great plan, that "it was the Lord's will to crush him and cause him to suffer" (v. 10), and that the suffering Servant "bore the sin of many and made intercession for the transgressors" (v. 12).

Much that happened at the cross is beyond our comprehension. Jesus' death was a great victory over sin and Satan. It was a wonderful example of suffering love. It was a window into the heart of a loving God. However, most of all, it was an act of substitution, when "God made him who had no sin to be sin for us, so that in him we might become the righteousness of God" (2 Corinthians 5:21). As a result there is full and free forgiveness for all who put their faith in Him. "In him we have redemption through his blood, the forgiveness of sins" (Ephesians 1:7). God does not merely dismiss our sins, waving them out of existence by an act of His sovereign power. He cannot simply condone our sins, declaring that they do not really matter. By so doing, He would violate His own fundamental holiness. Rather, God the Father sent His own Son, a willing and fully involved participant, to pay the penalty of our sins, thus satisfying the demands of His holy nature and making it possible for Him righteously to forgive those who put their faith in Him. The God against whom we have sinned chooses to pay the price so that we might go free.

Someone once described the gospel as an ocean in which children can play and elephants can drown. The simple truth is that Jesus, God's Son, took my penalty upon Himself, paid my debt, and

I am freely and fully forgiven, through faith in Him. But the profundity of that transaction staggers the most profound minds. Even in forgiving us, the holy God did not compromise His righteousness or trivialize our sinfulness. Rather, He took our sin and guilt upon Himself in the person of His Son, paid the full price, met all the demands of holy justice. The price was staggeringly high, but it was fully, freely, and lovingly paid. The demands of God's holy nature were utterly satisfied in the death of His Son. And His resurrection stamps the transaction as complete.

Our forgiveness is a costly forgiveness. We receive it as a free gift, through faith in the Lord Jesus, but it cost Jesus more than we can imagine. It is also a complete forgiveness. Jesus did not pay for some of our sins but for all of them. He did not offer a partial or a conditional forgiveness but a full and final one.

The Visa Isn't Hard to Get

Not long ago my wife and I flew to Europe to join a tour through the lands of the Reformation. Our first destination was Prague, the home area of Jan Hus. Getting there didn't prove to be easy. We encountered a wildcat strike at Heathrow Airport in London, a strike that threw travel connections to all European cities into total confusion. It took some ingenuity, a great deal of patience, and a night trying to sleep on a bench in the Paris airport, but we finally arrived in Prague. Along the way we had picked up three other tour members. Elizabeth preceded me to passport control. As the routine process dragged on, it became evident that something was wrong. Elizabeth and I are Canadians, and, as it turned out, Canada and the Czech Republic did not at that time have a reciprocal arrangement that waived the need for visas. No one had told us we needed a visa to enter the country. That seemed annoying but surely could be solved easily enough. Little did we know! We were sent over to the appropriate office. I was frustrated that this was going to eat up time, but I assumed that we would be given a way to deal with the problem. That wasn't to be. The immigration officer in charge had, I am convinced, failed whatever charm course such officials receive. His approach was very direct:

"You need a visa to enter the Czech Republic."
"We didn't know that. Nobody told us."
"Doesn't matter. Need visa."
"Can we get one here?"
"Not possible."
"But we're booked on a tour. We're only staying two days."
"Doesn't matter. Need visa."
"But the rest of our group got through."
"Doesn't matter. Need visa."
"Can we talk to anyone here?"
"Needed before you came. Too late here. Need visa."
"What are we supposed to do?"
"Doesn't matter. Stay in airport. Fly away. Need visa."

Whatever you may say about his style, he left no doubt about his meaning. We were not going to get into the Czech Republic. It didn't matter that we didn't know the rules. It didn't matter that we were sincere. It didn't matter that we were with Americans, looked like Americans, sounded like Americans (at least most of the time), lived with Americans, and were just as good and moral as Americans. Americans got in without a visa. We were Canadians, and Canadians didn't. We made calls: to the tour director, to the Canadian embassy, to Czech officials. The message was unanimous: We weren't getting in.

It wasn't the happiest moment of our lives. We were extremely tired because of the flight problems and the time change, and this just wasn't very much fun. I sat there in a country where I didn't speak the language, watching all kinds of people walk up to the counter, showing their passports, and getting in without a second look. As we sat there, trying to work out our plans, another woman sat down beside us, steaming with anger. It didn't take long for us to discover that she too was a Canadian, and she wasn't going to get in either. Misery didn't especially love company!

We ended up having to fly back to Germany. We met the tour when it arrived in Leipzig. It turned out to be only a brief glitch in an enjoyable trip. But I couldn't help but think of spiritual parallels as I sat watching others get in while I couldn't. It didn't matter one bit to that immigration officer what kind of person I was or how I measured up to other people who were going through. He didn't care how many degrees I had, what positions I held, what honors I had received or what testimonials I could produce from other people. He wasn't impressed by the stamps in my passport from other countries that had allowed me to enter. All that mattered was that I needed a visa for the Czech Republic, and I didn't have it.

I know that the analogy is far from perfect, but I could not help but think of what happens when we die. One day each one of us will stand, as it were, at Passport Control in heaven. Let me warn you ahead of time, so you will not be in the position I found myself in: a visa is required. Your passport must have a stamp that says, "Forgiven by God through faith in the Lord Jesus." The good news is, the stamp isn't hard to get! You can get it right now by putting your trust in the Lord Jesus as your Savior and Lord. He has made available, through the wonder of the cross, a costly forgiveness.

Chapter 3

FROM GUILT TO GRATITUDE

*W*hen Kay Lee married Tom Goetz, she was sure she had found her Prince Charming. Their courtship and wedding all seemed like a great fairy tale—a huge ring, an engagement announcement on the front page of the society section, a lavish wedding, and an exotic Bermuda honeymoon. However, real life made an abrupt entry on the honeymoon when Tom sat her down in their hotel suite and solemnly told her, "You are now Mrs. Frank Thomas Goetz, Jr., and there are things I don't like about you." He then proceeded to list her shortcomings, things that needed to change were she to be worthy of bearing his name. Tom was from a wealthy family, a gifted athlete who had attracted offers from several major-league baseball teams. But he declined the offers and entered the family business. Later, he accepted a commission in the navy. Despite his obvious potential, he seemed unable to find his place or to finish what he had started. Time would make it clear that he was battling manic depression.

Tom and Kay had two children, and Kay, a trained nurse, began a modeling career. To outsiders they seemed to be an all-American family, enjoying an almost ideal life. But behind closed doors, things were very different. The marriage was in trouble, and Kay was growing very unhappy: "I had a mink, I had money, and I was miserable." Although she professed to be a Christian, her Christianity was about being religious, not about knowing God in a personal way. And so a huge vacuum was growing inside her soul.

After six years she had had enough. She took her kids and left, spiraling into promiscuity and a long affair with a married man. Tom wanted her back, whining, "Kay, give me a reason to live; I'm thinking of killing myself." Her response wasn't exactly sympathetic, but she was also trying to shock him out of his self-pity: "Go ahead and kill yourself. I could use the money from the insurance." She was angry at God, blaming Him for her situation, going so far as to shake her fist at heaven and shout, "To hell with you, God. I'm going to find someone to love me."

But none of the men she became involved with and nothing else she tried could fill the emptiness. One night at a party, a friend told her, "Why don't you quit telling God what you want and tell Him that Jesus Christ is all you need?"

"Jesus is *not* all I need," she shot back. "I need a husband. I need a home. I need ___," and she walked away. The Holy Spirit, however, had no intention of letting her go. She had a restless, disturbed night, and the next morning, she found herself on her knees, crying out to the Lord: "God, I don't care what you do to me. Please, just give me peace!" At that moment, she says, "God gave me the Prince of Peace." Instantly she knew that she belonged to the Lord. She instinctively grasped who the Lord Jesus was and opened her heart to Him. As she says, "I went down on my knees a harlot, and I got up a saint."

The change was dramatic. Even as she stood up, she knew she could no longer dress in the provocative way she had been doing. It was the first of many changes, in her language, in her driving habits, but most of all in her new thirst to know God and to understand His Word. By this time the divorce was final, and Kay had no desire for reconciliation. However, after several months as a baby Christian, she became convinced that the Lord wanted her to try to restore the marriage. Sadly, she was too late. Before she could make contact, news came that Tom had hung himself. Her guilt was, at first, overwhelming. But now she had somewhere to take it. She took it to the cross and discovered in a new way that Jesus was her Sin-bearer. "He paid for all my sins, past, present, and future." A new love gripped her heart that led her to a Christian college to study

God's Word. There she met and married Jack Arthur. She served as a missionary for a time and then was enabled by the Lord to begin a Bible-teaching ministry, Precept Ministries, that now reaches around the world through study groups, radio, and television and almost a hundred books authored by Kay. But Kay Arthur has never gotten over the fact that she is a forgiven woman.[1]

Guilt is a universal human condition. Every one of us, without exception, has violated his own standards of right and wrong (never mind God's) and has wronged others, often unintentionally but sometimes intentionally. We have broken God's law. There is such a thing as false guilt, but true guilt is a fact of life. Wonderfully, so is the forgiveness God makes available through His Son. Forgiveness is not a commodity, something we receive in some kind of religious transaction in *Great forgiveness inspires great love.* exchange for our merit or our penance. It is a free gift of a gracious God that we receive through our relationship with the Lord Jesus Himself. As we have seen, it is a costly forgiveness, requiring our Lord's death on a cross. And it is a forgiveness that arouses deep love for our Forgiver. One way to measure whether we have understood and received forgiveness is to observe the depth of our response to the Savior. Great forgiveness inspires great love, as the Lord portrays in the passage we consider here, from Luke 7:36–50.

> *Now one of the Pharisees invited Jesus to have dinner with him, so he went to the Pharisee's house and reclined at the table. When a woman who had lived a sinful life in that town learned that Jesus was eating at the Pharisee's house, she brought an alabaster jar of perfume, and as she stood behind him at his feet weeping, she began to wet his feet with her tears. Then she wiped them with her hair, kissed them and poured perfume on them.*
>
> *When the Pharisee who had invited him saw this, he said to himself, "If this man were a prophet, he would know who is touching him and what kind of woman she is—that she is a sinner."*
>
> *Jesus answered him, "Simon, I have something to tell you."*

"Tell me, teacher," he said.

"Two men owed money to a certain moneylender. One owed him five hundred denarii, and the other fifty. Neither of them had the money to pay him back, so he canceled the debts of both. Now which of them will love him more?"

Simon replied, "I suppose the one who had the bigger debt canceled."

"You have judged correctly," Jesus said.

Then he turned toward the woman and said to Simon, "Do you see this woman? I came into your house. You did not give me any water for my feet, but she wet my feet with her tears and wiped them with her hair. You did not give me a kiss, but this woman, from the time I entered, has not stopped kissing my feet. You did not put oil on my head, but she has poured perfume on my feet. Therefore, I tell you, her many sins have been forgiven—for she loved much. But he who has been forgiven little loves little."

Then Jesus said to her, "Your sins are forgiven."

The other guests began to say among themselves, "Who is this who even forgives sins?"

Jesus said to the woman, "Your faith has saved you; go in peace."

Jesus consistently found Himself under attack from the religious leaders of His day. One of their most consistent complaints was that He persistently spent time with the wrong kind of people, the type the religious elite considered undesirable, untouchable, and unapproachable. He, they claimed, was "a glutton and a drunkard, a friend of tax collectors and 'sinners' " (Luke 7:34). He, of course, was neither a glutton nor a drunkard. But He certainly was a friend of tax collectors and sinners, making it a regular practice to spend time with the "wrong" kind of people. Religious people, then as now, can easily allow their concern for high standards to turn into a self-righteousness that looks with contempt on people of lesser religiosity or morality. Jesus refused to submit to their self-righteous standards. In fact, He often seemed to go out of His way to antagonize or shock such people. So it is somewhat surprising to read that a Pharisee invited Jesus to a dinner party in his home. Whatever the host's motives or intentions, his party was to take a turn he could never have imagined!

The Party: A Scandalous Expression of Forgiveness

Luke draws our attention to the fact that the host of this party is a Pharisee. He does this by calling him "the Pharisee" the first four times he's mentioned, and not until Jesus Himself addresses him do we learn that his name is Simon. To understand Luke's emphasis, we need to know some things about the Pharisees.

They were a group of highly dedicated laymen; that is, only men could belong, and they were not religious professionals such as priests. They set themselves apart from ordinary Jews (the very name *Pharisee* probably comes from a word meaning "separatist") being determined to live lives they felt would honor God. They did this by following a particular understanding of God's law. This led them to obey scrupulously not only the teachings of Torah, but also the growing body of tradition handed down from their predecessors. Those traditions had come to define for them righteous behavior. This meticulous religiosity won the grudging respect of the common people and made them the most influential of the various religious groups of the time. But this all too easily led to an attitude of spiritual pride and self-confidence, coupled with contempt for ordinary Jews. As well, Pharisees tended to a self-righteous legalism, and many came to believe that their behavior earned for them special favor with heaven. Their attitude both to God and to other people is marvelously captured in the prayer the Lord ascribes to a Pharisee in Luke 18:11: "God, I thank you that I am not like other men—robbers, evildoers, adulterers—or even like this tax collector." It was this group that often took the lead in opposition to Jesus.

One matter of special importance to the Pharisees was table-fellowship. Meals in Jewish culture were about far more than enjoyment of food. Sharing a meal was a symbol of friendship and community. People invited their social equals and their spiritual peers. The Pharisees were particularly concerned about ritual purity, even for ordinary meals, and had devised a set of careful preliminaries of washing and preparation. A specific amount of water, used in a specific ritual fashion, must be used to cleanse one's hands. The washing was not primarily about physical hygiene but about ritual and ceremonial "cleanness." This concern for proper preparation and appropriate companions meant that mealtimes were marker events that set boundaries about who was and wasn't religiously acceptable.

That makes Simon's invitation to Jesus to share a meal surprising, because Jesus was notorious for His openness to all kinds of people and His indifference to merely traditional practices. We cannot be sure of Simon's motivation. Was he genuinely curious to learn more about Jesus? Did he think he could win Jesus over to the Pharisaic mindset? Was he intending in some way to embarrass Him? Questions abound, but as the story unfolds it becomes clear that, although he welcomed Jesus, he did so with a cold politeness and a bare minimum of normal cultural courtesies.

We should be less surprised that Jesus accepted the invitation. It is true that some of the most biting things He said in His public ministry were directed at the Pharisees. He was repelled by their smug self-righteousness and spiritual arrogance. But He didn't do to them what they did to others. He did not exclude or boycott them; rather, He took the opportunity to be with them, even as He did with the disreputable and the irreligious. He had come to seek and to save even Pharisees.

The Jews had some intriguing customs for special meals. At a normal meal the family would sit. But at a special meal the invited guests would recline on couches around a low U-shaped table. The doors would be left open, and uninvited guests were allowed to enter and sit around the side of the room. They could listen to the conversation, a source of entertainment in such a culture, and perhaps collect some leftovers.

So it was not surprising that a woman would enter a room where a special meal was being held. But the identity of the woman was astonishing—"a woman who had lived a sinful life in that town" (v. 37). We can only guess about her past behavior. Clearly she had a reputation, most likely as a notoriously promiscuous woman, an adulteress, or even a prostitute. If there was anywhere that she was out of place, it was in the home of a Pharisee! Her very presence indicates her courage; she certainly knew what people would feel and say about her being there. And she was not content simply to take a seat at the edge of the room, making herself as inconspicuous as possible. She was a woman on a mission: "When [she] learned that Jesus was eating at the Pharisee's house, she brought an alabaster jar of perfume, and as she stood behind him at his feet weeping, she began to wet his feet with her tears" (vv. 37–38). Her display of emotion was genuine and spontaneous, but her action was carefully premeditated. She had come to honor Jesus publicly, for what He had come to mean to her.

Anyone who has traveled in the Middle East knows how carefully relations between men and women are structured, even today. The casual kinds of interaction we take for granted were unthinkable. A woman would not touch an unrelated man in public. She did not boldly enter the company of males, and she certainly did not let her hair down in their presence. In fact, in Jewish eyes a woman who took her hair down before a man to whom she was not related had given her husband grounds for divorce. There are even ancient accounts of men who boasted that that they had never seen their own wives' hair while it was let down! This may seem strange to us, but it helps us understand how people would have reacted when this notorious woman burst into the room and approached the feet of Jesus. If this was a shocking breach of conventional behavior, dissolving in tears and letting those tears soak His feet compounded the shock. But to take down her hair, wipe His feet with it, kiss those feet, and then break her alabaster flask and pour out her perfume on His feet—that was an outrage.[2]

The woman was emotionally overwhelmed. I suspect that she had intended to anoint the feet of Jesus as an act of love and respect. Perhaps she even had suspected that He would get a cold welcome in the Pharisee's house, and she wanted to set things right. But the overflowing emotions are evidence of a sense of gratitude so deep that she was unable to control her feelings. Note that Jesus did nothing to restrain or discourage her. He could have jumped immediately to His feet and ordered her to stop. But He didn't. Knowing full well that her actions would shock those present, He allowed her to do what she wanted.

Imagine the electric atmosphere in the room. Suppose a notorious local porn queen walked into a church service during the celebration of Communion, rushed to the front, and threw herself in tears at the feet of the pastor! No one present in Simon's house that day had ever seen such behavior. And the host recoiled in shock. He said nothing; he didn't need to. His body language gave him away. Yet, although the woman's behavior offended him, it was Jesus who bothered him much more. After all, He neither recoiled from the woman nor rebuked her, but allowed all this to happen. What kind of holy man would do this? Luke records the Pharisee's unspoken thoughts: "If this man were a prophet, he would know who is touching him and what kind of woman she is—that she is a sinner." Simon knew who the woman was—a dirty, untouchable, unacceptable sinner, the kind to be avoided at all costs. If he could see that, why couldn't Jesus? And if Jesus couldn't, how could anyone claim that He was some kind of prophet, a man uniquely in touch with God? Jesus' toleration of the woman's behavior was proof positive that He lacked even a good man's discernment, never mind a prophet's God-given special insight! Furthermore, Simon's training and experience taught him that good people maintain their goodness by protecting themselves from the wrong kind of people. Putting it all together, the entire episode confirmed his suspicions—whatever Jesus is, He is no prophet. That conclusion, so obvious to him, served to reinforce his own belief that he and his fellow Pharisees were people of spiritual righteousness and discernment, able to sit in judgment on others.

The fact is, of course, that Jesus knew exactly what kind of person the woman was. He also knew exactly what kind of person Simon was, seeing things in him to which Simon himself was blind. But rather than expose and embarrass Simon directly, the Lord Jesus chose to tell him a story, a parable about two debtors.

The Parable: The Amazing Gift of Forgiveness

Jesus introduces us to two men, both significantly in debt to the same moneylender. One man owed a debt of five hundred denarii. A denarius was a coin that paid the normal day's wage for the common worker, so his debt amounted to almost two years' wages, a very significant amount. The other man owed fifty denarii, only one-tenth the first man's obligation, but still a debt amounting to two months' wages. He may have owed less, but, in fact, both men shared the same problem: "Neither of them had the money to pay him back" (v. 42). In that sense, they were equal. If you have no assets, it really doesn't matter how much you owe: You are bankrupt. In the culture of the time, all they could look forward to was debt slavery or debtors' prison.

That's where Jesus' story starts, not where it ends. Jesus' parables usually contain a surprise, and in this case it comes from the moneylender. He does what moneylenders never do, whether in the first century or ours: "He canceled the debts of both" (v. 42). Lenders don't stay in business that way! It was completely unexpected. It was also completely undeserved, an act of pure grace. He didn't even require the debtors to work off even a portion of what was due. The debts were canceled in full, as a free gift. This is highlighted in the original text by the fact that the word translated as *canceled* is *charizomai*, a word built on the Greek word for *grace* (*charis*). But why? The reason lay in the forgiver, not the forgiven. He did it by making a gift, by choosing to pay himself what they owed. This is the very heart of forgiveness. The one owed the debt pays the debt and the debtor goes free. He didn't merely extend the repayment period. He didn't cut down the size of the obligation. He paid for them in full and set them free. At the heart of all forgiveness is a substitution. The offended pays so that the offender goes free.

As we have seen, this is the very heart of the cross, where the offended party in the person of the God-man took the debt of the sins we had committed upon Himself, and paid in full, so that we, His people, could go free.

The Lord usually allows His stories to speak for themselves. But on this occasion, He follows His parable with a question to Simon: "Now which of them will love him more?" (v. 42). The question is interesting, because it assumes that there is an inevitable link between forgiveness and love. Think of it: receiving a forgiveness we do not deserve because another has paid for us. Such a forgiveness may be free to you and me, but it is very costly to the forgiver. How can we be indifferent toward the person who has set us free from a burden we cannot carry? Observe that the Lord's question implies that forgiveness precedes love. The debtors did not love the moneylender before they were forgiven. Theirs had been a purely business arrangement. But forgiveness changed the whole relationship. Because they had been forgiven, they began to love. They had been forgiven by the lender, not because they loved him, but because they needed him.

How can we be indifferent toward the person who has set us free from a burden we cannot carry?

The answer to the Lord's question is obvious, but Simon approaches it warily and almost grudgingly: "I suppose the one who had the bigger debt canceled" (v. 43). He instinctively sensed that he wasn't going to like what Jesus would do with his answer! But for the moment, Jesus simply agreed with him and turned toward the woman.

The Pardon: The Clear Evidence of Forgiveness

Jesus' question, "Do you see this woman?" (v. 44), may seem like an exercise in the obvious, but, the fact is, Simon did not truly see her at all. At best, she was a stereotype, a member of a class to be avoided and shunned. She was a sinner, deserving only contempt. But the Lord saw something entirely different: an individual who, because of grace, had become a worshiper.

Jesus did not let Simon off the hook. He had a message to deliver. My mother taught me, as a young boy, to accept someone's hospitality for what it is and to avoid making comments on whatever deficiencies I find. Here in Luke 7 the Lord Jesus does not feel confined by my mother's concerns! He speaks directly to Simon, directly contrasting his cold formality with the effusive response of the woman. Simon has done only the bare minimum, coldly courteous, while the woman has shown overwhelming gratitude: "I came into your house. You did not give me any water for my feet, but she wet my feet with her tears and wiped them with her hair. You did not give me a kiss, but this woman, from the time I entered, has not stopped kissing my feet. You did not put oil on my head, but she has poured perfume on my feet" (vv. 44–46). In the culture of the time, the provision of water to cleanse feet (especially when one would be reclining at table), the kiss of greeting, and special oil, though not necessities, were the usual courtesies shown to valued guests. Simon's actions may not have been openly insulting, but they made it clear that Jesus was only marginally welcome.

The woman's response to Jesus has been the exact opposite—a culturally excessive overflow of heartfelt love. As Jesus here makes clear, her behavior was itself the clear answer to the question about which of the two debtors loved more: "Therefore, I tell you, her many sins have been forgiven—for she loved much. But he who has been forgiven little loves little." For the first time we are given a clue as to the earlier encounter between this woman and Jesus. Although we know nothing of the specifics, we know that the Lord Jesus had forgiven her, despite her abundant sins. She was forgiven not because she loved Jesus; she loved Him because He had forgiven her of her many sins.[3]

Jesus' words contain an implicit claim of great importance. He was claiming the right to forgive sins. Only the one sinned against can forgive a debt or a sin. If I owed you ten thousand dollars, and one of my friends forgave my debt, it would be nothing but a nice gesture. Only you can forgive my debt, because you alone are the one to whom I owe it. This woman had not sinned directly against Jesus the man. She had sinned against God. Only God could forgive her sins.[4] But because Jesus was, in fact, the God-man, He could and did declare her forgiven. It was a declaration that would inevitably lead Him to the cross where He would pay the debt of her sins by taking it upon Himself.

In 1987 Donna Rice found herself in a headline-grabbing scandal when she was caught in a sexual liaison with Sen. Gary Hart of Colorado, who was, at the time, running for the Democratic presidential nomination. Hart, a married man, had vehemently denied rumors that he was involved in "womanizing." Then very compromising photos became public of Hart and Rice on a pleasure cruise to the Bahamas. The headlines were sensational, and the ensuing scandal knocked Hart out of contention for the nomination. It also destroyed the reputation of Donna Rice, leaving her devastated. The media feeding frenzy followed her everywhere.

Raised as a Christian, a series of circumstances and compromises had caused her to wander far from her spiritual roots. Now the entire world saw her as a "bimbo." Encouraged by her mother to turn to the Lord, Donna did so. "God," she prayed, "it took falling on my rear in front of the whole world to get my attention. Help me to live life your way."

She says, "God answered my plea by flooding my heart with His presence and forgiveness and by surrounding me with Christian fellowship. . . . He died so that I might accept His love and forgiveness and have eternal life."

Hounded by the press, Donna retreated from the public eye. The Lord brought into her life a man who would love her, Jack Hughes, and they were married in 1994. When she did reappear in a public role, it was as the spokesperson and voluntary president of Enough Is Enough, an organization dedicated to stopping illegal pornography and making the Internet safe for children. Looking back on the scandal through the lens of her forgiveness, she observes, "God forgives us, but He doesn't grant us immunity from the consequences of our choices. However, when we mess up, if we ask His forgiveness, He'll redeem those choices. God has brought purpose to my pain."[5]

Great sinners become great lovers of Jesus when they grasp their forgiveness. There is a direct link between forgiveness and worship, made evident by this woman in the Pharisee's house. But if we trivialize sin, we will trivialize forgiveness and have little reason to pour out love for Jesus. *If we trivialize sin, we will trivialize forgiveness* In truth, there are no little sinners, people who are forgiven only a little. When the Lord says, "He who has been forgiven little loves little" (v. 47), He is not suggesting that such people really exist, any more than He meant that some people weren't spiritually sick when He said, "It is not the healthy who need a doctor, but the sick. I have not come to call the righteous, but sinners" (Mark 2:17).

The Pharisees imagined themselves to be "little sinners." But that was because they had carefully chosen which sins they would condemn. They did not feel the horror of the sins of attitude that dominated them, sins such as pride, arrogance, and anger. For them the sins of the flesh, which had long characterized this woman in Simon's house, were the only sins that really mattered. Simon, in fact, did not love Jesus at all, because he had not been forgiven by Him at all.

There is a fundamental spiritual principle involved here: *Love for Jesus is a prime evidence of a forgiven heart.* And such love is remarkably unself-conscious and intensely Christ-centered. This principle alone should have a profound effect on our private and public worship. The woman's encounter with Jesus had forever changed her. She was no longer a sinner to be avoided but a forgiven believer to be welcomed, cherished, and valued.

Having challenged Simon—intending to cause him to probe his own heart—Jesus then turned to the woman to assure her of the certainty of her forgiveness: "Your sins are forgiven," or more precisely, because He uses a perfect tense, "Your sins have been and remain forgiven" (v. 48). Her forgiveness was free; she certainly had not earned it by her past life, her repentance, or even her extravagant expression of love. Her forgiveness was final, not probationary. She did not need to maintain her status by her future course of behavior, although her encounter with Jesus had undoubtedly been morally transforming. Her forgiveness was total. He had forgiven her sins, not just one or two particular sins. And, although it is not the point here, her forgiveness was costly, not for her but for the Forgiver, who would "bear [her] sins in his body on the tree" (1 Peter 2:24).

The other participants in the meal, presumably many of them also Pharisees, immediately raised their objections to the Lord's declaration, echoing Mark 2. "Who is this who even forgives sins?" (v. 49). The answer is, of course, that He is both the One sinned against and also the One who will pay for sins. But the Lord would not be distracted. His focus was on the woman: "Your faith has saved you; go in peace" (v. 50). Her forgiveness was, in fact, the gift of salvation, and it came, as it does for us all, through faith in the Lord Jesus Christ. A great Scottish preacher and theologian captured the wonder of this woman's encounter with Jesus:

> Jesus knew what sin was more truly than any man. He saw it in its roots and its consequences. But he believed in forgiveness. He not only believed in it and proclaimed it, he embodied and bestowed it. . . . Jesus did not shrink from the sinful woman: He received her. He took her part against the

Pharisee. He spoke great and gracious words in her defense. "Her sins are forgiven, for she loved much." "Thy faith hath saved thee: go in peace." And as she went, she knew that friendless as she had been before she had now a friend with God; it is not too much to say, she knew that God himself was her friend. We see from this incident what a profound, thrilling, and far reaching experience reconciliation is. It is something which moves nature in all its depths, which melts it and casts it into a new mould. It regenerates the soul which passes through it, and it is accompanied with the sense of an infinite debt to Jesus.[6]

There is a significant message in this story. Jesus is the Forgiver, and our response to Jesus is the infallible evidence of whether or not we have understood and received forgiveness. We may be like one of the two debtors, the one owing five hundred denarii or the one owing fifty. We encounter Jesus with our personal account of guilt before a holy God. But the more

Our response to Jesus is the infallible evidence of whether or not we have understood and received forgiveness.

significant question is not the amount of our debt, but whether we resemble the woman or the Pharisee. If we have truly heard Jesus say, "Your sins have been forgiven. Your faith has saved you. Go in peace," our hearts have been captured by the wonder of that release, and the love that ensues drives us to His feet in adoration and worship.

John and Tonya, a couple in our congregation, both know the forgiveness of God in a very profound way. They have come to celebrate the reality of God's grace in their lives, a grace that knows the worst about them but provides for them through the Lord Jesus. The "perfume" they pour out on the Lord takes the form of their musical gifts that lead us in celebrating our forgiving God. Let me share the words of one of their songs that we, as a congregation, love to sing with them:

Awesome God

You truly love me, you truly do.
You pour yourself right into me,
And Lord, you see right through
All the secrets of my heart,
All my weakness
And everywhere I fall apart.
You truly love me.

What an awesome God you are!
What an awesome God you are!
You truly love me.

You still forgive me, you truly do.
I miss the mark a million times,
I fall so short of you.
All my worry, all my pride, all this envy
And all the things I wish I could hide;
You still forgive me.

What an awesome God you are!
What an awesome God you are!
You still forgive me.

I am crucified with Christ
And I no longer live,
But He lives in me.
Every breath I freely give;
I live through faith in Christ,
Who gave up Himself for me.

What an awesome God you are!
What an awesome God you are!
You truly love me,
You still forgive me,
You truly love me.[7]

Forgiven people are grateful people, overwhelmed by the gracious forgiveness of the Lord Jesus that has set them free of condemnation and guilt. So, if you count yourself among the forgiven, go ahead! Join the song. Or break the vase and pour the perfume at His feet in worship and thanksgiving.

Chapter 4

LIVING IN FORGIVENESS

One Sunday morning, after I had preached on the wonder of God's forgiveness, I suggested that some might find it helpful to write a brief note about an issue of guilt that the Holy Spirit had brought to mind that morning. I then encouraged them to come forward as we sang and place that note on the platform, as a symbol that they were laying that matter before the Lord. I keep many of those anonymous cards as a reminder of what many of us carry in our hearts. Here is a brief sampling:

I did a lot of things that I am ashamed of. I am still bound to a lot of it. But God is still faithful to forgive.

I need to ask for forgiveness of my gossiping, critical tongue! And go to my friend and confess my sin.

I need to let go of my sexual immorality.

Forgive my anger and bad thoughts when people do small things wrong to me.

Please forgive my sins as a result of my past alcohol abuse.

Forgive our anger and frustration in our home and with our children and each other. Help us to forgive and love each other.

I need to be forgiven of years of sexual sin. Images, old ways, and a current situation hold me in bondage.

I have failed in my marriage, in my parenting, in my walk—but Christ has forgiven me. I feel alone and confused and have found a million things surfacing that I have been holding on to.

Christ, forgive my adultery. Restore my relationship with my wife. I have stopped. I want better.

Although we only rarely reveal it in a way visible to others, each of us carries a need for forgiveness that sometimes becomes an almost unbearable burden. Forgiveness from all our sins is a wonderful gift that we receive when we come to Christ. All our sins are forgiven: past, present, and future. But at the same time, forgiveness is a continuing need in our lives, because sin is a never-ending reality. We do not need a repetition of the full and free forgiveness that made us members of the family of God through saving faith in Christ. But we do need the ongoing forgiveness that is part of being His children.

The movie *The Mission* depicts a conquistador slave trader, Roderigo Mendoza, who was responsible for the capture and killing of members of a South American Indian tribe, the Guarani, who lived "above the falls." He herded them into town for sale. While doing so, he discovered that his woman had left him for his own brother. Enraged, feeling his honor challenged, he killed his brother in a duel.

In prison he was overwhelmed with remorse for his actions. A Catholic priest came to meet him and called him to repentance, but Mendoza insisted there was no penance sufficient for the sins of which he was guilty.

The priest secured Mendoza's release on the condition that he would accompany the priest and others on a journey to a mission at a mountaintop Guarani village. When Mendoza agreed to go, the priest assigned the penance. He took a large net, filled it with Mendoza's heavy armor and weapons—the remnants of his former life—tied the load to the man's shoulders, and ordered him to drag it behind him on his trek up the mountain.

The climb was excruciatingly difficult—through jungle, up steep hills, along a river, and finally up a steep, slick bluff alongside a massive waterfall. Time and again Mendoza struggled and fell, constantly putting his life at risk. Finally one of the monks took a knife and cut the load free. Mendoza refused the kindness. He retrieved the bundle and tied it on again. At a later moment, the monks approached the priest to tell him that Mendoza had done enough. The reply is potent: "He doesn't think so. And until he does, neither do I."

Finally they reached the village, the very one Mendoza had plundered. As Mendoza collapsed in front of the mission, a Guarani man recognized him and angrily moved to confront him. But he seemed to recognize what Mendoza had endured, and he used his knife not to attack him but to cut free the burden and send it crashing down the cliff. As his liberator hugged him, Mendoza sobbed—his burden lifted, a grace extended that he did not deserve.

That burden is a powerful symbol of the guilt and remorse we can drag through life, guilt that is rightfully ours. The fact that only the Guarani could truly cut Mendoza free from his burden is a powerful reminder that forgiveness can come only from those who have been sinned against. But the idea that we deal with guilt and find forgiveness by penance and by undergoing an ordeal is profoundly contrary to the New Testament. Dragging our net full of armor through our daily jungle is not the path to forgiveness. As Phillips Brooks eloquently observed, "When there are questions to be feared and eyes to be avoided and subjects which must not be touched, then the bloom of life is gone." There is a better way and that is to understand God's provision for living in forgiveness.

The idea that we deal with guilt and find forgiveness by penance and by undergoing an ordeal is profoundly contrary to the New Testament.

It has become fashionable to speak about different kinds of intelligence: intellectual intelligence, emotional intelligence, relational intelligence, and so forth. We do not talk often enough about spiritual intelligence, the consistent application of basic God-revealed spiritual principles to our lives. One of the most important passages in this regard is found in 1 John 1:5–2:2, which indicates how people forgiven by the grace of the Lord Jesus live as forgiven people, experiencing the privilege of continuing fellowship with the triune God.

This is the message we have heard from him and declare to you: God is light; in him there is no darkness at all. If we claim to have fellowship with him yet walk in the darkness, we lie and do not live by the truth. But if we walk in the light, as he is in the light, we have fellowship with one another, and the blood of Jesus, his Son, purifies us from all sin.

If we claim to be without sin, we deceive ourselves and the truth is not in us. If we confess our sins, he is faithful and just and will forgive us our sins and purify us from all unrighteousness. If we claim we have not sinned, we make him out to be a liar and his word has no place in our lives.

My dear children, I write this to you so that you will not sin. But if anybody does sin, we have one who speaks to the Father in our defense— Jesus Christ, the Righteous One. He is the atoning sacrifice for our sins, and not only for ours but also for the sins of the whole world.

Almost every week, in the process of counseling and praying with different people, I am reminded why a proper understanding of forgiveness is so central to what the Lord wants to do in our lives.

Some believers are highly sensitive to their own sinfulness, haunted by a powerful sense of falling short of the standards of a holy God, standards they aspire to but feel they consistently violate. In the process, they feel joyless and defeated and wonder whether they will ever arrive at what they consider to be a normal Christian life. They need to receive God's good news of forgiveness.

At the other end of the spectrum are those who profess to be Christ-followers but who seem utterly unaware of their own need of forgiveness, whether from God or other people. They claim to have trusted Christ and to have been forgiven once and for all. But they live as if the whole issue of forgiveness is about someone else. They're doing just fine, thank you very much! In truth, they are people who need to see God's holiness and recognize their deep need to be forgiven. John's words in this passage are clearly written to give hope to the first group and a strong warning to the second.

Note that John is writing this, his first epistle, to people who are already Christians, people who have experienced the once-for-all forgiveness of the Lord Jesus.

> *I write to you, dear children, because* your sins have been forgiven *on account of his name* (2:12 emphasis mine).

Through faith in the Lord Jesus, every believer has been fully, finally, and freely forgiven of sins, by virtue of Jesus' substitutionary death on the cross. By the judicial decree of God the Father, our righteous Judge, we stand clothed in the perfect righteousness of Christ. But at the same time, we read in 1 John 1:9: "If we confess our sins, he is faithful and just and will forgive us our sins." If we have been forgiven, why do we need to be forgiven? The important answer to this question leads us to distinguish between two kinds of forgiveness in a Christian's life, a distinction that introduces us to a primary principle of Christian living.

Two Kinds of Forgiveness

Imagine with me that a relative has deeply wronged you in a way that could result in severe legal consequences. Although he fully deserves the full weight of the law to come down upon him, you choose, for reasons known only to you, to release him from all legal liability. He is judicially forgiven, and the relationship between the two of you is now clear of all legal impediments. That does not mean that problems will never arise between you. Such personal issues may put a serious strain on your personal relationship, but they do not jeopardize his legal status. *Judicial forgiveness does not remove the need for relational forgiveness.*

The analogy is far from perfect, but it establishes an important distinction. By God's grace in Christ, we are the recipients of *judicial forgiveness*, which means that we have perfect standing with God. We are members of His forever family. But *family forgiveness* is about my ongoing enjoyment of a warm, intimate relationship with my Lord Jesus. I dearly love my children and my grandchildren. Nothing they could do would make me disown them. But, because we are sinners, things sometimes happen that damage our enjoyment of one another and that, left unresolved, could do serious damage to our relationships with one another. A healthy family relationship requires the consistent extending and receiving of forgiveness.

The same principle applies to our relationship with our heavenly Father. As our Judge He pardoned us once for all, when we trusted the Lord Jesus. But as our Father He forgives us many times, as we deal with the sins that enter our lives. In other words, 1 John 1 presupposes judicial forgiveness and describes the family forgiveness that enables us to experience the privilege of living in fellowship with our Lord. The same distinction lies behind the often misunderstood words of the Lord's Prayer:

> *Forgive us our sins, for we also forgive everyone who sins against us*
> *(Luke 11:4; see Matthew 6:12).*

We must remember that the so-called Lord's Prayer is, in fact, a believer's prayer, taught by the Lord to His followers as their distinctive prayer. We must not view it as a generic prayer that could be authentically prayed by anyone, regardless of their relation to Christ. It is for those who have already been forgiven through faith in Christ. But we are still to pray for a forgiveness that is all about our fellowship with the Father. It stands to reason that, if I refuse to forgive my fellow-believer who is also a beloved child of the Father, I cannot expect my relationship to our mutual Father to be unaffected, any more than I would expect my dad to be unconcerned if I were in the midst of a nasty squabble with one of my brothers. My status in the family would not be at stake; my fellowship in the family would be.

Judicial forgiveness is unconditional, grounded on the finished work of Christ. It is once-for-all forgiveness. But just as the petition in the Lord's Prayer is for daily bread, not a once-for-all provision of food, the petition for forgiveness is also about daily forgiveness as a daily need. I need forgiveness daily because I sin daily! And the forgiveness I seek is parental, not judicial. This parental forgiveness is conditional, based upon my relationship with others. This is a sobering challenge to every Christian: "If you forgive men when they sin against you, your heavenly Father will also forgive you. But if you do not forgive men their sins, your Father will not forgive your sins" (Matthew 6:14–15). These dynamics of forgiveness *within* the spiritual family are very important. Such forgiveness requires forgiving-ness.

The Character of God Sets the Terms of Fellowship

The first major truth John lays out is that *the character of God sets the terms of fellowship*. The affirmation found in verse 5 determines everything about the spiritual life: "This is the message that we heard from him and declare to you: God is light; in him is no darkness at all." Light is a powerful biblical symbol that represents the perfection of God's character.

To say that God is light is to speak of His *moral purity*, the total absence of sin or moral imperfection. He is the holy One, set apart from all that is corrupt or contaminating. As light, He cannot and will not coexist with the darkness of moral evil and sin.

To say that God is light is also to speak of His *perfect truth*. Darkness often symbolizes ignorance or error in the Bible. But such things find no place in the person of the perfect God.

To say that God is light is also to affirm that He has *life-giving power*, since life flourishes in the light.

All of this is intended to remind us that the *character* of God determines the ground rules of spiritual fellowship. God is God.

Because He is perfect, He cannot change for the better, and He will not change for the worse. The conclusion is obvious: If we are to have fellowship with Him, we must adjust to Him, not vice versa. The Christian life is radically God-centered, not human-centered. He is the Sun around whom all else revolves.

But some will not accept that. They live with the illusion that we set the conditions of our relationship with God, that God adapts to us. John constructs our featured passage around three repetitions of the statement: "If we claim . . . " (vv. 6, 8, 10). These are, in fact, false claims that distort the fundamentals of living in fellowship with God.

These claims are put in unique first-century language, but it is not difficult to find their twenty-first century counterparts. The first, in verse 6, says, "Sin in my life is no big deal; I can tolerate it (and so can God)." The second declares, "Sin isn't really my fault; I can just ignore it" (v. 8). The third contends, in verse 10, "Sin isn't my problem; I've redefined it."

I have never heard anyone use the exact words of the first of these claims, but the concept, "If we claim to have fellowship with him and yet walk in darkness . . ." is surprisingly common. Here is a professing Christ-follower who, although he or she emphatically claims to be experiencing fellowship with the God who is light, is living a lifestyle contrary to what God has revealed about His character and His will. To "walk in the darkness" is to engage in activities contrary to and outside the realm of light. *Walking* also indicates that this is a sustained pattern of conduct, a lifestyle, not just a momentary lapse. Surely you've had the experience of entering a dark building after being in bright sunlight and finding yourself momentarily unable to see. But your eyes quickly adjust to the lack of light, and the darkness becomes comfortable. Sadly, the same thing happens in the spiritual realm. We make choices that put us in the realm of darkness, and so we find ourselves accustomed to walking outside the realm of God's presence. The realm of moral or spiritual darkness is disorienting at first. But all too soon we adjust.

The claim that we are in fellowship with the God of light while we are walking in moral and spiritual darkness amounts to a claim that sin doesn't matter. There is a New Age spirituality that counsels us to trust and follow our own inner voice. Spirituality becomes a matter of connecting with "the deepest truth within," but such spirituality has no necessary connection with morality. A news story in the *Los Angeles Times* on the contemporary merging of religious ideas quotes Scott Bartchy, director of the Center for the Study of Religion at U.C.L.A.:

> People are picking out the cherries that interest them [in various religions]. . . . People who come up with their own kind of spiritual mix don't have to contend with the "constraints" and "demands" of major religions. You are told that God loves you or that the spirit of the cosmos thinks favorably of you, or as some Hindu teachers love to say, "My goodness, all of you are recycled stardust."[1]

That empty notion of "spirituality" has settled like a fog on our society, and many professing Christians have unknowingly inhaled it. Or others will contend, "The Lord is so loving; all He's concerned about is my happiness!" (an idea that usually means that I can do whatever I want, because "He's cool with it"). Or others tell us that "God doesn't sweat the small stuff," while categorizing as "small stuff" a remarkable number of things the Bible would call sin.

But neither the apostle John nor the Holy Spirit will allow us to play such games. If that is our claim, "we lie, and do not live by the truth" (v. 6). The idea that we can tolerate sin in our lives while we enjoy fellowship with God is a direct contradiction. We may deceive others, and we may even deceive ourselves, but the truth is clear: We are not living in the truth or light of God. People who hold to this view of truth will obviously be blind to their need of family forgiveness.

It is God, and God alone, who sets the terms of fellowship. We can have fellowship with Him only if we are where He is. God cannot and will not change His standards. He will never compromise His essential character to accommodate us. He cannot enter darkness without opposing and destroying it. Light is not just where

It is God, and God alone, who sets the terms of fellowship. God is; it is *who* He is. As light, He exposes the darkness of sin, opposes it, and ultimately destroys it. So all fellowship with Him must be in the light. And the truth of God's essential nature leads to a promise: "If we walk in the light, as he is in the light, we have fellowship with one another, and the blood of Jesus, his Son, purifies [or cleanses] us from all sin" (v. 7).

"Walking in the light" does not mean living a perfect or sinless life. Otherwise we would have no need for the blood of Jesus to "keep on cleansing us from all sin." We are to live in the sphere of God's truth and holiness, walking "in" the light, if not "as" the light. God never ignores sin, but He does forgive it. However, denial of sin always produces distance. I can be in the family but out of harmony with the Father, if I persistently refuse to deal with those things He patiently and persistently reveals, things out of step with our family values.

Human families work in the same way. My children are always my children, but, even now, when they have children of their own, I would not permit them to come into our house with wet, mud-covered hands and feet that could soil our furniture. No one loves his grandchildren more than I do. But if they were to try to come to the dinner table covered with dirt, they would quickly discover that this isn't an option. They need cleansing, and it will do them no good to remind me that I love them or that they aren't as dirty as I claim.

Cleansing is the condition of table-fellowship. But provision for that cleansing is close at hand. In fact, when my children were young, I would lead them to the sink and do the cleansing for them. I want them to join us at the table, but on my terms, not theirs—terms of light, not darkness.

In the same way, the Father has made advance provision for our cleansing through the work of His Son on our behalf. He doesn't ignore sin; He forgives it at great price. His blood paid the penalty for our sins (*blood* being a vivid biblical metaphor for His life poured out in violent and sacrificial death). The death of Christ is the complete provision for my relationship with the triune God, not only for justification and salvation in terms of my legal standing, but also for continual cleansing from daily sins that disrupt my fellowship. His blood has continuing power because we have continuing need before Him.

Confession of Sin Is the Means of Fellowship

In this 1 John passage the apostle presents a second truth, that *confession of sin is the means of fellowship.* Once again he begins with a false claim made by a professing Christ-follower: "If we claim to be without sin . . . " (v. 8). The expression is literally, "If we say we have no sin." Although it is possible that John has in mind a person who flat out denies that he has sinned, we should probably understand his statement in a somewhat different way. The apostle John uses the expression "to have sin" four times in his gospel (9:41; 15:22, 24; 19:11). Each time it suggests the idea of *having guilt*, not just of having done something wrong. For example, in John 9:41, Jesus confronts the Pharisees with the accusation, "If you were blind, you would not be guilty of sin [literally, have sin]; but now that you claim you can see, your guilt remains." The phrase rendered "you would not be guilty of sin" is the same as that found in 1 John 1:8: "to have no sin." John 19:11 reads, "The one who handed me over to you [i.e., Pilate] is guilty of a greater sin [has greater sin]." Thus, for John, the expression "to have sin" has the connotation of having guilt.

The person who claims to "have no sin" is therefore not claiming to be sinless but to be guiltless. He is not saying that he has done no wrong, but that what he has done does not produce guilt. In contemporary terms, "It's not my fault." Someone else is to blame. If such an idea was present in the ancient world, we need to admit that it is almost omnipresent in ours! We have perfected rationalizations, explanations, and excuses. Psychologists and lawyers have mastered the art of proclaiming that people who have done wrong are not thereby guilty. Theirs was a mistake, not a sin; a sickness or a syndrome, not a moral fault; a habit or an addiction, not a transgression. In a million and one ways, we train ourselves to avoid, evade, or explain why we do not bear guilt for what we have done. We are all victims, not violators! Even Christians are not immune to this cultural disease.

On April 13, 2001, a man named Luther "Luke" Casteel walked into a pub in Elgin, Illinois, with four guns. Determined to repay an insult, he opened fire while laughing and shouting, "I'm the king!" and "I'm a natural-born killer." Within moments, two people were dead, and sixteen others lay wounded. His victims were total strangers. At his trial, he was asked if he had any remorse. "Any feeling I have in that regard I'll keep between myself and the Lord," he said. "As ironic as this sounds, I'm a passionate, giving person. I like to think I'm a pretty good person. I'm not the one to hurt anyone that doesn't provoke me."[2] The message is clear: "I'm not guilty, because I was provoked." No wonder Jeremiah 17:9 proclaims,

> *The heart is deceitful above all things,*
> *and beyond cure. Who can understand it?*

Self-deception is precisely what John tells us is involved in the claim that we have no guilt: "we deceive ourselves and the truth is not in us" (v. 8). Such self-deception puts us in a worse state than the deceiver of verse 6, because a self-deceived person has lost touch with reality, having shut truth out of her life. If I can look at things in my life clearly contrary to God's character and revealed will, dismissing them with the assertion that they're not my fault, I am afflicted with a serious spiritual disorder. The Father, like any loving parent, loves us too much to allow us to stay in darkness and self-deception. He will do whatever it takes to discipline us so that we will face and deal with the reality of our sins, a process vividly described in Hebrews 12:4–13.

There is, however, an alternative to self-deception. Spiritual intelligence means a return to reality about ourselves: "If we confess our sins, he is faithful and just and will forgive us our sins and purify [or cleanse] us from all unrighteousness" (v. 9). This simple statement has proven to be of tremendous help and direction to many Christians and deserves careful consideration. What does it mean to confess our sins? Because the context is describing fellowship with God, it almost certainly refers to confession to God, rather than to other people. I had memorized this verse as a teenager. But when I was learning Greek and reading this verse in the original language for the first time, a light went on. The word translated *confess* has the root meaning "to agree, to say the same thing." Suddenly I saw "confession" in a different light. It wasn't just admitting that I had done something wrong. Rather, it was agreeing with God about my behavior, saying the same thing He does about what I have done. When I confess, I side with God as a witness against myself, seeing my actions as He does, saying about them what He says, and responding to them as He does. It is the attitude modeled by David in his brokenhearted outpouring of confession to his Lord in Psalm 51:3–4:

Spiritual intelligence means a return to reality about ourselves.

> For I know my transgressions.
> and my sin is always before me.
> Against you, you only have I sinned
> and done what is evil in your sight,
> so that you are proved right when you speak
> and justified when you judge.

Robert Packwood represented the state of Oregon in the United States Senate for twenty-six years. Then, in 1992, shortly after he had narrowly held his seat in an election, the *Washington Post* published a lengthy front-page story outlining the senator's unwanted sexual advances to ten women, mainly former staff members and lobbyists. Initially Packwood emphatically denied the charges, attacking the credibility of his accusers. But sixteen other women soon came forward with similar accusations. Under mounting pressure Packwood reversed his position and apologized for his behavior: "I never intended to make anyone feel uncomfortable. . . . I will seek professional help to see if alcohol caused the alleged misbehavior." Whatever else can be said about that statement, it falls considerably short of authentic confession. "I didn't mean it, and it really wasn't I but alcohol."

Confession of sin is not an occasional event for a Christian, but a continuing lifestyle.

We have become used to such guarded and calculated declarations, carefully crafted by lawyers. But such "confessions" are laughable in the presence of the all-knowing God, who reads our hearts. Authentic confession causes us to bring into the light those things the Father already knows about us and consciously to see them as He does, standing alongside Him as He sees our actions. But it is not simply the knowledge that God already knows that propels our confession. It is also the recognition that, when we are in the presence of the Father, we are in a place of grace. Mark McMinn puts it beautifully:

> In the presence of grace we can afford to open our eyes to our brokenness and honestly confront our sin. Sometimes we assume that places of grace begin with open and frank confession. Maybe we have it backwards. Maybe open confession begins with the promise of grace. . . . In places of grace such as this we can dare to tell the truth to ourselves and to the other.[3]

Confession of sin is not an occasional event for a Christian, but a continuing lifestyle. All confession begins with the exposure of our sin, sometimes by the Word of God, perhaps by the inner conviction of the Spirit of God, or perhaps through the insight of another person. We are to live with the mindset expressed in Psalm 139:23–24:

> *Search me, O God, and know my heart;*
> *test me and know my anxious thoughts.*
> *See if there is any offensive way in me,*
> *and lead me in the way everlasting.*

When sin is exposed, it needs to be confessed, in the first place to the Lord, and then, as necessary, to others.

The promise to those who confess their sins is clear and unambiguous: "he is faithful and just and will forgive us all our sins" (v. 9). This forgiveness isn't arbitrary but is grounded in the provision of the Lord Jesus on the cross. As we have already read in 1 John 1:7, "the blood of Jesus, his Son, purifies us from all sin." He forgives what we confess. But the verse goes on to say that He does more than that: "[He will] purify us from all our unrighteousness." We are never fully aware of all those things in our lives that are outside of and contrary to the will of God. Such knowledge would be a crushing burden that we could not bear. But when we confess the sins that God reveals to us, He not only forgives those sins but also cleanses all other areas of unrighteousness in our lives. As a result we are made totally fit for fellowship with the God who is light. To receive the gift of salvation, we confess Jesus as Lord (Romans 10:9–10); to experience the joy of fellowship salvation makes possible, we confess our sins to the Father.

The Cross of Christ Is the Basis of Fellowship

The third spiritual truth that John lays out is that *the cross of Christ is the basis of fellowship.* Once again, we hear a claim made by some professing Christ-followers: "If we claim we have not sinned . . ."

(v. 10). Apparently some were living so far into the darkness of self-deception that they denied that they had any personal history of sin. Such people must either radically redefine sin or find a way to rationalize it. Over the years I have talked with people in pastoral situations who have engaged in the most amazing acts of redefinition and rationalization. Such people often admit that in most cases their action—adultery or theft—would be wrong. But not theirs. They had prayed, and the Lord had given them peace about their adulterous relationships. Or their employer had mistreated them, and they had taken only what was rightfully theirs. So, in their cases, sin wasn't sin. In fact, it was the will of God!

One can only pray for such people. John has no patience with such foolish talk. If we say such things, "we make [God] out to be a liar and his word has no place in our lives" (v. 10). God's standards are not made of plastic, to be twisted in whatever shape we desire to meet the desires of our heart or the dictates of our culture. All too often the media informs us that some major denomination has met and declared some new standard of moral or sexual behavior, a standard that overturns or ignores clear biblical affirmations. But such declarations impugn the integrity of the God of truth and make it clear that a tragic proportion of the modern church has cut itself loose from the authority of God's eternal Word. A famous psychotherapist once boasted, "I teach my patients never to feel guilty about anything." I'll bet he made them pay in advance, so he would be sure to collect his fees! The denial of guilt and sin is nothing less than a denial of reality, and there is no fellowship with God in the land of make-believe.

In his first epistle John wants us to understand that, because God is light, sin is always unacceptable: "My dear children, I write this to you so that you will not sin" (2:1). But Scripture is always intensely realistic. Although sin is never acceptable, it is nevertheless inevitable. Until we receive our resurrected bodies, we will fight one long battle with sin, and we will not always be victorious. We should not sin, but we do. That is why John immediately continues: "But if anybody does sin. . . ." The way he expresses himself makes it clear that we will sin. But God's provision for sin is the person and work of our Lord Jesus Christ. John uses two remarkable pictures to describe our Savior.

First, He is our legal Advocate, who represents us before the eternal throne, "one who speaks to the Father in our defense." John borrows a term used to describe a legal defender, an attorney, who would come alongside a person in a court of law to represent him and plead his case. Satan is the great "accuser of our brothers" (Revelation 12:10), who incessantly defames God's people and points out their many faults and failings, seeking to disqualify them from salvation or from the privilege of fellowship with God. But our court-appointed defense attorney, the Lord Jesus Christ, meets each of His accusations with a perfect response. He has impeccable credentials, since He is "Jesus Christ, the Righteous One" (2:1). But He does not plead the innocence of His clients. Rather, He declares the perfection of His work on our behalf.

How and why? This leads to the second picture. Jesus is "the atoning sacrifice [literally, the propitiation] for our sins, and not for ours only, but for the sins of the whole world." Behind the word *propitiation* is the idea of the wrath and anger of a holy, righteous God against all sin. God cannot simply ignore sin; it is an offense against His essential being. A propitiation is a sacrifice that settles the claims of justice. As the perfect sacrifice, the Lord Jesus met all the righteous requirements of a holy God against us. We can enjoy fellowship with the righteous God, not because He ignores our sin, but because He forgives it, based upon the atonement made through the death of the Lord Jesus. His is a death sufficient for all possible claims made against it, because it is "not only for our sins but also for the sins of the whole world" (2:2). All are not forgiven, but it is not because the death of Christ was insufficient!

The basics of the Christian life set out by John in this remarkably helpful passage are very simple. Our Christian life begins when, through the gracious work of God within us, we see our need, own our sin, and confess Jesus as our Lord and Savior. The call to salvation is a call to the God who is light. The blood of Christ brings us into the light of a life with God, and our entire Christian life is to be lived in the light. Yet, sinful as we are, we continually veer off into the darkness. When sin enters, God graciously exposes it to us. If we deny what he shows and we see, we head off into the darkness. But if we own it and confess it, we experience the gracious cleansing of our defilement by our Father through the work of His Son on our behalf, receive His family forgiveness, and maintain our walk in the light.

So, where are you walking right now?

Chapter 5

FROM FORGIVEN TO FORGIVING

*S*ometimes distant news hits close to home. This was the case when I heard that a Moody Bible Institute alumna, a young missionary named Bonnie Witherall, had been killed by a terrorist attack in Lebanon. When she had answered the door of the prenatal clinic where she worked, she was shot in the head three times by a man brandishing a pistol. My daughter and son-in-law both graduated from Moody, apparently at about the same time as Bonnie, so I called Heather with the news. She didn't immediately recognize Bonnie by her married name, but she soon realized that Bonnie and her husband Gary had been her classmates. In fact, my son-in-law Cat had often played soccer with Gary. Instantly, remote events and the seemingly endless spiral of violence in the Middle East had become very personal.

Bonnie's killer has never been apprehended. He almost certainly was a fanatical Muslim, angered by the presence of Christians serving needy people in the area. He vanished into the refugee camp. When her husband Gary heard the news, he immediately rushed to the clinic. He tried to enter to see his wife, but police were now treating the area as a crime scene. Two soldiers tackled him and pushed him to the floor. They confined him to a room next door for several hours while his bride's body remained on the floor of the clinic, and police officials dealt with the evidence. What a traumatic experience! Yet two days later he sent an emotional e-mail to family and friends around the world. "While lying on the floor in grief near Bonnie I felt God's presence and a deep desire to just forgive whoever did that. It is a forgiveness that seems to cost everything that I am but I recognize God's forgiveness of the sin in my life."

C. S. Lewis once wrote, "Everyone says forgiveness is a lovely word, until they have something to forgive."[1] On a more mundane level, a man in our congregation told me, "Forgiveness is like passing a kidney stone. It hurts like crazy at the time but feels so good when it's gone!" I've never had a kidney stone, but I have had to forgive, so I can understand at least part of his comparison.

Many of us live with a list, written in our minds if not on paper, of people we believe have wronged, hurt, misused, misjudged, or mistreated us. Sometimes there are no specific names—just generalized feelings of bitterness or anger that erupt in unpredictable ways. We live in a world in which people are capable of doing horrific things to one another, usually in the name of "getting even." There is not even one of us who does not have something to forgive, as well as some things for which we need forgiveness. Every week the media is full of accounts of terrible acts committed by people in retaliation or revenge for something done against them, real or imagined. An unforgiving spirit inspires war, traumatizes entire nations, destroys marriages, divides families, ruins friendships, splits churches, and poisons communities. The effect is also intensely personal. As Everett Worthington observes, "Unforgiveness is a jumble of emotions. Resentment, hostility, hatred, bitterness, simmering anger and low-level fear interlace in the tapestry of unforgiveness."[2]

"Everyone says forgiveness is a lovely word, until they have something to forgive."

C. S. LEWIS

The Lord Jesus obviously believed that forgiveness, both from God and of other people, is one of the most significant issues in human life. He talked about it directly and often, gave His life to make it possible, and taught that His people were not only forgiven, they were also to be forgiving. One of the most powerful places He does that is in the passage before us in this chapter, the parable of the unforgiving servant, found in Matthew 18:21–35.

Then Peter came to Jesus and asked, "Lord, how many times shall I forgive my brother when he sins against me? Up to seven times?"

Jesus answered, "I tell you, not seven times, but seventy-seven times.

"Therefore, the kingdom of heaven is like a king who wanted to settle accounts with his servants. As he began the settlement, a man who owed him ten thousand talents was brought to him. Since he was not able to pay, the master ordered that he and his wife and his children and all that he had be sold to repay the debt.

"The servant fell on his knees before him. 'Be patient with me,' he begged, 'and I will pay back everything.' The servant's master took pity on him, canceled the debt and let him go.

"But when that servant went out, he found one of his fellow servants who owed him a hundred denarii. He grabbed him and began to choke him. 'Pay back what you owe me!' he demanded.

"His fellow servant fell to his knees and begged him, 'Be patient with me, and I will pay you back.'

"But he refused. Instead, he went off and had the man thrown into prison until he could pay the debt. When the other servants saw what had happened, they were greatly distressed and went and told their master everything that had happened.

"Then the master called the servant in. 'You wicked servant,' he said, 'I canceled all that debt of yours because you begged me to. Shouldn't you have had mercy on your fellow servant just as I had on you?' In anger his master turned him over to the jailers to be tortured, until he should pay back all he owed.

"This is how my heavenly Father will treat each of you unless you forgive your brother from your heart."

Matthew has constructed his gospel around five major blocks of the Lord's teaching.[3] Matthew 18 is the fourth of these, and its theme is the relationships Christ-followers are to build in the new community of kingdom citizens, the church. Let us now consider the parable found in verses 21–35. Later, we will consider the preceding section of verses 15–20, with its special emphasis on difficult relationships. I recognize that taking it in this order reverses the sequence of the text and weakens or obscures the connection that inspires Peter's question in verse 21. But I have chosen this method because this parable sets out in graphic form the central message that moves us forward in our understanding of the larger subject of forgiveness: *Forgiven people must be forgiving people.*

The Problem of Forgiveness: Keeping Score

The concern of Jesus in the immediately preceding verses is "regaining a brother," a fellow believer who has sinned against us. Although the Lord had nowhere used the word *forgiveness* in this section, Peter was alert enough to recognize that forgiveness is precisely what Jesus had been speaking about. Regaining an offending brother meant forgiving him. But Peter also knew, perhaps from hard personal experience, that forgiveness is not an easy matter. It is all well and good to talk about "gaining a brother," but just how much forgiveness does Jesus expect? Surely there are limits to the number of times you have to forgive someone who keeps on doing you wrong! Peter would also have known that the rabbis of his time debated this very issue. Their conclusion, later recorded in the Talmud, was that a person could and should be forgiven, but only three times: "If a man commits a transgression, the first, second and third time he is forgiven; the fourth time he is not forgiven."[4] Peter intuitively knew that his Lord would have a higher standard than they would, so when he blurted out the question that had bothered him, he upped the ante: "Lord, how many times shall I forgive my brother when he sins against me? Up to seven times?" (v. 21).

The concept of forgiveness lies at the heart of the Christian gospel. But there is a danger that we talk about it glibly, without considering how complex and challenging an issue it can be. Too often, we reduce one of the greatest challenges of life to a simple "just do it."

Solomon Schimmel, writing from a Jewish perspective, reminds us that it is not quite so simple.

> It is easier to preach glibly the virtues and pragmatic value of forgiveness and reconciliation than it is truly to understand why, when, whom, and how to forgive. Forgiveness is a complex phenomenon. It is affected, among other factors, by the nature and extent of the injury we have suffered, our relationships with the person who has hurt us, our sense of self, and whether or not the person whom we contemplate forgiving has expressed remorse for his deed or sought to repair the emotional, physical, or material damage he has wrought upon us. Mature forgiveness entails difficult emotional and intellectual work. It is a skill that needs to be cultivated, a virtue that needs to be acquired by self-training. When practiced thoughtlessly or simplistically, it is ineffective and counter-productive and can even be dangerous to oneself, to the person forgiven, and to society.[5]

So give Peter credit. He recognized both the importance of the issue and the higher standards Jesus would bring to the discussion. He more than doubled the forgiveness standards of the respected religious leaders of his time. But because his question—"how many times shall I forgive my brother when he sins against me?"—provides the basis of the parable that follows, it is worth considering carefully.

First, the specific issue is the action of a brother, a fellow believer, rather than of a stranger or an outsider. He is talking about those who are close to us, the very kinds of people it is often hardest (but most important) to forgive. Any list of people we need to forgive will begin with family members, close friends, fellow church members, and people with whom or for whom we work. These are the people with the most capacity to hurt us, as well as those whose friendship matters most.

Second, Peter's question is about someone who has sinned against us. A real wrong has been done, not just a misunderstanding or an accident. Forgiveness operates in the realm of sin. As G. K. Chesterton observed, "Charity [Christian love] certainly means one of two things—pardoning unpar-

Forgiveness is one of the hardest things we are called to do, not something we dispense wholesale.

donable acts, or loving unlovable people."[6] Third, in the light of the preceding discussion in Matthew 18, Peter's question assumes that the wrongdoer has repented. He has owned what he has done and turned from it. The relationship between forgiveness and repentance is of great importance, and we will return to it in a later chapter.

Peter is perceptive. He knows that forgiveness is one of the hardest things we are called to do, not something we dispense wholesale. True forgiveness is costly, not cheap. We live in a fallen world, where people fail and hurt one another, often intentionally. He also knows that the way of Christ rises far above the normal patterns of the world and continually pushes us out of our comfort zone into the realm of grace and compassion. His suggestion that Christ's followers are to forgive "up to seven times" is itself an incredibly high standard that pushes all of us way past our natural instincts.

I'm sure Peter was dumbfounded by the Lord's response: "I tell you, not seven times, but seventy-seven times" (v. 22). The *King James Version* gives the more familiar rendering "seventy times seven times." The translations differ because the Greek expression is ambiguous and could be translated either way.[7] In one sense the distinction is not important. The Lord is not making a mathematical statement. His point is that our forgiveness is to be unlimited, not carefully counted. However, the translation "seventy-seven times" alerts us to an Old Testament passage that contains exactly the same expression in the Greek translation, the Septuagint. There is good reason to believe that Jesus has Genesis 4:23–24 in mind and that He is intending a direct contrast with the infamous song of Lamech:

Adah and Zillah, listen to me;
wives of Lamech, hear my words.
I have killed a man for wounding me,
a young man for injuring me.
If Cain is avenged seven times,
then Lamech seventy-seven times.

If Lamech is celebrating revenge, in Matthew 18:22 the Lord is commanding forgiveness. The contrast is intentional and important. The alternative to forgiveness is revenge. The antidote to revenge is forgiveness.

Our natural response to sins committed against us involves rage, retaliation, revenge, getting even. Revenge takes many forms, from open retaliation to silent punishment. But it is all about paying back. My college rugby coach drilled it into us: "Don't get mad; get even." There's a lot of Dirty Harry in all of us: "Go ahead. Make my day." That is the way of the world. "You'll pay for this." And when we do, we find ourselves playing a very dangerous game. We are inevitably self-serving in our damage assessment. Almost invariably I will judge that you have hurt me far more than I could possibly have injured you. As a result, when I will strike back, I will follow the pattern of Lamech and strike a little (or a lot) harder.

Even as I write, the hockey world is reeling from a brutal on-ice attack by one of its star players on the member of another team. The injured player had given the first team's best player a concussion in an earlier game, in what the first team considered a dirty play. They came into the next game between the two teams talking about "payback time." When it came, it was in the form of a brutal blind-side attack that left the recipient with career-threatening injuries and the offender with a season-ending suspension. The attacker was full of contrition, but there can be no doubt that a revenge mindset led to the play. Revenge tends to set in motion an ever-escalating spiral of retaliation, with an ever-increasing infliction of pain. Revenge enjoys seeing another suffer, receiving what we believe he deserves.

The more he suffers, the greater our pleasure. But somewhere we cross a line and find ourselves in a terrible place. There is another danger. Revenge leads me to generalize beyond my particular experience, to extend the range of my anger. I know of cases in which a woman hates virtually all men because of the appalling acts of just one man, as well as cases in which a man despises all women because one woman mistreated him. Other people seethe with fury at all members of a particular ethnic or religious group because of the evil acts of one or a few. So racism and sexism flourish. Such is the song of Lamech. But the Lord calls us to something very different. Under His lordship, unrestrained revenge gives way to unlimited forgiveness.

One of my favorite stories concerns a man who was bitten by a dog, later found to be rabid. This was at a time when medical science could do very little for such a condition. The man was transported to the hospital, where he was given a battery of tests. The tests, unfortunately, revealed that he had contracted rabies. When the doctor came into the room to break the news, he was both troubled and compassionate: "Sir, we will do all we can to make you comfortable. But I cannot give you any hope of recovery. I would advise you to put your affairs in order as quickly as possible." The man sank back into his bed in despair. But some time later he rallied his energy and asked for pen and paper. He then began to write feverishly, filling sheets of paper with names. When the doctor returned, he found his patient hard at work and commended him for working on his will. He was startled by the reply: "This ain't no will. This is a list of people I'm going to bite before I die."

As tasty as revenge seems at first bite, it inevitably turns bitter. What results is an endless cycle of retaliation, seen on a world scale in the battle between the Palestinians and the Israelis and on a smaller scale in far too many families. The Lord fully intends to take our breath away, to stop us in our tracks, by calling us to forgive, whether seventy-seven times or seventy times seven times. He is not giving us a literal number so we can keep count. He is calling us to a new way of life, challenging our natural instincts and putting us on an entirely different path. His people are forgiven people, who must become forgiving people, dispensing God's astounding grace to others. Such forgiveness opens the door to new ways of relating.

The Parable of Forgiveness: The Unforgiving Servant

To drive home His point, the Lord launches into a story. The parable takes us into the workings of a great empire, a powerful king, and his high officials. For reasons that aren't disclosed, the king decides to audit his affairs and require an accounting from each of his officials. One of his men, a powerful governmental official in his own right, given the amount of money under his authority, is summoned before him. The accounting has revealed that the man owes "ten thousand talents." Rendering financial currencies into another time and language is difficult, but we need to recognize that this is a truly astonishing amount. Ten thousand (*myrioi*) represents the highest Greek number, while a talent was the largest unit of measuring wealth. One talent was composed of six thousand denarii, a denarius being a day's wage for the average worker. Ten thousand talents, then, amounts to about two hundred thousand years' wages for the average worker or billions of dollars in modern terms. He could have owed so much money only by a massive misappropriation of funds, draining off royal resources at an astonishing rate. Sadly, recent scandals in the corporate sphere have made us aware that such behavior also occurs in real life—even today.

This man obviously has not misappropriated such a massive amount of money overnight. He has been engaged in a deliberate, determined, and carefully devised fraud. He is like a modern Third-World dictator, plundering and impoverishing his country, while living lavishly and squirreling a fortune in an off-shore bank. He is a predecessor of the modern overpaid corporate executive who votes himself a huge salary and stock options and then cashes in his stocks, while the company goes bankrupt. This man, however, is neither a king nor a chief executive. He is in a position of accountability and responsibility. His misuse of funds on such a scale must have inflicted suffering on a great number of people. But he hasn't saved anything. He has squandered it, and now nothing is left. He cannot make even partial repayment. His debt is incomprehensibly large and his resources are nonexistent. There is a spiritual application we should not miss. The king represents God, and I am the evil servant. My sin makes me criminally guilty and spiritually bankrupt before a holy and righteous God.

The servant's debt is astronomical, his guilt is inescapable, his resources are completely inadequate and his doom is certain. The king could order him executed for such dereliction of duty and personal betrayal. However, he does not. Instead, he orders his guards to sell the family—the man, his wife, and his children—into slavery, "to repay the debt" (Matthew 18:25). His actions not only defrauded his king, they have now victimized innocent members of his own family. Sin has a way of doing that. It inevitably brings unintended collateral damage. Selling people into slavery for their debts was common practice in the ancient world, where legal protections such as bankruptcy did not exist. Certainly the king had no hope of recovering even a small percentage of his debt by selling the man's family. This was an act of punishment, intended as a warning to his other servants. And it is a punishment richly deserved.

Desperate, the man begins to beg for mercy. Falling to his knees before the king, he pleads for time: " 'Be patient with me,' he begged, 'and I will pay back everything' " (v. 26). The suggestion is laughable. Because he has squandered all his resources and defrauded his king, he has no possibility of meaningful employment. The debt is so enormous that no amount of time would be sufficient. But, amazingly, "The servant's master took pity on him, canceled the debt and let him go" (v. 27). This is a marvelous picture of forgiveness.

First, it reminds us that *forgiveness is about the forgiver not the forgiven*. The king is motivated purely by his own mercy, not the man's merit. The king chooses to grant forgiveness simply because he takes "pity"; the evil servant clearly has not earned it and does not deserve it. The king is moved by compassion, just as a holy God, being the gracious God He is, chose to initiate the plan of salvation and provide forgiveness through faith on the basis of the sacrificial death of His Son, the Lord Jesus Christ. In the final analysis, forgiveness is about the character of the forgiver.

Second, *the forgiver pays what the forgiven owed*. The king has a rightful claim on the ten thousand talents. It is his money. By forgiving the debt, he forfeits all claims on it. In fact, he is paying the debt so the offender can go free. Not only is the man not imprisoned, but his debt is forgiven. He "canceled the debt" (v. 27) can be rendered he "erased, wiped out, forgave the debt." The king, in fact, absorbs the loss. He doesn't establish any kind of repayment plan. He takes the cost on himself. This is of great importance. *Forgiveness is free to the forgiven, but costly to the forgiver, because the forgiver pays.*

This is an insight that brings us to the heart of the gospel. At its heart, forgiveness involves a substitution. The offended pays the debt owed by the offender. That is why the One who took our place on the cross was not an innocent third party whom God made to pay for our sin; it was the very God against whom we had sinned who took the price upon Himself. We owe an unpayable debt to a holy God; the Lord Jesus paid an infinite price. God does not simply dismiss our sin; He pays for it through the Lord Jesus. We are forgiven people because our triune God has paid an amazing price! We cannot earn forgiveness, but we can receive it as a gift through faith in Jesus.

That would seem to be the end of the story, but it isn't. The wicked servant leaves the presence of his king a free man. One would imagine that such an experience would indelibly mark his character, forever changing his attitudes and relationships. Unfortunately he goes out from the king with his debt cancelled but his heart unchanged. That becomes evident when he sees a fellow servant who owes him money—a hundred denarii. That is a significant amount of money, one hundred days' wages. But it is a mere one–six-hundred-thousandth of the debt he had owed the king! Surely he could overlook such a debt in the glow of his own forgiveness.

But he can't or won't. He refuses simply because he is not willing. His own forgiveness has given him neither humility nor empathy toward a person whose failing is a paltry imitation of his own. Instead he confronts the man, seizes him by the throat, and demands, "Pay back what you owe me!" (v. 28). Amazingly the man falls before him and uses words almost identical to those the evil servant himself used before the king: "Be patient with me, and I will pay you back."[8] But those words find no response in the servant's hard heart. He refuses him completely, and "went off and had the man thrown into prison until he could pay the debt" (v. 30). By throwing the man into prison, where he could do nothing to repay the debt, the servant is not only being unforgiving, he is being vindictive. He makes the man's condition worse and transfers the burden to other members of the man's family, who are the only ones in a position to find the money that would set him free.

Several things should be noted. The man had a legal right to act as he did. The law was on his side. The second servant had failed to meet his obligations. But he had no moral right to receive forgiveness gratefully for his own debts while spitefully refusing to extend it to others. We should also notice that an unforgiving spirit shrivels the soul. It turns us into hard, cruel people. Ken Sande makes some very helpful observations about the dynamics of forgiveness:

> If someone has sinned against you, part of their debt is also owed to you. This means you have a choice to make. You can either *take* payments on the debt or *make* payments. You can take or extract payments on a debt from others' sin in many ways: by withholding forgiveness, by dwelling on the wrong, by being cold and aloof, by giving up on the relationship, by inflicting emotional pain, by gossiping, by lashing back or by

seeking revenge against the one who hurt you. These actions may provide a perverse pleasure for the moment, but they exact a high price from you in the long run.[9]

Even by pagan standards, the servant's behavior is reprehensible. Other royal servants, who must have been astonished when this guilty man was pardoned, are now stunned to hear of his present behavior. They are not interested in analyzing his behavior. Rather, they are so upset by the obvious inappropriateness of what they have witnessed that they approach the king to report on his conduct. Their king has shown himself to be a ruler of grace and compassion. This man's behavior has violated the values of his sovereign's kingdom. They knew that the servant was a forgiven man. They expected him therefore to be a forgiving man. Their response is a stark reminder of the watching world's response when followers of Christ, who proclaim to the world that they have been fully forgiven by a holy God at a costly price, refuse to forgive those who have wronged them. They rightly see the behavior as nauseatingly hypocritical.

An unforgiving spirit poisons the community in which it lives, and an unforgiving, forgiven person becomes an open scandal. Jerry Sittser knows the issue of forgiveness from the inside, since his mother, wife, and daughter were all killed in a collision caused by a drunk driver crossing the center of the highway. He writes out of his own experience:

> It is easy to spot unforgiving people. They leave a trail of evidence everywhere. They take offense easily, and they caress hurts that sometimes go back years, even to childhood. They rehearse the wrongs done to them as if reciting a script. They are absolutely convinced that they were—and are— victims. . . . Unforgiving people become so preoccupied with the wrong done to them—which may be and often is severe and painful—that they cannot see the wrong in them. Obsessed by their own pain they become oblivious to the pain

that they inflict on others—on their children, their spouses, their friends, even God.[10]

Such people destroy the churches, the marriages, the families, and the friendships in which they live.

Hearing the news of his servant's appalling behavior, the king immediately summons the man. His anger is clear: "You wicked servant. I canceled all that debt of yours because you begged me to. Shouldn't you have had mercy on your fellow servant just as I had on you?" (vv. 32–33). The king calls the man "wicked," not because of the debt he had accrued and been unable to repay, but because of the forgiveness he refused to extend. That is a powerful statement. For a forgiven person to be unforgiving is not merely unfortunate or inappropriate, it is wicked! Forgiveness is free, but it creates an obligation. "Shouldn't you?" is literally "didn't you have an obligation to?" God does not pour His grace into us so that we will become a Dead Sea, taking in His blessings but not giving them out, but so that we will become a conduit of grace to others.

The parable ends with a powerful description of the king's response: "In anger his master turned him over to the jailers to be tortured, until he should pay back all he owed" (v. 34). The "jailers" are literally "the torturers." Torture was not allowed in Jewish prisons, but it was a common practice in the Roman world and in Judah under Herod. Obviously the man could never pay back his massive debt, and torture would only worsen his condition. He has condemned himself to a life sentence. If we turn this parable into an allegory, where every detail has a direct correlation to some spiritual truth, we find here a situation where God employs a band of torturers and where our forgiveness can be forfeited by our refusal to forgive others; we may even invent a concept such as purgatory. But parables are not allegories, and such an interpretation would contradict what the Lord teaches elsewhere about both the character of God and the finality of our forgiveness. However, what this closing picture does show is the complete incompatibility of a forgiven person with an unforgiving spirit. Even more profoundly, it forces the question of whether a person who refuses to forgive has ever really experienced in a personal way the forgiving grace of God. Can an unforgiving, unchanged heart have truly met the heart-changing God? Could a true Christ-follower act as this man did?

The imagery of the torture chamber suggests another important fact about an unforgiving spirit. When I refuse to forgive another, I allow that person and that past event to have a controlling influence on my life. I never get rid of it. I remember one young man who told of the heart-chilling moment when his angry father said he wished that this son had been the one who died, rather than the child who had died

When I refuse to forgive another, I allow that person and that past event to have a controlling influence on my life. I never get rid of it.

in infancy. Those poisonous words festered in that teenager's heart, producing first anger and then hatred, a hatred that poisoned many of his following years. His father's words and attitude were nothing less than evil. No other word will suffice. Yet that young man will continue to be tortured by them, until he chooses to let them go to the heavenly Father. Many of us who feel pain fail to recognize it as having a source in our unforgiveness. Everett Worthington eloquently describes the process we often follow:

> Practicing unforgiveness is a trap. We start into the trap
> of unforgiveness by thinking it's a safe place to be. We worm
> our way inside inch by inch. We pass sharp wires that face
> the center of the trap. When we are inside, practicing habitual
> unforgiveness, we do not want to go back. To forgive, we must
> face the jabs of confronting our unforgiving character traits
> and the stabs of trying to change. We can wallow miserably in
> guilt and self-condemnation. Or we can face the jabs.[11]

The Principle: Forgiven People
Must Be Forgiving People

Jesus concludes His parable with a pointed word to His disciples, Peter most of all: "This is how my heavenly Father will treat each of you unless you forgive your brother from your heart" (v. 35). The Lord makes it clear that the authentic community of His followers is composed not only of forgiven people, but also of forgiving people. We have been forgiven a massive debt by a holy God through the work of Christ, and although others may be guilty of serious sins against us, their debt is trivial compared to what we have been forgiven by a holy God. To the extent that we realize this truth, we will understand that we have been called to a lifestyle of forgiveness that cannot be limited to three or seven or seventy-seven or even seventy-times-seven occasions.

As we saw in chapter 1, God's Word consistently declares that God's forgiveness is full, free, and final.

As far as the east is from the west,
  so far has he removed our transgressions from us (Psalm 103:12).

For I will forgive their wickedness
  and will remember their sins no more (Jeremiah 31:34).

"Son, your sins are forgiven" (Mark 2:5). We are forgiven on the basis of the work of Christ upon the cross, not on the basis of our performance or even of our forgiving of others. But Christians are not merely forgiven; they have been regenerated by the Holy Spirit and been made new people in Christ, not only with a new standing but also with a new heart. Therefore a forgiven person has the nature of his Father; although we may struggle to forgive others, the indwelling Spirit will push us to a lifestyle of forgiving. It would seem that a truly unforgiving person has never truly been converted, because his or her heart remains unchanged. Yet only God knows the reality of a person's salvation. But it is clear that a believer who refuses to forgive will come under the disciplining hand of God. The central message is very clear: *Forgiven people must be forgiving people.*

The parable challenges me to recognize that an unforgiving spirit is hateful to our forgiving God. To celebrate my forgiveness but to see no implications for my treatment of others is to be blind to the meaning of the crucifixion. The very experience of being forgiven should produce in us profound humility. I deserve something entirely different from what I actually receive *The very experience of being forgiven should produce in us profound humility.* from my heavenly Father. How can I face others with a self-righteous arrogance or a determined closing of my heart? To have been forgiven means that I have rejected any idea of moral or spiritual blamelessness. I have failed, and receiving forgiveness means that I have faced my failures and received the gracious deliverance of my God. An unforgiving spirit is so profoundly contrary to the way of Christ that even pagans can see the incongruity. Forgiveness from God should produce in me empathy toward those who need my forgiveness. There are many consequences to unforgiveness—broken relationships, resentments and bitterness, hardness of heart. But the most important of all is an estrangement from the heart of a gracious God.

Forgiving others is a response to God's forgiveness. We need to remind ourselves of the extent of our debt to a holy God; we need to understand the great cost of our own forgiveness through the Lord Jesus. Because we have been forgiven by the King, we need to be forgiving of those who have sinned against us. Such forgiveness is not an option but an obligation, a choice to obey God by an act of the will. The final phrase of Matthew 18 adds another thought: "forgive your brother from your heart." Forgiveness is not a perfunctory act, but a heart-searching, heart-felt gift that we extend to others in the name of Christ.

The cross is where we both receive and learn forgiveness. Forgiveness at such a price humbles our hearts and softens our spirits.

We see our own need of God's grace. Then as the Spirit of God flashes across the screens of our minds the names and faces of those who have wronged us—spouses, parents, children, friends, or acquaintances—there is a call to go and do likewise. We recognize that they too stand in need of grace, and we become willing to give to them what we ourselves need from our Father. We live out our forgiveness not only in thankfulness but also in forgivingness. We forgive because we know that we both need and have received what we do not deserve: forgiveness.

My friend Rob tells the story of God's grace at work in and through his life:

> My father died when I was eight months old, and my mother remarried just after my third birthday. My stepfather was at first aloof, and as I grew older, I saw him to be obsessive and controlling. When I was about twelve, my stepfather called me one day, in a real temper over a trivial task that I had not done to his satisfaction. He completely lost control of himself and punched me in the face, breaking my nose and laying me out unconscious. That day, fear turned to hate. As I grew stronger, the day drew inevitably nearer when some incident would spark an argument between us, and I would take my revenge.
>
> Thankfully, I found Christ in my middle teen years and became his follower. One of the first things he did was to overwhelm me with his love, unconditional acceptance, and forgiveness. One of the first things God asked of me, almost as evidence of my changed heart, was to give up my bitterness toward my stepfather although his behavior had become increasingly irrational and the marriage to my mother failed. In the light of the forgiveness I had received, this was easy.
>
> As an adult I continued to send Christmas cards and basic family news even long after I had moved away. I never heard anything in return. Then two summers ago, I was contacted by

a hospital when my stepfather had been admitted following a stroke. I arranged to visit and found a dejected little old man. At our first meeting, he cried and said he was sorry for the way he had treated me as I grew up. I was finally able to tell him how I had been able to forgive him because of how Jesus had forgiven me. While I had lived in freedom down the years, the guilt of his actions had obviously been gnawing away at him. I was finally able to set him free too. We haven't grown close since, but meet every once in a while. I keep praying that he will also find the forgiveness of Jesus himself before his earthly days are done.

Chapter 6

LEARNING TO FORGIVE

*I*n 1944 young Simon Wiesenthal was a prisoner in a concentration camp located on the outskirts of the town in which he had been raised. One day his work detail was marched through the town where he had once lived. Along the way his group passed a military cemetery, with a sunflower planted on each grave. He could not help but contrast that careful remembrance with the mass grave that almost surely would be his destiny, with other corpses piled on top of him, unmarked and unknown. They finally came to the high school Wiesenthal had attended, a building full of memories of anti-Semitic harassment now turned into a makeshift hospital for wounded German soldiers. Wiesenthal's group carried cartons of rubbish out of the hospital. While working on this detail, he was approached by a Red Cross nurse. "Are you a Jew?" she asked. When he indicated yes, she summoned him to follow; she led him to the bedside of a young German officer covered with bandages, barely able to speak. He had asked her to find a Jew to whom he could speak, and Wiesenthal had arbitrarily become that person. The officer said his name was Karl. He knew he was dying, and before he died, he needed to talk about something that was torturing him. As he summarized the story of his life and military action, Wiesenthal tried to leave three times, but the man reached out to grab his arm each time. He needed to tell him the story. Finally he told of an atrocity he'd participated in while pursuing the retreating Russians. Thirty German soldiers had been killed in booby traps set by the Russians. In an irrational act of revenge against the innocent, he and his men rounded up a group of three hundred Jews, herded them into a house, doused it with gasoline, and set it on fire with grenades. They then shot anyone who tried to escape. He recounted with great emotion his memory of hearing the screams, of watching terrified women and children jump from the building, and of his own gunfire. One scene in particular haunted him: a desperate father and mother jumping with a child with black hair and dark eyes, only to be riddled with bullets. The man kept talking, recounting a later battle, when he had been given orders to shoot a similar group of unarmed Jews. That time he wouldn't or couldn't squeeze the trigger; as he froze in place, a shell exploded, giving him the wounds that were now taking his life.

His story told, he pleaded with Wiesenthal:

> I cannot die . . . without coming clean. This must be my confession. . . . I am left here with my guilt. In the last hours of my life you are with me. I do not know who you are, I only know that you are a Jew and that is enough. . . . I know that what I have told you is terrible. In the long nights while I have been waiting for death, time and time again I have longed to talk about it to a Jew and beg forgiveness from him. Only I didn't know whether there were any Jews left . . . I know what I am asking is almost too much for you, but without your answer I cannot die in peace.[1]

Wiesenthal stood there in silence, wrestling with what he should do. "At last I made up my mind, and without a word I left the room."

The officer died, unforgiven by a Jew. But that was far from the end of the story for Wiesenthal. He anguished about his response. Had he made the right choice? He discussed it with his fellow prisoners in the death camp. After the war he visited Karl's mother in Germany, trying to judge the authenticity of the young officer's remorse. Finally, twenty years after the end of the war, Wiesenthal, now an international figure as a Nazi hunter, felt compelled to write the story. He ended it with two plaintive questions: "Was my silence at the bedside of the dying Nazi right or wrong?" and "What would you have done?" He then sent it to theologians, moral and political leaders, and writers for their answers to those questions. The story, with thirty-two responses, was published in 1969 in a book titled *The Sunflower*, which was then reissued years later with thirty-two new responses and eleven retained or revised from the first edition. The responses are fascinating. The vast majority of contributors agreed that Wiesenthal did the right thing. The Jewish respondents were unanimous; Wiesenthal did not have any obligation, or even any right, to forgive the man. Only the victims could forgive the perpetrator of such an atrocity, and the man did not display the marks of true repentance as defined by Jewish tradition, which includes reparation. Others contended that the entire notion of asking for and granting forgiveness was dangerous. Herbert Marcuse, a Marxist philosopher who was very influential in the troubled decades of the sixties and seventies, wrote, "One cannot, and should not, go around happily killing and torturing and then, when the moment has come, simply ask, and receive, forgiveness. In my view, this perpetuates the crime. . . . I believe the easy forgiving of such crimes perpetuates the very evil it wants to alleviate."[2] A few of those who identified themselves as Christians did suggest that the Christian ethic called for a person to forgive, even in such a situation.

A book such as *The Sunflower* takes the issue of forgiveness out of the realm of the idealistic and the sentimental and makes us face the ugly realities of life in a fallen world. At times issues related to forgiveness become anything but theoretical. Anytime I stand before a congregation to proclaim God's Word, I know that in the congregation there are marriages that will disintegrate if some do not find a way to forgive, families that will unravel, friendships that will collapse, and groups that will split. I also know that some listeners have been done great evil by marriage partners, parents, employers or employees, supposed friends, or complete strangers. And I know that you may be reading this book because you feel a deep need to forgive or to be forgiven. Others have watched sadly as a friend's life has unraveled over an inability or unwillingness to forgive or to admit the need of forgiveness.

In recent years researchers have devoted a great deal of attention to questions of forgiveness. Much of their work, done in purely secular terms, is extraordinarily helpful. It is not hard to see the escalating damage caused by unforgiveness on the large scale of international crises in the Middle East, the Balkans, Ireland, and the subcontinent of India-Pakistan. But researchers have also documented that unforgiven or unforgiving people have higher rates of stress-related disorders, cardiovascular disease, and clinical depression, as well as lower immune system function and higher divorce rates. Unforgiveness is deadly, in more ways than one!

But what does forgiveness look like? Is it something we do automatically? Do we do it immediately? Is it a single act or a process? Do we wait until we feel ready to forgive? Do we require the other person to repent, or is forgiveness personal and internal, something we do for ourselves? If we forgive, does that mean we must immediately return to a persistently abusive relationship? These and a host of other practical questions require good answers. As always, the best answers begin to come when we listen carefully to the master Forgiver, our Lord Jesus.

Perhaps the most compressed, succinct statement about forgiveness found on the lips of Jesus is recorded in Luke 17:3–4. His words deserve careful attention and need to be read in the larger context of verses 1–10:

> *Jesus said to his disciples: "Things that cause people to sin are bound to come, but woe to that person through whom they come. It would be better for him to be thrown into the sea with a millstone tied around his neck than for him to cause one of these little ones to sin. So watch yourselves.*
>
> "If your brother sins, rebuke him, and if he repents, forgive him. If he sins against you seven times in a day, and seven times comes back to you and says, 'I repent,' forgive him."

The apostles said to the Lord, "Increase our faith!"

He replied, "If you have faith as small as a mustard seed, you can say to this mulberry tree, 'Be uprooted and planted in the sea,' and it will obey you.

"Suppose one of you had a servant plowing or looking after the sheep. Would he say to the servant when he comes in from the field, 'Come along now and sit down to eat'? Would he not rather say, 'Prepare my supper, get yourself ready and wait on me while I eat and drink; after that you may eat and drink'? Would he thank the servant because he did what he was told to do? So you also, when you have done everything you were told to do, should say, 'We are unworthy servants; we have only done our duty' " (emphasis mine, vv. 3b–4).

In Luke 17 Jesus is setting forth kingdom values for His followers. Strikingly, His message is built around a warning: "So watch yourselves" (v. 3). On the one hand, we need to guard against causing others to sin. On the other, we need to resist the temptation to keep those who have sinned against us in an emotional penalty box, making them serve endless hard time for their offenses. The message is not especially hard to understand, but it is penetrating and convicting. In fact, the statement about forgiving seven times a day was so counterintuitive that it caused the Lord's hearers to cry out: "Increase our faith!" (v. 5). The disciples instinctively know that they can obey the Lord's directions only by depending on Him.

True Forgiveness Begins by Dealing with Sin Honestly

The Lord's initial words are deceptively simple: "If your brother sins, rebuke him" (v. 3). But they are extremely important and communicate at least three foundational aspects to the giving and receiving of forgiveness. Jesus is not giving us a simple recipe that we are to follow in rote fashion, but He is giving us the essentials that must be present.

Define the Offense Carefully

First, *we must define the offense carefully:* "If your brother sins. . . ." The use of the term *brother* puts this in the context of kingdom relationships and reminds us that the primary place where forgiveness needs to be lived out is within the community of faith, the band of Christ-followers who are called to obey and imitate their Lord. This is not to suggest that the Lord's words do not apply outside the church; it is to say that they are of first importance within the church. Christians, more than any others, are to forgive one another. That, of course, applies with special force to Christian marriages, families, and churches.

Equally important is the obvious, but essential, recognition that the Lord Jesus is talking about sin, specifically about someone who "sins against you" (v. 4). This must not be passed over quickly. Many things may irritate, annoy, or upset us about someone else. Those things may require enduring; they do not involve forgiving. In a later chapter we will discuss what it means to be forbearing. Sometimes we feel that someone has wronged us. But the truth is that jealousy, insecurity, or ambition easily distort our perspective. In the Bible, Miriam was jealous of Moses, and Saul of David, but in neither case was the feeling justified. Someone disagreeing with us or hurting our feelings does not necessarily bring us into the realm of forgiveness. Not all wounds are created equal, which is why Proverbs 27:6 tells us that

> *Wounds from a friend can be trusted,*
> *but an enemy multiplies kisses.*

Forgiveness operates in the realm of sin, when there is violation of God's standards of behavior in my relation with another.

Forgiveness never minimizes the reality of sin. This means that forgiveness cannot mean ignoring the reality of evil. *Forgiveness cannot be our first response.* John Ensor reminds us of the priority of wise love, as he vividly portrays the foolishness of some suggested responses to evil:

If I come across a man raping a woman, I cannot love both of them in the same way. . . . Love is inherently *moral* in character and demands a moral force that is as much opposing as it is defending. I can't go up to the struggling, terrorized woman and the overpowering assailant and say, "I love you both just the same, and so does God. He doesn't want you to harm this girl, but please don't think He is angry at you right now. Because God is love, He doesn't get mad. Isn't such love amazing?" The woman would denounce my love as sick and worthless, even cowardly and evil. She would know that love must have a *passionate commitment* to right over wrong. It must be willing to vindicate and disarm; to reward and to punish. To act in love in this situation I must hate what the attacker is doing and push him aside, scream my lungs out for help, grab the woman, and run.[3]

Therefore, forgiveness does not involve *excusing* an act. If it can be excused, it needs to be understood, not forgiven. Forgiveness is about the inexcusable.

Nor does forgiveness involve *ignoring* or denying sin, turning a blind eye to the misdeeds of another, pretending it didn't happen. Such a response indulges sin, rather than dealing with it surgically by the hard work of forgiveness. By keeping it in the darkness, we allow the evil to remain unchallenged, putting others at risk.

Forgiveness is not *trivializing* sin, trying to put it in the best possible light. C. S. Lewis said it well: "Real forgiveness means steadily looking at the sin, the sin that is left over without any excuse, after all allowances have been made, and seeing it in all its horror, dirt, meanness, and malice."[4]

The Lord is not talking about *burying* sin, under the naïve assumption that "time heals all wounds." Untended wounds do not automatically heal. As Mark McMinn says, "Time heals clean wounds. Soiled wounds fester and infect."[5] The same thing happens both in our inner being and in our relationships when we attempt to suppress

Those denied offenses have a way of continuing to pump their poison into the systems where they live.

the sins done to us. Those denied offenses have a way of continuing to pump their poison into the systems where they live.

Note that the Savior is not talking about simply *forgetting* sin, as is suggested by the naïve cliché "forgive and forget." Often such an idea gains credence by quoting the biblical idea that God "forgets" our sins. That language is certainly used, for example, in Hebrews 10:17:

> *Their sins and lawless acts*
> *I will remember no more.*

But we must not misread that to mean that our sins are somehow erased from God's memory. If so, He could hardly be the all-knowing God! He would know almost nothing of human history. How could He have inspired the Bible, which graphically records the failures of even the greatest of saints? He didn't forget their sins; He recorded them so that all future generations would know about them and learn from them. So when God says that He does not remember our sins, it means that He does not remember them *against* us, that He does not treat us on the basis of our sins. Besides, our minds do not function like computers with their convenient "delete" function. We *do* remember the bad things others have done to us. The central issue is not that I forget, but what I do when I remember how the person has wronged me. Gregory Jones puts it well:

> It is largely a mistake to say, "Forgive and forget." Rather, the judgment of grace enables us, through the power of the Holy Spirit, to remember well. When God promises to "blot out [Israel's] transgressions" and "not remember [Israel's] sins" (Isaiah 43:25; see also Jeremiah 31:34), God is not simply letting bygones be bygones. Rather, God is testifying to God's own gracious faithfulness.[6]

It is possible that we genuinely do not remember what some-one has done against us. On the one hand, that may mean that the incident was relatively trivial, hardly amounting to the level of an act requiring forgiveness. On the other, the human mind can some-times deal with profound pain by hiding it in some deep recess of one's being. About such "forgetting," Lewis Smedes wisely writes, "The pains we *dare* not remember are the most dangerous of all. We fear to face some horrible things that once hurt us, and we stuff it into the black holes of our unconsciousness where we suppose it cannot hurt us. But it only comes back disguised; it is like a demon wearing an angel's face. It lays low for a while only to slug us later, on the sly."[7] In such a case, the only way to forgive is by remembering. It is impor-tant that we do not make a simplistic connection between forgiving and forgetting. True forgiveness requires a careful look at what has actually happened to us.

> *It is important that we do not make a simplistic connection between forgiving and forgetting. True forgiveness requires a careful look at what has actually happened to us.*

Perhaps here, in this discussion of defining the offense, we should briefly note two things that are said about forgiveness: first, that we may need to forgive God; second, that we need to forgive ourselves.

I do not want to quibble about words, but it is extremely impor-tant that we think clearly about this first point. Forgiveness always involves sin. Because God can never sin, it is always wrong to speak about forgiving Him; He has not, cannot, and will not ever sin against us. I have met many people who blame God for what has happened to them, but the blame is misplaced. Behind it is the sense that we are somehow entitled to some things from His hand. We may need to come to terms with what the sovereign God has permitted in our lives. We may even feel the need to vent our anger to God or our disappointment with how He is working. The Psalms, the book of Job, and the writings of Jeremiah carry many illustrations of such outbursts. But in nearly every case the writer follows with an acknowledgment that his anger is misplaced. The language of forgiveness does not apply. Faith does not mean that we necessarily understand God's ways or purposes, but it does mean that we are to trust His goodness and submit to His purposes.

The concept of "forgiving myself" is somewhat different. Logically, if I have sinned, I am the offender, the perpetrator, not the victim of my actions. Clearly I have no moral right to "forgive myself" for what I have done. On the other hand, my actions have harmed me, because sin always boomerangs. The harm may be severe, and I may feel a combination of guilt, shame, disappointment, and anger at myself. When people speak about forgiving themselves, they nearly always are talking about alleviating such feelings. Let me note several things. First, such talk often carries the underlying assumption that I, somehow, am better than other people and should be above such behavior. There is a significant element of pride in this. ("I can see why others would do this, but not why I would.") Second, there is danger of turning forgiveness inward, so that my focus is on how I feel rather than on what I have done. My goal should be deep repentance and character transformation more than emotional release. Most important, what I need to develop is a robust confidence in God's forgiveness and a grateful reception of the forgiveness of the other person. I do not need to forget what I have done as much as I need to face what I have done, building a firewall of protection against recurrence and walking in self-doubt and God-reliance. Thank God that genuine repentance and God's forgiveness do bring the restoration of joy! When David, in Psalm 32:1, writes,

> *Blessed is he*
> *whose transgressions are forgiven,*

his joy comes not from the fact that he has forgiven himself, but that God has forgiven him.

Confront the Sin Courageously

The second implication of the Lord's words is that *we must confront the sin courageously*. When the Lord commands, "If your brother sins, rebuke him" (v. 3), He is clearly telling us that we must hold people accountable for their behavior. This obviously requires that we have carefully and prayerfully determined that the other person's behavior is truly sinful. In such a case, we are not called to ignore the behavior or simply to endure it. The word the Lord uses calls us "to speak seriously, to warn, to challenge."

I don't think it is possible to overstate the importance of this step. It means I am to speak *to* the person directly, not *about* him to others. We are not to criticize or to nurse grudges, but rather honestly to confront the offender with the sin involved in her behavior. This introduces a very important distinctive of biblical forgiveness. It is not simply an internal process that I engage in for my own sake; it is also an interpersonal process that I engage in for the larger good, of both the other person and the community in which we participate. To forgive without confronting short-circuits the process. The goal of such confrontation is not to express our anger or to get something off our chests, but to bring about repentance, restoration, and reconciliation. It also is for the benefit of others who will be victimized if this behavior is not challenged for what it is. In calling us to this behavior, Jesus is reflecting the instructions of the Old Testament, such as those found in Leviticus 19:17–18:

> *Do not hate your brother in your heart. Rebuke your neighbor frankly so you will not share in his guilt.*
> *Do not seek revenge or bear a grudge against one of your people, but love your neighbor as yourself. I am the Lord.*

Most of us will find the Lord's words tremendously challenging. When we have been mistreated, the last thing we want to do is to face the offender. It is much easier to complain about him to others or to bear the wrong in silence, while we avoid and withdraw, or perhaps to put on a good public face, despite what we are feeling inside. We have an instinctive fear of the potential unpleasantness of confrontation, and we realize that going to the other person may resemble walking through a field strewn with landmines. But the Lord leaves us no option; He calls us to the risky business of challenging the person about his sin.

Honesty requires us to admit that some people enthusiastically jump on a command like this. They seem to relish the task of rebuking others for their sins and shortcomings. If we enjoy the prospect of rebuking another for her sin, we need to remember that the Lord Jesus condemns a judgmental, critical spirit, a subject we will return to in a later chapter. But we should not miss the point: True forgiveness requires an honest confronting of sin. Anything less cheapens and short-circuits the process.

Confront the Sin Properly

Although the Lord does not expand on the process of rebuking here, in the light of what He teaches elsewhere, we need to understand a third foundational aspect: *We must confront the sin properly.* In a closely related passage in Matthew 18:15, Jesus expands on the process: "If your brother sins against you, go and show him his fault, just between the two of you. If he listens to you, you have won your brother over."

It has become common to emphasize the therapeutic benefits of forgiveness. Lewis Smedes writes of "our need to forgive for our own sakes. Every human soul has a right to be free from hate, and we claim our rightful inheritance when we forgive people who hurt us deeply."[8] Another writer goes so far as to say, "Make a commitment to yourself to do what you have to do to feel better. Forgiveness is for you and not for anyone else."[9] I do not want to deny the therapeutic benefits of forgiving another or miss the obvious point that, if the other person rejects my gift of forgiveness, I am the only one to benefit by the process. But we do need to decentralize it. Forgiveness must not be reduced to a simply internal and personal process. It is not just about me. The Lord Jesus did not forgive us for His sake, but for ours! And I must remember, walking in the steps of His love, that forgiveness is not "for me and not for anyone else." Although it certainly benefits me in a host of ways, it is not just about me and my healing. The hope is to gain my brother, the very one who wronged me, to bring him back to spiritual health too. It is also about the larger good: the protection of others and the promotion of the community's well-being.

Before we move on, we need to return to the word the Lord uses, translated "rebuke." The standard Greek lexicon defines it as follows: "express strong disapproval of someone, *rebuke, reprove, censure* also *speak seriously, warn* in order to prevent an action or bring one to an end."[10] It is a strong word, but it reminds us that there are times when it is appropriate to inflict pain. This stands against some ideas. One writer suggests that "This then is total forgiveness: not wanting our offenders to feel guilty or upset with themselves for what they did and showing there is a reason God let it happen."[11] He also suggests that, because many of the people who have hurt us will not believe that they have done anything wrong at all (an observation I am sure is completely true), we should usually forgive them in our hearts and say nothing to them. I think that his suggestion is sentimental, but not scriptural. It is clearly wrong to "confront" someone with a goal of hurting that person. That is revenge, not constructive confrontation. But the Lord does insist that I am to confront him. Furthermore, it strikes me as somewhat dangerous to give the reason "God may have let it happen." Although we occasionally may be able to discern this (as Joseph did in Genesis 50:20), such talk is significantly out of place before the person has repented (as the brothers had, in the Genesis passage).

Several passages do give us a handle on how we should approach a sinning brother and how best to go about "speaking the truth in love" (Ephesians 4:15).

- We should do it privately, not publicly. "If your brother sins against you, go and show him his fault, just between the two of you" (Matthew 18:15).
- We should do it humbly and repentantly, not arrogantly and self-righteously. "Why do you look at the speck of sawdust in your brother's eye and pay no attention to the plank in your own eye? How can you say to your brother, 'Let me take the speck out of your eye,' when all the time there is a plank in your own eye? You hypocrite, first take the plank out of your own eye, and then you will see clearly to remove the speck from your brother's eye" (Matthew 7:3–5).
- We should do it spiritually, not carnally. "Brothers, if someone is caught in a sin, you who are spiritual should restore him gently. But watch yourself, or you also may be tempted" (Galatians 6:1).
- We should do it reluctantly, not gleefully.
- We should do it restoratively, not punitively.

True Forgiveness Requires the Offender to Own Sin Repentantly

The Lord's next phrase (Luke 17:3) tells me not only how I am to respond if I have been sinned against, but also how I am to respond if I have been the offender. The simple words contain a wealth of significance: "and if he repents. . . ." The way I respond to the courageous confrontation of someone who cares enough to challenge the sinful behavior in which I have engaged is character-defining. In fact, the book of Proverbs makes it clear that my response to appropriate rebuke is an index of my wisdom. One of the best-known verses in Proverbs (9:10) is introduced by Solomon's description of the response to rebuke:

Whoever corrects a mocker invites insult;
whoever rebukes a wicked man incurs abuse.
Do not rebuke a mocker or he will hate you;
rebuke a wise man and he will love you.
Instruct a wise man and he will be wiser still;
teach a righteous man and he will add to his learning.
The fear of the Lord is the beginning of wisdom,
and knowledge of the Holy One is understanding (9:7–10).

Genuine repentance goes deeper than apology or the expression of regret. Chapter 11 will delve into the subject of repentance, but here I note that the biblical words describe a change of mind that produces a change of direction. Repentance involves more than a feeling of wrongdoing or regret, and it produces more than an apology. Suppose that on a visit to my home, you accidentally spill something on my new carpet. Clearly you ought to apologize. But you would not need to repent. Or suppose you realize you should end a romantic relationship. You will almost certainly hurt the other person. This may cause regret.

Genuine repentance goes deeper than apology or the expression of regret.

And you may need to apologize for the awkward way you handled the breakup. But the breakup itself does not require repentance (although wrong behavior in the relationship may!). I return to an earlier point. If someone has hurt me, that does not necessarily mean the person needs to repent. Repentance is the way we deal with sin. It is deeper than regret, because it involves a determination to change. But repentance can be genuine, even if it does not instantly produce complete change. After all, Luke 17:4 suggests someone could repent seven times in a day! Also note that the repentance described here is not merely felt, it is expressed (if he "comes back to you and says, 'I repent' . . .").

It's important to recognize that *without repentance, the process is broken.* The Lord Jesus says, "If he repents, forgive him." True forgiveness flows toward repentance. The ideal is clear: I am sinned against; I confront the offender; he sincerely declares his repentance; I declare my forgiveness. That is the way it is supposed to work. The fact is, however, that sin contaminates everything. Too many times, there is no repentance. Sometimes the offender will not admit the sin, no matter how clear the facts. ("I didn't do anything wrong.") Sometimes he has no regret for the sin. In fact, he may celebrate the evil he has done. ("You had it coming.") At other times, the person cannot repent; he has died or is too ill to respond. What do we do then? Do we forgive anyway, even when the offense sits there, like a huge elephant, in the middle of the relationship? We must return to this important question at length. At this point, it is sufficient to observe that we need to let go of the offense, even when the other person won't. Romans 12:19 says, "Do not take revenge, my friends, but leave room for God's wrath, for it is written: 'It is mine to avenge; I will repay,' says the Lord." That process takes us beyond Luke 17:3–4. In this context, Jesus *does not* tell us to declare our forgiveness to an unrepentant offender. In fact, were we immediately to forgive this unrepentant person, we may well only harden his conscience and accelerate the repetition of the sin.

True Forgiveness Is Given Graciously and Generously

The Lord Jesus does not turn aside to discuss the case of the unrepentant. His command is clear: If he repents, forgive him. *To forgive is to wipe the slate clean, graciously to cancel a debt.* The word for *forgive* that Jesus uses has various meanings. It means "to set free, release" and in certain contexts "to wipe away, release." A forgiven person has been set free from his past behavior and had his record wiped clean.

The Lord underlines the amazing nature of forgiveness by His words of clarification in verse 4: "If he sins against you seven times in a day, and seven times comes back to you and says, 'I repent,' forgive him." We can stumble on this if we dwell on puzzling over how a person could truly repent, not merely apologize, seven times a day. Clearly the Lord is not encouraging cheap words of regret, but He is saying that His followers are to imitate the amazing grace of God, which pursues us in the midst of our determined sinfulness and waywardness. Forgiveness is not earned but given, and, in imitation of our Father, it is to be given generously and graciously.

Note that only the wronged party can forgive. This was part of my problem with the prayer of forgiveness for Osama bin Laden and the September 11 terrorists, mentioned in the introduction. Who were we in southern California, thousands of miles away from the scene of the atrocity, to forgive Osama for what he had done to people on the East Coast? We weren't the ones desperately making the rounds of hospitals hoping to discover a missing loved one or searching the rubble for whatever remains could be found. We weren't the ones sitting by a phone anxiously waiting for a call that would never come. On more than one occasion I have had people confess to me a sin that was directed against another person or an organization and then ask for my forgiveness. But if I'm not a party to the offense, how can I forgive? I can assure them, if they have dealt with the matter biblically, that God has fully forgiven them. If their actions in some way cast a shadow over me, I can forgive them for that. But in most cases the sin isn't mine to forgive, and I need to direct them to go to those who are the victims of their behavior. Forgiveness must come from those who have been wronged, and we must be careful that we do not short-circuit the process that God intends in a desire to alleviate the pain of the person who has come to us.

I had a second, and more obvious, problem about September 2001. The Lord commands me to forgive the repentant. But Osama was taking delight in what he had done and was actively planning further atrocities. For him, the slaughter of noncombatants was a moment of high victory, not an act of sin over which he grieved. How could we declare him forgiven under such circumstances? We will return again to these questions.

We should not, however, miss the point. Jesus requires us to forgive the repentant. To forgive is to win one's brother, to reclaim him from the bondage of sin. It means to release the desire to get even or the "right" to require him to pay for what he has done. To forgive is to say, "You are free. Your debt is paid. I'll pay; not you." Forgiveness doesn't mean forgetting to remember, but remembering to forget. That sounds like a paradox, but it isn't. We *do* remember what has happened, probably every time we meet the offender. When I declare, "I forgive you," I am not engaging in an act of willful amnesia. I am committing myself not to treat you on the basis of what you have done, even though I remember very well what it was. Time may dull the pain, but it is unlikely ever to be erased completely from memory. Desmond Tutu, who led the nation of South Africa through a national process of forgiveness and reconciliation, put it well: "Forgiveness and being reconciled are not about pretending that things are other than they are. It is not patting one another on the back and turning a blind eye to the wrong."[12] Forgiveness looks sin in the eye and nevertheless speaks costly words: "I forgive you."

> *Forgiveness doesn't mean forgetting to remember, but remembering to forget.*

At the same time, we must recognize that forgiveness doesn't necessarily restore the status quo. Forgiveness isn't the same as reconciliation. Forgiveness clears the ledger; it does not necessarily instantly rebuild trust. Forgiveness is given; reconciliation is earned. Forgiveness cancels all debts, but it does not eliminate all consequences. In the Luke 7 parable we considered in chapter 3, the Lord tells of a king who forgave one of his servants of a huge debt. But he does not suggest that the king's intention was to keep the servant in his position or to lend him more money! This is extremely important. A wife who has been abused by her husband may forgive him, but she is very unwise to allow him to return to her home, unless there is clear evidence, over time, of deep change. A husband may genuinely forgive his adulterous wife, but that may not mean that the marriage can be restored. In chapter 10 we will consider the hard work of reconciliation that follows forgiveness. Here it is enough to observe that the two are related, but quite distinct.

In short, *forgiveness involves both a choice and a process.* True forgiveness cannot be reduced to a simple formula, but it is useful to consider four steps.

Face the Facts

As we have indicated, authentic forgiveness requires that we identify what has happened. There are four diagnostic questions:

- How serious was the offense? As we shall see in chapter 7, all offenses are not created equal. Some things require forbearance more than forgiveness. If I turn every offense into a Luke 17 issue, I will devastate my relationships with my intensity and self-absorption.
- How raw is the wound? This is not an issue of time alone. It is possible that I am "picking the scab" to keep it open.
- How close is the person?
- How significant is the relationship to me?

Feel the Feelings

There is a danger of "quick forgiveness," a hasty verbal declaration that keeps me from processing the violation involved. If we are in a period of emotional numbness or even denial, as we try to make sense of the violation we have experienced, we are in no condition to declare the work of forgiveness finished. Ironically, our desire for quick closure may actually prolong the process. The other extreme is the temptation to "slow forgiveness," an ongoing "I don't feel ready yet," which can be a disguised way of inflicting punishment on the offender, by consigning her to an emotional purgatory. Between these two extremes, there is an appropriate time to grieve the loss of what might have been. This will be a grief mixed with anger over the wrong done to us. But that anger, justified as it may be, must be carefully monitored in view of God's clear command: " 'In your anger do not sin.' Do not let the sun go down while you are still angry" (Ephesians 4:26).

Forgive by Making a Decision and a Declaration

Forgiveness is ultimately an act of the will, not a stirring of the emotions. For a Christ-follower, it is a choice to obey God and let it go. This is an inward choice that produces a declaration given, a promise spoken: "I forgive you." When I speak those words, I declare that the issue between us is dead and buried. I'm saying, *I will not rehearse it, review it, or renew it. When it comes to my mind, I will take it to the Lord and to the foot of the cross, not to you.*

There is an old story of a man who complained to his counselor: "Every time we argue, my wife gets historical."

"Do you mean hysterical?"

"No. I mean historical. She drags up everything I've ever done wrong!"

No. Saying "I forgive you" means I shut the door on such behavior. Some of my saddest counseling experiences have come when someone who declared, with apparent sincerity, "I forgive you," later chose to go back and reopen the file on the wrongdoing. The violation of trust that occurred in such cases made all attempts at reconciliation virtually hopeless. On the other hand, when I was fifteen, I talked my dad into letting me drive the car home from church one Sunday. However, I lost control of the car at a corner and hit a light pole, doing hundreds of dollars worth of damage to the car. I was both ashamed and afraid. As steam hissed out of the radiator, before we even left the car, my father turned to me and said, "It's okay, Gary. I forgive you." Never once, for the rest of my life, was that event ever mentioned by my father, even though it cost him a great deal of money. (I did remind him of it years later, to thank him.) And he gladly let me use the car when I did get my license. What a wonderful thing it is to be forgiven, and not to be constantly hit over the head with your past failure!

Refresh It

Forgiveness may be a decision but it is not a one-time decision. I remember, when I had forgiven someone who had hurt me deeply, how much I struggled with my feelings over the following days and weeks. I had said, "I forgive you," and meant it, but I had to remind myself repeatedly that I needed to hold on to that commitment. The sin certainly wasn't erased from my memory; in fact, I had a tendency to dwell on it, to ruminate on it over and over. So I fought an inward battle, and it was only by continually bringing it to the Lord and relying on His help that I could keep from bringing it out in the open again. Otherwise, it becomes what someone has called "hollow forgiveness," a statement without any substance, if we go on harboring our grudges. C. S. Lewis wisely observed, "To forgive for the moment is not difficult, but to go on forgiving, to forgive the same offence every time it recurs to the memory—that's the real tussle."[13] Clarissa Pinkola Estes rightly observed, "Forgiveness has many layers, many seasons. The important part of forgiveness is to begin and to continue. The finishing of it all is a life work."[14]

I have found encouragement in the story of Clara Barton, the nursing hero of the Civil War and the first president of the American Red Cross. A friend mentioned something cruel that another person had done to her and asked her, "Don't you remember?" Barton's answer is classic: "I distinctly remember forgetting that."

As Martin Luther King, Jr., said well, "Forgiveness is not an occasional act. It is a permanent attitude." That is why a declaration of forgiveness needs to be accompanied by a commitment to loving acts toward the forgiven person, regardless of how much we struggle with unloving feelings.

In 1947 Corrie ten Boom went back to Germany to preach the gospel. Her family had been caught hiding Jews. She and her sister had been sent to Ravensbruck, one of the Nazi death camps, where she had watched her sister and many others die.

After the war, in one of her meetings, she had spoken about the forgiveness of God. After the service, a long line of people waited to talk to her. She saw, standing in line, a terribly familiar face—a man who had been one of the cruelest guards in the prison camp. As she saw him, a score of painful memories flooded her mind.

The man came up to her, stuck his hand out, and said, "A fine message, Fraulein. How good it is to know that all our sins are at the bottom of the sea." Corrie didn't take his hand but fumbled in her purse. Her blood froze. She knew him, but he obviously didn't recognize her. That was understandable. After all, she was only one faceless prisoner among tens of thousands. Then he said: "You mentioned Ravensbruck. I was a guard there. But since then, I have become a Christian. I know God has forgiven the cruel things I did there, but I would like to hear it from your lips as well." Again he stuck out his hand: "Fraulein, will you forgive me?"

How could she, after all that had happened? Her hand wouldn't move, yet she knew that the Lord wanted her to forgive him. All she could do was cry inwardly: "Jesus, help me. I can lift my hand, but you'll have to do the rest." Woodenly, mechanically, she raised her hand to take his. She was acting out of obedience and faith, not out of love. However, even as she did, she experienced God's transforming grace. She writes,

> "I forgive you, brother!" I cried. "With all my heart!" For a long moment we grasped each other's hands, the former guard and the former prisoner. I had never known God's love so intensely, as I did then. But even then, I realized it was not my love. I had tried, and did not have the power. It was the power of the Holy Spirit.[15]

Chapter 7

FORGIVING OR FORBEARING?

*D*wight Eisenhower was not only the thirty-fourth president of the United States; he was also the supreme commander of the Allied Forces in Europe in World War II. In both positions he encountered more than a few challenging and difficult people, and he devised his own way of dealing with them:

> I make it a practice to avoid hating anyone. If someone has been guilty of despicable actions, especially towards me, I try to forget him. I used to follow a practice—somewhat contrived, I admit—to write the man's name on a piece of paper, drop it in a bottom drawer, and say to myself, "That finishes the incident, and, as far as I am concerned, that person." That drawer became over the years a sort of private wastebasket for crumpled up spite and discarded personalities. Besides, it seemed to be effective and helped me avoid harboring useless black feelings.[1]

Only an Eisenhower expert would be qualified to evaluate how successfully his method of dealing with problem people worked for him. But any of us can understand his reasoning. All of us encounter difficult people whom we would just as soon eliminate from our lives, even though we usually can't. Some are people who have harmed us or continue to sin against us, often in terrible ways. But most of us know a lot of people who don't so much harm as annoy or frustrate us. We would rather just avoid them and have as little as possible to do with them, keeping them at arm's length. To update President Eisenhower's method, we would gladly push the "delete" buttons on our computers' address books and consign them to our recycle bins.

However, President Eisenhower isn't our model; the Lord Jesus is. He calls us to an entirely different way of relating to people, including those who harm or annoy us. Besides, trying to discard people doesn't work. They have a way of crawling out of wastebaskets and reemerging in our lives. Even if we were successful, a life full of discarded people begins to resemble a landfill full of toxic waste. Inevitably the contamination seeps into the groundwater of our lives and poisons almost all of our most valued relationships. Some people's actions call us to the highest levels of forgiveness. Most others fall into a lesser category. They may irritate us, annoy us, or be difficult to live with, but they don't really sin against us. How do we deal with those things in other people that set our teeth on edge? God's Word speaks to that issue as directly as it does to the issue of forgiveness. One such passage is Colossians 3:12–14, where we are introduced to the "well-dressed Christian."

> *Therefore, as God's chosen people, holy and dearly loved, clothe yourselves with compassion, kindness, humility, gentleness and patience. Bear with each other and forgive whatever grievances you may have against one another. Forgive as the Lord forgave you. And over all these virtues put on love, which binds them all together in perfect unity.*

A Christ-follower is an intriguing paradox. When I trust Christ, I become genuinely new in Him. I have a new identity and a new capacity: "If anyone is in Christ, he is a new creation; the old has gone, the new has come!" (2 Corinthians 5:17). Although I am genuinely new in Christ, I am not yet completely new. In fact, complete newness awaits the redemption of my body, at Christ's return. In the meantime, God is at work, through His Spirit, to bring substantial change as I am being renewed in the image of Christ. So every Christian is both new and being renewed.

One way Scripture describes this is in terms of putting on clothing. In one sense, we are new people, wearing old clothes. Perhaps today Paul would use the model of an "extreme makeover." The essential surgery has been done, and now we need to live in a way consistent with our new identity. That means we are to take off the clothes of the old life and put on the clothes of the new person in Christ. That is Paul's picture in Colossians 3. Having described the clothes we are to "put off" in verses 5–11, Paul describes the new clothes we are to "put on" in verses 12–14. Those new clothes are the character qualities and relational practices that are patterned after Christ, rather than after the world or our "natural selves." Forgiveness and forbearance are essential garments of the well-dressed Christ-follower.

Wearing the Clothing of Forgiveness

Paul's central command in this passage is "Forgive as the Lord forgave you" (v. 13). This parallels a similar directive in Ephesians 4:32: "Be kind and compassionate to one another, forgiving each other, just as in Christ God forgave you." How did He forgive us? Generously, upon our repentance. By definition, every Christian is a forgiven person. The Christian life begins when we own our sins and failures in the presence of a holy God and understand the amazing price the Lord Jesus paid to set us free. Forgiveness is a gift we are given, not a status we attain. In both verses Paul makes it clear that forgiveness is a past event: "God forgave you." Forgiveness trumps justice. With justice, the offender pays; in forgiveness, the offended pays and sets the offender free! Forgiveness doesn't change the past; my sins don't disappear. But forgiveness does change the power of the past to control my present and my future.

Forgiveness doesn't change the past . . . but forgiveness does change the power of the past to control my present and my future.

The power of forgiveness is made clear by the terms used to describe us as God's new people: "God's chosen people, holy and dearly loved" (v. 12). God's work in Christ has bestowed upon us an entirely new identity, and we are to live on the basis of who we now are, not who we once were.

I'd like to share the story of a friend, a member of our congregation who has put on the new wardrobe of being forgiven and forgiving.

When our pastor announced he was going to do a series on forgiveness, my ears picked up. I hoped silently that I might understand how I could live "with the knowledge of God's forgiveness."

Understanding why I was struggling with such a question can be understood only as I explain a little of my need to be forgiven. The story of my life may be condensed to one basic feeling, the feeling of inferiority, a desire to fit in, a need for acceptance and a desire to have people view me as a gifted, talented, and humble Christian worker. Needless to say, such motivation is not conducive to effective Christian ministry. In fact, I was constantly seeking new places to have these feelings met. Sometimes I was more aware of these needs than at other times. I quickly became dissatisfied with my present place of ministry and often found a reason to move on to new ministries and new places. As I look back now, I "needed" to be the new boy on the block, where people would respond with the acceptance, compliments, and trust that a new minister experiences.

As years went by, this mode of operation became less and less possible and my soul was starving to death. Pretending to believe "Truth," which I found not to be working in my life, I began feeling that I had missed out on things in life, because I grew up in a Christian home, went to Christian colleges, and into ministry. I came to believe Satan's oldest lie, that God had held out on me.

I gradually allowed my thought life to grow into actions, which were both clearly unbiblical and destructive to my life, my marriage, and my ministry. I tried to deal with my series of moral lapses personally, quietly between God and me. While in a small group, I felt increasingly that I could no longer live with my duplicity. With the advice of two men of God, and the help of a Christian counselor, I confessed to my wife, family, and church, knowing I was risking losing them all. Then reconstruction began.

My heart was slowly melting, but I was "doing" what was right because it was right, not because I "felt" like it. I wanted to do what is right. It was a matter of willpower and choice, doing what I believed in my head. (Looking ahead in light of eternity, there was eternal truth.) I made the commitment, that even if I would never have my "felt" needs met by God, I would never deliberately move away from him again. My wife was especially used of God to authentically live forgiveness toward me, knowing I didn't deserve her forgiveness or love.

There is more to the story, but let me interrupt it to make Paul's point: Forgiven people are to be forgiving people. We might even go further. Forgiven people will never really lay hold of the fullness of their forgiveness by God until they become forgiving toward others. When Paul in Colossians 3:13 calls us to "forgive whatever grievances you may have against one another," he is writing about the realities of life in a fallen world.

The word *grievance* is used only here in the Greek New Testament, and it indicates not merely a personal complaint or grievance but a moral fault or wrong, a complaint grounded in objectively sinful behavior, not just in my personal sensitivity. Whenever two fallen people come in close contact for an extended time, they will have complaints against one

> *Forgiven people will never really lay hold of the fullness of their forgiveness by God until they become forgiving toward others.*

another, some trivial and others significant. Whether we are talking about families, friendships, or churches, the fact is that sinners comprise these relationships.

Forgive Because the Lord Has Forgiven

So we are commanded to forgive *because the Lord Jesus has forgiven us*. This comes as a command, not an option. Not so long ago, the media was full of the news of a dentist in Houston convicted of running over and killing her philandering husband, when she discovered him in the act of once again violating his promise to break off an affair. She not only ran him down; she backed up and did it three or four times! I was struck by the televised comment of her father-in-law: "I forgave her because I have been forgiven. I will not turn away from her." That kind of forgiveness is an act of trust in and obedience to the Holy Spirit, not simply the product of natural feelings. I show that I trust my God when I do what He says.

Imagine for a moment that you go to your doctor with a medical complaint, and he prescribes a course of treatment. However, you persistently choose not to follow his directives. A few weeks later, when you return to him with the same complaint and report your noncompliance, he once again prescribes the same treatment. You continue to disregard it. Were you to return to him with the same complaint and the same report of noncompliance, he would almost certainly address you very directly: "If you won't do what I say, find a doctor you can trust!" Or he could say, "Find a doctor you will obey." There is a direct connection between faith and obedience. Trust is seen by obedience. Faith in Christ is shown by a willingness to do what He says. That means that a primary reason I am to forgive is because my Lord has commanded me to.

People who are struggling with an issue of forgiveness often complain, "But I don't know how." My response is based on a fundamental principle: *We become forgiving by forgiving.* For years members of our church staff gave me a hard time about my computer illiteracy. I stubbornly defended my yellow-pad lifestyle, but actually I was intimidated by the process of becoming computer literate. I had never learned to type, and I didn't know how I could find time to learn in an already busy schedule. Besides, I was doing fine the way I was. So I adopted what I felt was a bulletproof response. When friends extolled the virtues of the computer and encouraged me to give it a try, I responded, "I don't type, and I don't have time to learn." Others would attempt to entice me with accounts of the massive amounts of information available at my fingertips through the Internet; it would enhance my research resources. My answer was tediously familiar: "I don't type." "But a word processor would make doing your next book much easier." "I don't type. If I could, I would." Finally, someone cut through all my excuses: "Gary, the way you learn to type is by typing." "But I don't know how to type." "So, start typing." There was no good answer. Finally, the truth sank in: You learn to type by typing. What a profound insight! So I decided to learn to type by typing, and the book you are reading is the fourth I have done by myself on a computer. Apparently, although a leopard can't change his spots, a Canadian can, at least sometimes!

The point here is the same. *You learn to forgive by forgiving.*

"But I'm not a forgiving kind of person."

"So forgive. The way you become forgiving is by forgiving."

"But you don't understand. I've never known how to forgive."

"So do it anyway. The way you learn to forgive is by forgiving."

"I'm not sure I'm ready yet."

"It's OK. The way you learn to forgive is . . ."

There is a point where to not forgive is to sin. We need to face what was done to us and feel the wrong of it. But there comes a time when, in response to God's gracious forgiveness, I must let go, both to the Lord and to the offender, of the wrong that was done to me. I am not suggesting that this is easy. As Miroslav Volf observed, "Forgiveness itself is a form of suffering. . . . When I forgive, I have not only suffered a violation but also suppressed the rightful claims of strict retributive justice."[2] It is not easy, but it is necessary.

Forgive as the Lord Has Forgiven

We are to forgive not only because the Lord has forgiven us, but *as the Lord has forgiven us*. His forgiveness was costly, not cheap. Ours will be as well. Forgiving may be one of the hardest things we ever do. Recently I watched a strong man's eyes fill with tears as he spoke of how costly it had been to forgive. To pay the price of another's sin can be agonizing. Imitating Christ and the way of the cross, we also realize that forgiveness is full and final, not partial or provisional. I will never forget a long, intense counseling session that climaxed when the wife turned to her husband and declared that she forgave him of a wrong he had committed years earlier. Something about the condescending way she said it touched a raw nerve. He exploded:

Forgiveness delayed is often forgiveness denied and punishment exacted.

"Forgive me? You've made me pay for it every day for ten years. I've paid with compound interest. There's no way you can tell me now that you're forgiving me. I don't want your forgiveness." Despite the evident hostility of the encounter, he had a valid point. Forgiveness delayed is often forgiveness denied and punishment exacted. You cannot continually extract psychological payment, and then, at a time you deem valid, claim, "I forgive you." Forgiveness is all about forgoing repayment.

The Lord's forgiveness of us is full and final and therefore freeing. That is to be the pattern of our forgiving as well. And when we forgive, our own forgiveness often becomes even more real than before. Let me continue my friend's story. (The church he mentions is the one I pastor, and I like the music.)

> I had a growing desire to be the kind of man my wife would want to marry all over again. I worked hard at being transparent, without bruising the fruit, at loving her in language she understood, and making my focus not what I felt I needed but what she needed. I was focusing on doing what was right.

Through the years that followed, I retrained for a different career, entered elementary teaching, and began attending Trinity [church]. As I sat there, I often HATED the music. I said it was because it wasn't done well, but the reality was that the song was not in my heart. With a passion I avoided pretending. I, therefore, would not participate in the music but always looked forward to our gifted pastor's teaching of the Word of God. In keeping with the question I believed I needed answered, I waited to see how Gary would answer it. I knew the answer was there, in the Word of God, so I listened and waited.

One Sunday Gary preached about those we needed to forgive. I thought I had forgiven everyone—I had dealt with those issues—but a name kept coming to mind. I really didn't like this person, but I thought I had dealt with my feelings about him. Our pastor finished by asking us to write on a card the name of the person we needed to release. So I wrote that name on the card.

Some weeks later my wife noticed I was singing, a little bit, during worship time. She, I'm sure, didn't know if she should ask about it, but we eventually discussed it. What happened was a surprise. I thought I needed to know how to live with the knowledge of God's forgiveness. What I got, I was not asking for or expecting. He healed my heart. It seems as though I, for the first time, am touched in the deepest recesses of my heart by his love, grace, mercy, and forgiveness. I still don't know for sure what the answer to my original question is, but it really doesn't matter so much. I do know he has touched my heart in ways I had given up feeling he ever would. I have a deep sense of his love for me, largely because my wife modeled for me how to love as he does. I can genuinely say he does change a man's heart!! He still is, changing it that is.

I find it so refreshing to live life watching as God moves from the inside, making necessary changes there, and giving the Holy Spirit to help live it out so others can see the change, for His glory and the good of others.

Wearing the Clothing of Forbearance

There is another phrase in Colossians 3:13 that deserves our careful attention: "Bear with each other." The *King James Version* uses an expression we don't encounter much in modern speech, but it is worth resurrecting: "forbearing one another." *Forbear* or *forbearance* isn't very romantic or inspiring; in short it means "to put up with, to endure." The same word is found in a similar exhortation in Ephesians 4:2: "Be completely humble and gentle; be patient, *bearing* with one another in love" (italics mine). It may not sound very spiritual to say that we have to "put up with" some kinds of people, but that is exactly what our Lord is requiring. Some people and some things we need to forgive. Many more, we need to grit our teeth and put up with and endure. A wise person is careful to make a distinction between forgiving and forbearing. If I turn every grievance into a forgiveness issue, I will become a very lonely person. I will appear to others to have a chip on my shoulder, and they will avoid me.

Dictionaries give a variety of definitions of *forbearance*: "a delay in enforcing rights, claims, or privileges"; "an indulgence toward offenders"; and my personal favorite, "a good-natured tolerance of delay or incompetence."

Forbearance is also a legal term, a usage I had not known before I found it on the Internet (remember: you learn to type by typing!). There it occurs in a discussion of student-aid loans, where "forbearing" refers to the postponing or reducing of payments on a loan, though the interest keeps accruing and the loan is still due. It is important to recognize that this is precisely *not* what Paul has in mind: "I may not make you pay now, but your day is coming and the interest is growing!" Forbearing is not about postponing repayment, but rather involves putting up with the weaknesses, frailties, and failings of others, without charging it to their account or making it a big issue. It is an oil that lubricates the places where relational gears mesh, so that friction is minimized, not maximized.

Paul is intensely realistic. We are usually convinced that it is other people, not us, who possess irritating mannerisms, annoying habits, bad manners, and unattractive personalities. Why do they seem to enjoy such bad music (not my kind, the good stuff), demand special attention, act immaturely, and have poor hygiene? Why are their accents so unusual and their customs so strange? Of course they probably feel the same way about me! One of the great surprises of the first year of marriage is how many unexpected things you discover in the person you once viewed only through the misty lens of romantic love. But marriage, family, and church exist in the harsh world of reality. A church isn't a nice little club of mutually compatible people; it's a group of often difficult, in-process people filled with quirks, idiosyncrasies, failures, and personality shortcomings who are in constant need of the grace of God, just as we are.

The call of God is to "bear with them," not in the sense of "barely tolerate them" but in line with God's call for us to be His people—compassionate, kind, humble, gentle, patient, and, above all, loving. To forbear is to grit your teeth and to put up with differences, mistakes, and failures in an attitude of grace, because we are deeply and humbly aware of our own need of grace. Forbearance is all about enduring discomfort in the name of love. It is the spirit shown by the great missionary leader Hudson Taylor, when he was challenged by the incompetence of some of his missionaries: "My greatest temptation is to lose my temper over the slackness and inefficiency so disappointing in those on whom I depended. It is no use to lose my temper—only kindness. But oh, it is such a trial!"[3] The Lord Jesus models that kind of grace continually, not only with His disciples while on earth, but also with us on a daily basis. It is all about making allowances for the weaknesses of others, just as we desire others to do for us. As C. S. Lewis wrote to a friend: "May God's grace give

you the necessary humility. Try not to think—much less speak—of
their sins. One's own are a much more profitable theme. And if, on
consideration, one can find no faults on one's own side, then cry for
mercy: for this *must* be a dangerous delusion."[4]

Forbearance is a continuing theme of Scripture. Proverbs 17:9
tells us that

> *He who covers over an offense promotes love,*
> *but whoever repeats the matter separates close friends.*

This is echoed in the great chapter on love, where we are told
that love "keeps no record of wrongs" (1 Corinthians 13:5). These
passages are not calling us to a secretive dealing with sin. As we have
seen, the Lord's words in Luke 17:3 do not allow such a response,
and the recent history of church leaders and company officials who
protect themselves by covering over sin remind us of how evil such
behavior can be. But there are offenses that do not need to be uncov-
ered but love-covered. Let us again turn to the wisdom of the book
of Proverbs, where we find a helpful corrective to our scandal-loving,
exhibitionist, gossip-ridden culture:

> *A man's wisdom gives him patience;*
> *it is to his glory to overlook an offense (19:11).*

Our concept of personal glory often involves "telling it like it is,"
letting the chips fall where they may, standing up for one's rights and
showing that we won't be "dissed" by anyone. God's concept of personal glory is very different. One insightful commentator expounds
Proverbs 19:11:

> [This] is more than a forgiving temper; it includes also
> the ability to shrug off insults and the absence of a brooding
> hypersensitivity. It is the ability to deny to an adversary the
> yelp of pain even when the words have inflicted a wound, of
> making large allowances for human frailties and keeping the
> lines of communication open. It contains elements of toughness

and self-discipline; it is the capacity to stifle a hot emotional rejoinder and to sleep on an insult.[5]

The New Testament continues the theme. Some things are just not worth fighting over, worrying about, or losing sleep over. As Peter exhorts, "Above all, love each other deeply, because love covers over a multitude of sins" (1 Peter 4:8).

The call to forbearance has great practical significance. As Lewis Smedes wisely wrote, "Not every hurt calls for forgiveness, any more than every cut needs stitching."[6] Not everything is about forgiveness. We need to accept others. We are not going to like everything about the people with whom we live. Some of that is about them; much of it is about us. We need to learn to put up with differences, mistakes, and failures. That does not mean that we never raise our concerns, or that we set aside our moral discernment. But it does mean that we give others the benefit of the doubt and surrender many of our concerns to the Lord. Imagine all that the Lord Jesus had to forbear in the lives of His disciples and those He came to serve! But He loved them, and His enemies complained that He was "a friend of sinners." He companied with fallen people without condoning their sin.

> *Not everything is about forgiveness. . . . We need to learn to put up with differences, mistakes, and failures.*

Although Ken Sande uses the term *overlooking* rather than *forbearing*, he is discussing the same thing:

> Overlooking is not a *passive* process in which you simply remain silent for the moment but file away the offense for later use against someone. That is actually a form of denial that can easily lead to brooding over the offense and building up internal bitterness and resentment that will eventually explode in anger. Instead, overlooking is an *active* process that is inspired by God's mercy through the gospel. To truly overlook an

offense means to deliberately decide not to talk about it, dwell on it, or let it grow into pent-up bitterness. If you cannot let go of an offense in this way, if it is too serious to overlook, or if it continues as part of a pattern in the other person's life, then you will need to go and talk to the other person about it in a loving and constructive manner.[7]

Forgiveness and forbearance are both garments that a well-dressed Christ-follower should wear. Some offenses are relatively trivial; wise people choose to forbear. Some offenses are strictly personal; wise people often choose to turn the other cheek. Some offenses are damaging and destructive; wise people choose to walk the path of true forgiveness.

Clarifying Questions about Judging Others

Discussions of forgiveness and forbearance usually provoke questions: Didn't Jesus tell us not to judge others? Doesn't all this talk about forgiving and forbearing call us to do exactly what the Lord opposed? Who are we to go to people and rebuke them for their sin? So we need to consider the statement of the Lord that is often turned on its head to mean something He never intended. The first rule of understanding any statement is to be sure that we honor the context in which it is found. Otherwise, we can twist it to mean anything we desire. The Lord's statement about judging is found in the Sermon on the Mount.

"Do not judge, or you too will be judged. For in the same way you judge others, you will be judged, and with the measure you use, it will be measured to you.

"Why do you look at the speck of sawdust in your brother's eye and pay no attention to the plank in your own eye? How can you say to your brother, 'Let me take the speck out of your eye,' when all the time there is a plank in your own eye? You hypocrite, first take the plank out of your own

eye, and then you will see clearly to remove the speck from your brother's eye" (Matthew 7:1–5).

"Who are you to judge? Didn't Jesus say, 'Judge not'?" has become the mantra of a permissive, anything-goes generation whenever anyone challenges a particular action or way of life. Tolerance has become the familiar buzzword in a society that celebrates diversity and open-mindedness. But did the Lord Jesus really intend us to suspend moral judgment and ethical discernment? Although a superficial reading of Matthew 7:1 could lead to that conclusion, a little more serious examination makes it clear that the Lord's concern was not the fact of judging, but the manner of judging. He was not condemning discernment. In fact, throughout the Sermon on the Mount, He insists upon it. He has no patience for a critical spirit, but He insists that His followers must live lives of moral discernment.

When Jesus commanded His hearers in Matthew 7:6 not to give what is holy to dogs or pigs, He was certainly encouraging them to ponder the moral and personal qualities of those with whom they were interacting. In Matthew 7:15 He tells us to "watch out for false prophets," assuring us in verse 16 that "by their fruit you will recognize them." The famous story of the two men, one who built on a sand foundation, the other on one of rock (Matthew 7:24–27) makes the judgment that one is wise, the other foolish. This certainly involves moral and spiritual discernment. As we discussed earlier, in Luke 17:3 Jesus commands us to confront a brother who sins against us. How could we do any of those things if we are not to judge others in any way? Such an interpretation makes nonsense of Jesus' words. Our Lord's concern is not with *whether* we judge, but *how* and *why*.

So what does the Lord mean? Part of the answer is found in the word Jesus uses, which can mean "to judge" but often conveys the more specific sense of "to condemn." He used a verb tense that indicates an ongoing attitude and practice, not just an occasional event. An accurate rendering of the statement *Do not judge* would be something like "Stop constantly condemning, criticizing, and finding fault." He is prohibiting *judgmentalism*, an attitude that continually sits in judgment on others, usually from a position of self-assigned superiority. A critical spirit is often the "vice of the virtuous," the response of people who care deeply about truth and moral standards. But it is a perilously small step from moral discernment to a judging spirit that focuses on the negative in others. The huge danger of judging others is pride, arrogance, and blindness to our own faults. We must not surrender our need to develop a discerning spirit. In our morally relativistic, permissive, indulgent culture, few skills are more needed than moral discernment. At the same time, we must cultivate a humble, caring spirit, and starve all tendencies to a critical, judging spirit that is so destructive, wherever it is found. Those of us who love God's truth and value His holy standards must recognize that judgmentalism is a weed that too often flourishes in the garden of God's people. Too many who carry the name of Christ are just plain mean to other people, and too many churches are more judgmental than they are discerning.

It is a perilously small step from moral discernment to a judging spirit that focuses on the negative in others.

The Lord wants us to understand that a critical spirit is sinful. The command is clear: Stop judging and fault-finding. Historian Will Durant once wisely observed, "To speak ill of others is a dishonest way of praising ourselves; let us be above such transparent egotism. If you can't say good and encouraging things, say nothing."[8]

A critical spirit is also dangerous: "Do not judge or you too will be judged. For in the same way you judge others, you will be judged, and with the measure you use, it will be measured to you" (Matthew 7:1–2). This may suggest that others will be at least as hard with us as we are with them, an obvious pattern of human behavior. But it suggests far more. The judgment of God is in view, and the Savior seems to be saying that the Lord Himself will hold us to the standards we put on others. That reminds me of David's plea to the prophet Gad:

"Let us fall into the hands of the Lord, for his mercy is great; but do not let me fall into the hands of men" (2 Samuel 24:14). People can be very cruel, as most of us know only too well.

The Lord also wants us to recognize that a critical spirit is ridiculously self-deceived. Jesus' picture is comical: A man with a huge beam protruding from his own eye seeks to remove the speck from another's eye, an act that is not only foolish but also dangerous.

The Lord's point is clear: I can be amazingly blind to my own failings, while I obsess about the wrong things I am convinced I can see in the lives of others. The "beams" of pride, arrogance, and self-deception are far too prevalent. Unfortunately those most critical of others are often in complete denial about their own sins and shortcomings and blithely unaware of the danger they pose to others. They are often "black and white" people, blind to their own prejudices, elevating their preferences to the level of divine principles and stubbornly sure of the rightness of their opinions. And it really isn't "they." I have been this person far more than I want to admit.

The Lord is not denying that there really is a speck in the brother's eye. But, as a person who has had several eye surgeries, I have great appreciation for the delicacy and sensitivity of the eye. Probing someone else's eye is a precarious task. Irreversible damage can be done very quickly. The problem is not correction but premature and improper correction. The Lord wants me to understand that I am in no condition to help my brother until I have allowed the Lord to do surgery on me, to remove the beam lodged there. This adds another step to the process the Lord laid out for forgiveness in Luke 17:3. I may see my brother's sin, and I may need to confront him in grace. But before I do, I need to go into the presence of my Lord, to humble myself before Him, submitting to His surgery. The great evangelist D. L. Moody was once asked to comment on someone else's behavior. He commented, "Right now, I'm having so much trouble with D. L. Moody that I don't have time to find fault with the other fellow." When I have allowed the Lord to remove my "beam," I may be in a position to approach my brother humbly, gently, lovingly, and very carefully. As someone has said, "Christians are unusual people: They are called to be hard on themselves and gracious to others."

Wearing the Overcoat of Love

All of this means that the well-dressed believer, clothed with forbearance and forgiveness, will understand the exhortation of Colossians 3:14: "And over all these virtues put on love, which binds them all together in perfect unity." Gordon MacDonald has described our calling well:

> I can hardly think of a more important function than the giving of grace to the man or woman who has never learned of the love of Christ and his reclaiming grace. To the young or struggling believer who seeks a Christlike faith and the joy of experiencing reforming grace. And to the broken-world person who has so disappointed his brothers and sisters in faith and needs restorative grace. Where there is grace, there is hope, hope for a broken world to be rebuilt.[9]

Chapter 8

WHEN THERE'S NO "I'M SORRY"

*A*uschwitz is a terrible place. The worst of the Nazi death camps, more than a million people lost their lives there, under the most appalling conditions. It was created in 1940, under Hitler's orders, to deal with people considered undesirable, such as Polish patriots and gypsies. When the Nazis launched their hellish "Final Solution," a horrific attempt systematically to exterminate the Jewish people, it became their primary death camp. Even today, almost sixty years after its liberation, a palpable sense of evil hangs over the camp.

When Elizabeth and I were in Europe to visit a missionary friend, we went to Auschwitz. Visitors are greeted by the unbelievably cynical sign that hung over the front gate, *Arbeit macht frei* (Work makes us free)—this slogan over a place where many would be gassed immediately, where those who escaped the gas chambers would die in less than a year from their forced, hard labor. The entire journey was a horrifying look into the deepest recesses of evil latent in the human heart. As we walked through the now-empty barracks, once crammed with suffering people, or witnessed the places of punishment or execution or stood in the gas chambers and crematorium, we struggled to find anything to say to each other. What could one say? How could people, especially those from one of the world's most "advanced civilizations," do such things? We stood in front of displays containing piles of shoes, clothing, and eyeglasses, even one containing more than a ton of women's hair, all these stripped or shorn from the bodies of those gassed, before their corpses were burned or dumped in a common grave. The hardest place to stand was before piles of little suitcases and of clothes and shoes, the last possessions of hundreds of thousands of children who had been told they were going to a country camp but ended up in gas chambers. I am grateful for the opportunity to have been there, but even now it is hard to grasp that we saw what we did. The experience was both deeply disturbing and profoundly moving.

When he was fifteen, Elie Wiesel and his family were marched as prisoners through the gates of Auschwitz. They had been hauled there in cattle cars, along with other Jews from Romania. He never again saw his mother and younger sister; by the time he was liberated, fifteen months later, his father also had died. In 1995 Wiesel returned for the fiftieth anniversary of the liberation of the camp. The night before the official ceremony, Wiesel and others gathered at the crematorium for an unofficial ceremony, where Wiesel articulated his feelings:

> Although we know that God is merciful, please God do not have mercy on those who have created this place. God of forgiveness, do not forgive those murderers of Jewish children here.
>
> Do not forgive the murderers and their accomplices. Those who have been here . . . remember the nocturnal processions of children and more children and more children. . . . If we could simply look at one, our heart would break. Did it not break the heart of the murderers? God, merciful God, do not have mercy on those who had not mercy on Jewish children.[1]

I cannot pretend to understand what Wiesel had endured or even to imagine what he felt as he stood in that place of such personal horror. But what a burden to carry through life!

Wiesel wasn't merely speaking on his own. His words reflect ancient rabbinic teaching, found in the Talmud: "The Day of Atonement atones for sins against God, not for sins against man, unless the injured party has been appeased."[2] Simply put, there is no forgiveness possible for a murderer or for something like the Holocaust. Only victims can forgive, and then only after repentance and restitution. Dead victims obviously can't forgive their victimizers. If forgiveness is impossible, what do you do with the toxin building up inside you?

That is one extreme. On the other hand, we have people going around after a terrible act of evil, declaring the perpetrator "forgiven" before he has shown any remorse or the victims have been buried. In such cases forgiveness turns into a kind of automatic, immediate response that seems to trivialize the offense and minimize the profound hurt that has been inflicted on the victims.

Not long before she died in 1988, Marghanita Laski, one of the best-known secularists in England, said, "What I envy most about you Christians is your forgiveness; I have nobody to forgive me."[3] Christians are forgiven people because of the Lord Jesus Christ. And we are called and commanded to be forgiving people. That is hard under any conditions. But what if the offender does not, will not, or cannot repent? Do I forgive anyway? Doesn't that merely encourage her in her sinning? That is anything but a theoretical question. Many offenders have no intention of either stopping or repenting. That is the issue we want to address in this chapter, and we will begin by returning to a section of Scripture we visited earlier, Jesus' words that immediately precede the parable of the wicked servant in Matthew 18.

What if the offender does not, will not, or cannot repent? Do I forgive anyway?

> *If your brother sins against you, go and show him his fault, just between the two of you. If he listens to you, you have won your brother over. But if he will not listen, take one or two others along, so that "every matter may be established by the testimony of two or three witnesses." If he refuses to listen to them, tell it to the church; and if he refuses to listen even to the church, treat him as you would a pagan or a tax collector.*

I tell you the truth, whatever you bind on earth will be bound in heaven, and whatever you loose on earth will be loosed in heaven.

Again, I tell you that if two of you on earth agree about anything you ask for, it will be done for you by my Father in heaven. For where two or three come together in my name, there am I with them (vv. 15–20).

As we previously observed, Matthew 18 contains teaching from our Lord on kingdom relationships. In the preceding verses, Jesus has recounted His familiar story of the faithful shepherd who left the ninety-nine sheep to find one lost sheep that had wandered away. This seeking shepherd is a portrait of the Father's heart: "In the same way your Father in heaven is not willing that any of these little ones should be lost" (v. 14). But what is to be my response to that wandering sheep, especially if his wandering has included sin against me? And what if I seek to bring her back, and she doesn't want to come? That question is our concern here.

Classic Forgiveness:
When Forgiveness Meets Repentance

There is a close similarity between what Jesus says here and what is recorded in Luke 17:3–4. The repetition provides an opportunity for us to review the basic pattern of forgiveness set out by our Lord.

Forgiveness begins with *the problem: We have been sinned against.* Living in a fallen world means that each one of us has been sinned against, just as certainly as we all have sinned against others. The Lord makes it very clear that the issue is sin, not just a mistake, accident, or misunderstanding. In Matthew 18:15 He says, "If your brother sins against you. . . ." Sin is a violation of God's standards, not merely something that upsets me or causes me problems. This seems obvious enough, but, as we have observed, many things can upset us about others that don't lie in the realm of another's sin. Not every issue requires formal forgiveness, and, therefore, forbearance is a primary

Christian virtue. The manager of a prize fighter was once asked why he had turned down a fight that would have made his man a considerable amount of money. His response was memorable: "My fighter only has so many fights in him, and we're not going to use one up on this opponent." That is good advice. For some issues it's not worth putting on the gloves. The "sin against you" suggests that this is an act that is serious enough to break or threaten a relationship. The later statement that you would "win your brother" suggests that a significant relationship was in danger of being lost.

> *"Nothing is so cruel as the tenderness that consigns another to his sin. Nothing can be more compassionate than the severe rebuke that calls a brother back from the path of sin."*
>
> DIETRICH BONHOEFFER

Just as He had in Luke 17, the Lord here in Matthew 18 establishes *the process: We must bring sin into the light.* The Lord's command could not be more clear. We are not to complain about the behavior to others or to stuff our feelings inside, making the best of a bad situation. We are to "go and show him his fault, just between the two of you" (v. 15). If this advice were followed, an immense number of problems would be dealt with before they reached the level of ugly, festering sores. It is tempting to harbor grudges rather than deal with them. Conversely, we may leave evil unchallenged by a misunderstanding of forgiveness that skips the step of confrontation. As Dietrich Bonhoeffer trenchantly observed, "Nothing is so cruel as the tenderness that consigns another to his sin. Nothing can be more compassionate than the severe rebuke that calls a brother back from the path of sin."[4]

Not long ago a few of us were talking about some forgiveness issues, and a woman, obviously deeply hurt by an offense, mentioned a book she had been reading about forgiveness. She said, "I've learned that, whatever he's done, I'm not supposed to talk about it to him, but to take it to the Lord and forgive him." I felt constrained to quote this passage to her, and to remind her that for his sake, as well as for hers, she should not be silent. She needed to go to him and "show him his fault."

We need to balance what the Lord says here with what He says in Matthew 5:23–24, where He sets out the other side of the coin: "Therefore, if you are offering your gift at the altar and there remember that your brother has something against you, leave your gift there in front of the altar. First go and be reconciled to your brother; then come and offer your gift." So then, whether I feel that I have been sinned against or am convicted that I have done something wrong, I am to initiate a meeting with the other person. As Gregory Jones observes, "We need to seek out those against whom we have sinned and be willing to be sought out by those who have sinned against us."[5] The person who becomes aware of the breach in relationship is to take the initiative to deal with it.

The Greek word the Lord uses to describe this encounter, which the *New International Version* renders "show him his fault," is particularly difficult to render into English. The word is the same one the Lord uses in John 16:8 to describe the work of the Holy Spirit: "When he comes, he will *convict* the world of guilt in regard to sin and righteousness and judgment" (emphasis mine). In such a context, the word describes the process of bringing facts into the light, not for the purpose of making someone feel guilty, but to make the issues clear. When I go to my brother in obedience to the Lord, my purpose must not be to unload my feelings or to pour out accusations. It must be to clarify the truth. The phrase *show him his fault* is accurate as far as it goes, but it has a dangerous connotation. It encourages a less humble, more accusatory encounter than the Lord suggests. To "convict" is to be an act of love not of animosity. This attitude is underscored by a passage in the Old Testament that encourages the same response, a passage that includes the statement that Jesus called the second "great commandment":

Do not hate your brother in your heart. Rebuke your neighbor frankly so you will not share in his guilt.

Do not seek revenge or bear a grudge against one of your people, but love your neighbor as yourself. I am the Lord (Leviticus 19:17–18).

In the same way, the New Testament encourages us to loving but firm confrontation: "Brothers, if someone is caught in a sin, you who are spiritual should restore him gently. But watch yourself, or you also may be tempted" (Galatians 6:1).

The purpose of this encounter is repentance, restoration, and reconciliation. Matthew 18:15 continues, "If he listens to you, you have won your brother over" (more literally: you have gained your brother). Obviously, to "listen" in such a context means more than merely hearing what is said. It is to hear in such a way as to respond appropriately, in true repentance. To "gain the brother" means that forgiveness is offered and received, and that a door is opened for the restoration of the relationship. David Augsburger notes the importance of the purpose: "For Jesus, this is the goal—the central focus, the true meaning of forgiveness. The primary issue is not inner peace for oneself, not moral rightness with one's own conscience, not assurance of one's own salvation."[6] This may not mean that everything instantly returns to the way it was before. Forgiveness may have been given, but trust needs time to grow. Repentance may open the door, but entrance into the house requires taking off your dirty shoes!

The hope is that the two individuals will be able to work out the problem on their own, without involving anyone else. However, Jesus is a total realist. He knows that sinful people often deny, rather than respond to, the light and defend even their most horrendous behaviors. It would be nice to imagine that everyone listens and responds with repentance when confronted with personal wrongdoing. But successful confrontations are probably the exception rather than the rule. That said, we are not to abandon the process simply because the first effort fails.

Frustrated Forgiveness:
When the Process Breaks Down

"But if he will not listen" to you (v. 16) takes us to the second step. We are not told that we are to forgive him anyway, even if he refuses to repent. Nor are we just to forget the issue and move on, writing that person out of our lives. The Lord Jesus treats us with patient grace, and that is to be our model. We are responsible not to give up; the next step is a group encounter, to "take one or two others along."

There are probably several reasons for this. One is indicated by the statement, "A matter must be established by the testimony of two or three witnesses." This is an Old Testament legal principle (Deuteronomy 19:15), and it suggests the seriousness of what is taking place. Wisdom suggests that we take with us people of discernment, spiritual maturity, and objectivity, not just people the other person may feel are there to gang up on him. Wisdom also requires us to be sensitive to the situation. I remember when a group of us met with a couple to deal with a delicate situation. Unfortunately, the wife was the only woman present, and, even though that was far from our intention, she felt somewhat isolated and intimidated. Obviously, a group of men are not the ones to meet with an unaccompanied woman. Nor is an encounter in a public place appropriate. However, granted such practical wisdom, the presence of several people is important. It enables the parties to clarify the issues; as they hear both sides, probe for the facts and the underlying issues, try to determine whether sin really is involved, whether the fault is shared or singular, and what future steps could be followed. The presence of a group also increases the pressure on the offender to deal with the problem and not just pass it off as a trivial issue. Whatever happens, the goal of the encounter is that the brothers and sisters come to a place of repentance and restoration. What a great time it is when true healing occurs!

But "if the offender will not listen," the offended person is, once again, not just to forgive, forget, and move on. The Lord now calls us to "tell it to the church." This is only the second time the Lord speaks of "the church" to His disciples. (The first is the famous declaration in Matthew 16:18, "I will build my church, and the gates of Hades will not overcome it.") His disciples would have understood Him to be speaking of the gathered community of Christ-followers, and it is a reminder that, in the Lord's family, interpersonal disputes do not always remain private business. We live in a culture characterized by intense individualism, and we protect our privacy fiercely. So when the Lord commands us to bring such issues to the church, many modern Christians instinctively complain, "What business is it of theirs?" Church discipline sounds like a relic of the Dark Ages to many Christians, who have bought into our culture's consumer mindset. But Christ-followers are to form their practices upon the commands of their Lord, not the passing whims of culture. We cannot escape it. The Word of God and the Lord of the church call us to "tell it to the church."

We should not read this carelessly. The Lord Jesus has used the term *church* only once previously in Matthew (16:18), and, as far as we can tell, He has given no instructions about what its organizational structure was to be. We should not infer that He intended such issues to be raised and discussed in a general congregational meeting. That is not an appropriate forum for discussing private and confidential issues. More likely, the church is portrayed as acting through the involvement of its elders or church leaders. Mature, seasoned leaders should hear the issues, protect the individuals, and come to a conclusion in a context of deep prayer and careful consideration. Their mandate is once again clear: repentance, restoration, and reconciliation.

Even here the process may hit a dead end. Sadly I've observed that by the time an issue has reached this point, most people are entrenched in their positions. They are determined on their course of action and so refuse "to listen even to the church" (v. 17). If that is the outcome, church discipline is to be carried out: "treat him as you would a pagan or a tax collector."

Again, we need to read this carefully. First, this is the last step, the end of what is usually a long process, taken only when it is evident that the violator has hardened his or her heart. Second, Jesus never taught His followers to treat others, be they pagans, tax collectors, or anyone else, in an abusive way. Nor does He call His followers to avoid all contact with such people. We are, in fact, called to win them by showing love. John MacArthur has wisely observed, "This is no license for hostility or contempt. In fact, Christ's treatment of heathens and tax collectors is notable chiefly because of how He reached out to them in love. A similar kind of compassionate evangelistic pursuit should characterize our treatment of those who have been excommunicated in this manner."[7] Having said that, they are now to be seen as outsiders, people no longer in good standing in the community of Christ-followers. At a minimum, such people are to be considered as being outside the family. We cannot pretend that it is "business as usual." This is a biblical act of tough love, a calling of kingdom people to kingdom standards in their relationships. Interpersonal sins and relational brokenness are the very opposite of what the Lord Jesus came to bring into being among His people.

This point is a stark reminder that achieving forgiveness is not an easy process. People may stubbornly refuse to do the right thing, no matter how gracious the approach, how careful the process, or how spiritual the pressure brought upon them. We are to forgive repentant offenders as fully and freely as possible. But we are not simply to forgive, forget, and move on when people refuse to repent. For the sake of both the offender and the offended, we are to pursue truth and a process of restoration.

Unilateral Forgiveness: Letting Go of the Burden

So what now? I have sought to forgive, but the other person will not repent. She is blind to what she has done, despite what many others have said, and she steadfastly refuses even to consider admitting the wrong of her behavior. Perhaps she doesn't regret her behavior at all, feeling pleased at what she has done. "After all, you had it coming." Television news recently carried the sentencing of a terrorist, responsible for the death of hundreds of people in a bomb attack. As he received his death sentence and was led out of the courtroom, his entire demeanor was one of defiance, sneering at the relatives of his victims and raising his hand in a gesture of victory. Through his lawyer, he announced that the sentence was good news because he had always wanted to die as a martyr. What do you do with someone like that?

Others must deal with the fact that their victimizers are unable to express repentance, perhaps because they have died or have a medical or mental condition or are confined to prison and legally prevented from making contact. Recently a woman revealed to me that she had been raped at gunpoint by a relative, when she was a child. She had been too young and too ashamed to say anything about it, and he had lived in the family as if nothing had ever happened. Decades passed, and he had died, taking his secret with him to the grave. Now he could never express repentance for his awful act, even though he had never given the slightest suggestion that he would. What was she to do with this unresolved and unresolvable evil?

There are two common responses to such scenarios. Some suggest that we cannot, indeed must not, forgive, unless the person repents. There is strong logic in this, but it also leaves the offender in control. The wronged person is left carrying the load, waiting for the other person's response while she fights a continual battle against bitterness.

Others give the opposite counsel. We are to forgive unconditionally and immediately, whatever has happened, simply because the Lord commands us to do so. I respect the sincerity of such a position, but it is not without significant problems. Is it, in fact, what Jesus requires? What about the clear call in the New Testament to confront sin and to work toward repentance? There are also some very practical issues, well captured by Don Carson in a set of hard and probing questions:

> Should a woman forgive the man who brutally raped her? If so, when? On the spot? Two years later? Only when he repents? Should a man forgive the father who abused him? While he is abusing him? Only later? Only if he repents? Should the survivors of the Holocaust forgive the Nazis? Should they have done so during the Holocaust? . . . If we should forgive Osama bin Laden, does that mean we are not to go after him militarily? Suppose we know that he is planning another attack. Do we simply absorb it on the other cheek, as it were? . . . What do love and forgiveness demand if while walking home on dark streets, you see four toughs brutalizing a woman? Should you try to stop them? Or forgive them on the spot? Or wait until they are finished and then forgive them for what they have done?[8]

Just to raise some of those questions is to go a long way toward answering them. Love is not blind. It must make a calculation about what its primary responsibility is in any situation. It would be a violation of God's heart of just love to stand back and forgive perpetrators, while they are in the very act of ravaging another person. Yet, even in such situations, a believer is commanded to practice enemy love, to avoid repaying evil for evil, to avoid revenge, and to overcome evil with good (Romans 12:17–21). There is also an important distinction between the mandate God gives His people to "not take revenge, my friends, but leave room for God's wrath" (Romans 12:19) and the responsibility of governmental authorities to act as "God's servant, an agent of wrath to bring punishment on the wrongdoer" (Romans 13:4). It is not only permissible, it is obligatory for a government to pursue evil doers with the intent of terminating their evil actions. That is involved in Paul's affirmation that a political leader "does not bear the sword for nothing" (Romans 13:4). To forgo the pursuit of justice and the restraint of evil is to abdicate governmental responsibility. On the other hand, for an individual Christ-follower to pursue revenge or to dispense forgiveness indiscriminately is to abdicate the way of Christian love.

In the 1980s, as Solomon Schimmel tells the story, a nun in New York City was brutally raped by two men, who also cut seventeen crosses into her body with a nail file. The brutality outraged even a city as hardened to reports of violence as New York. However, the police found themselves handcuffed. Although they had found and arrested the perpetrators, they could charge them with only minor offenses. Although the men were obviously guilty, police could not charge them with rape and aggravated assault, because the nun, the only witness, refused to testify against them. She said that she had no desire for revenge and hoped that, by forgiving them, she would make them sensitive to their wrongdoing and motivate them to change their ways.

I am impressed by the love and courage of that nun. But I have serious questions about her wisdom. Had she called the men to repentance? Did she think about the other women who would be put at risk, if men capable of such atrocities were set free? What role does civil justice have in such matters? Schimmel, writing from a Jewish perspective that insists on repentance and reparation prior to granting forgiveness, asks some hard questions Christians must not avoid:

> Did the nun do what her Christian faith requires of Christian women who are raped and tortured? If you are a Christian woman, would you do the same if you were raped and tortured? If you are a Christian man and your wife, mother, sister, or daughter were a victim of such a crime, would you think that they, like the nun, should not press charges? Do you feel that what the nun did was unethical because, though she might have *personally* been able to forgive those who assaulted her, from the *societal* point of view she had no right to do so?[9]

Obviously these are probing and challenging questions. But they must be faced if we are to avoid discussing forgiveness in superficial and even harmful ways. Forgiveness, as we have seen, is intended to be an interpersonal and bilateral process, when a wronged person extends forgiveness to a person who has sinned against him, on the basis of the offender's repentance. This is the only forgiveness that opens the possibility of reconciliation. But the Bible also suggests that, when attempts at interpersonal forgiveness have come to a dead end, a Christ-follower is not stymied. There is such a thing as personal or unilateral forgiveness, when the offended party lets go of an offense by giving it over to the Lord, and committing herself to act in love, regardless of the other's response. Three passages are especially helpful in illustrating how we are to respond when there is no "I'm sorry."

The first of these passages is Mark 11:25, which concludes a saying by the Lord about faith:

> *"Have faith in God," Jesus answered. "I tell you the truth, if anyone says to this mountain, 'Go, throw yourself into the sea,' and does not doubt in his heart but believes that what he says will happen, it will be done for him. Therefore I tell you, whatever you ask for in prayer, believe that you have received it, and it will be yours.* And when you stand praying, if you hold anything against anyone, forgive him, so that your Father in heaven may forgive you your sins" (vv. 22–25, emphasis mine).

When the Lord Jesus described the process of forgiveness in Matthew 18:15 and Luke 17:3–4, He envisioned an encounter between an offended person and the sought-out offender. However, this Mark 11 context is quite different. A believer is standing in prayer (a common Jewish prayer posture, whether in public or private), when he realizes that he is carrying something in his heart against his brother. Strikingly, he is not commanded to go to the brother and confront him with his sin. Rather, he is to forgive him (the Lord's use of the word makes it clear that sin is involved), right where he is. This would seem to indicate that the procedure given in Matthew and Luke is no longer possible or has proven futile. Because the context is prayer, this is a vertical transaction, a releasing of the person and the matter to God. Apparently this form of forgiveness goes something like this: "Lord, this is now in your hands, not mine. I surrender any desire or attempt to get even in any way. I abandon any perceived right to bitterness and complaining. I entrust this person to you in your grace and justice. I will follow your command not to repay evil for evil and to overcome evil with good." It is important to recognize that this takes place in a very different arena than that of interpersonal forgiveness. It is distinctive in that it is personal and internal, carried out between an individual and the Lord.

This subjective or personal forgiveness is substantially different from the declared, interpersonal forgiveness that is God's ideal. And it should be noted that the latter is still the goal toward which we work and pray, so that full restoration is possible. But, in the meantime, while I wait, I release to the Lord any supposed rights endlessly to recycle feelings of anger, resentment, or bitterness; I commit myself to act in wise love (after all, I am called to love even my enemies, Matthew 5:44); I resign the effort to make sure the person pays for what was done; I choose to wait for the Lord's vindication, whenever He chooses to settle all accounts (Romans 12:19).

Such forgiveness, the Lord tells us, is key to our ongoing enjoyment of "family forgiveness," "so that your Father in heaven may forgive you your sins." We have encountered this idea earlier, in the distinction between judicial forgiveness, which establishes our relationship with God, and family forgiveness, which enables our experience of fellowship with our Father. Wayne Grudem elaborates on this idea, found not only here, but also in the Lord's Prayer (Matthew 6:12, 14–15):

> Our Lord does not have in mind the initial experience of
> forgiveness we know when we are justified by faith, for that

would not belong in a prayer that we pray every day. . . . He refers rather to the day-by-day relationship with God that we need to have restored when we have sinned and displeased him. In fact, Jesus commands us to build into our prayers a request that God forgive us in the same way that we have forgiven others who have harmed us (in the same "personal relationship" sense of "forgive"—that is, not holding a grudge or cherishing bitterness against another person or harboring any desire to harm them). . . . If we have unforgiveness in our hearts against someone else, then we are not acting in a way that is pleasing to God or helpful to us. So God declares (Matthew 6:12, 14–15) that he will distance himself from us until we forgive others.[10]

The second passage comes in the midst of the climactic moments of the Savior's life, as He was being nailed to the cross. He had already experienced terrible physical abuse and had stumbled under the weight of the cross. He had been thrown to the ground and stripped naked; nails were driven through His wrists as He was fastened to the crossbeam. His Roman executioners roughly raised Him into the air, yanked His legs together, and drove nails through both ankles, impaling Him in agony. All the while the Jewish leaders led the rabble in an orgy of mockery and verbal abuse.

In this context the Savior spoke His first words from the cross: "Father, forgive them, for they do not know what they are doing" (Luke 23:34).[11] His executioners, whether Jewish leaders or Roman soldiers, were, at that moment, in no way repentant. Some were callously indifferent; others were celebrating the success of their efforts to rid the nation of Him. Although they were ignorant of what they were really doing, their ignorance wasn't innocence (or they would have had nothing to forgive). However, Jesus, rather than cursing His enemies, prayed for them, just as He had taught His followers to do (Luke 6:35).

I am impressed that here Jesus did not do what He had done on all the other occasions when He had forgiven someone. Previously, He had spoken directly to the individual, declaring, "your sins are forgiven" (Luke 5:20; 7:48). But from the cross, He prayed to the Father on their behalf, putting them in the Father's hands. He did not ask the Father to avenge Him but to forgive them. This was not a blanket forgiveness, granted to people whether or not they wanted it. It would become theirs only as they came in repentant faith to see the cross in an entirely different way. Even as He prayed this grace-filled prayer, their hearts were untouched. The soldiers indifferently gambled for His garments, while "the rulers even sneered at him" (Luke 23:35).

The third passage shows us that Stephen, the first Christian martyr, was deeply influenced by this example of his Lord. When he was called to account for his preaching of the good news of Jesus, he stood before his nation's leaders, and, with great courage, called them to repentance because "You always resist the Holy Spirit! . . . And now you have betrayed and murdered [the Righteous One]" (Acts 7:51–52). Their response was exactly the opposite of repentance; "they were furious and gnashed their teeth at him" (v. 54). Imitating his Master, Stephen prayed, even as he was being stoned to death: "Lord, do not hold this sin against them" (v. 60). Once again, note that he did not say to his unrepentant killers, "I forgive you." Rather, he entrusted them into his Father's hands. He could not declare their forgiveness in the midst of their rebellion, but he could give them over to the Lord. Remarkably, one of the answers to his prayer was found in a man who was "giving approval to his death" (8:1). Saul, better known as the apostle Paul, would not only come repentantly to the Lord, but also become the Lord's agent of forgiveness throughout the Mediterranean world.

In summary, not every case of interpersonal forgiveness is the same. The ideal is bilateral forgiveness, where an act of sin is followed by courageous confrontation on the part of the wronged person and sincere repentance on the part of the offender. But, even when repentance does not immediately occur, an obedient Christ-follower does not abandon the process. He continues to pursue the offender, seeking his restoration. And, when all efforts for the present have seemed to fail, he lets the issue go to the Lord in an act of unilateral forgiveness.

Some Good Lessons from a Bad Example

We have seen how the process ought to work. However, sometimes we learn best by looking at a bad example. Sadly, one of the Bible's great men gives us a case study in how not to deal with the failures of others. David was a great king who had experienced God's profound forgiveness. But when his own children engaged in a series of terrible acts against one another, David's actions only made a bad situation worse. He illustrates what can happen when we don't do forgiveness God's way.

As we have continually seen, *forgiveness means that we need to deal with sin honestly.* True forgiveness holds people accountable for their behavior, and if we attempt to deal with sin by ignoring it or by only partly forgiving it, we will cause greater damage. God fully and freely forgave David's sins—adultery with Bathsheba, followed by his arranged killing of Uriah—when David came to the place of confession. That forgiveness did not, however, cancel the tragic consequences that David had

True forgiveness holds people accountable for their behavior, and if we attempt to deal with sin by ignoring it or by only partly forgiving it, we will cause greater damage.

unleashed in his family. One of his sons, Amnon, raped his own half-sister, Tamar (2 Samuel 13:1–22). "When David heard all this, he was furious," we are told (v. 21). But rather than confronting and punishing Amnon, David avoided him. In so doing, he failed as a man, as a father, and as a king. Such an act called for severe punishment—exile, imprisonment, or even capital punishment. David's passivity was to yield a very bitter harvest. Tamar's brother Absalom was infuriated at Amnon's sin and David's tolerance. He burned with a deep hatred toward his half-brother, but he bided his time. Two years later his anger came to full flame in a carefully planned execution-style killing of Amnon, his half-brother (13:23–33). David was once again filled with grief, this time not only for his dead son, Amnon, but also for his lost son Absalom, who had fled for his life into a neighboring country. "King David mourned for his son every day" (13:37). For three years Absalom lived in exile. Finally David's general, Joab, persuaded David to allow Absalom to return. David agreed, but with a condition: "He must go to his own house; he must not see my face" (14:24). So Absalom's sin was never challenged; David's forgiveness was never offered; and reconciliation between the two was obviously never achieved. Absalom's appeal is pathetic: "I want to see the king's face, and if I am guilty of anything, let him put me to death" (v. 32). But when they did meet, David "kissed Absalom" (v. 33). It was an empty gesture, because the massive issue between them was never addressed. It was not forgotten. Absalom's anger festered and grew until it erupted in a civil uprising, in which Absalom came very close to taking both his father's throne and his life.

David's story, as well as the Lord's continued call for us to be forgiving people, is a reminder that *we need to guard carefully against an unforgiving spirit.* Anger can become a kind of security blanket to which we cling. But in the process, we become our own worst enemy, so that we become angry, embittered, and wounded people. An unforgiving spirit distorts our entire view of life. David's withholding of forgiveness was, it seems to me, an attempt to punish his son, although he lacked the courage to challenge his sin directly. Jeff VanVonderen observed,

> For some people, unforgiveness serves a very practical purpose. One reason why people don't or won't forgive is because it is a way for them to have the upper hand over another; it holds the other in a position of owing a debt they cannot repay. And feeling held in a constant state of being unforgiven keeps some people scrambling to discover what

good behavior it will take on their part to make up for what they have done. In a very real and devilish way, unforgiveness becomes an effective tool to control another's behavior.[12]

Whatever David's intentions, his response clearly didn't work. Absalom's response is a reminder that if people are left scrambling for too long, their hearts may harden, and scrambling will become retaliating.

Laying Down the Load

In the final analysis, the call of the Lord is that we need to let the issue go to Him. We need to put the person and the problem into the Lord's hands. Some years ago my wife and I were visiting friends at their beautiful lakeside vacation home. Elizabeth was deeply troubled by the way she believed some other people had mistreated me, people who steadfastly refused to imagine that they had done anything wrong. She believed she had dealt with her feelings, but her faithful friend listened to her conversation and finally called her on her attitude: "You're still angry."

"No I'm not. I've let it go."

"Then why do you keep talking to me about it over and over? You're carrying a load of rocks."

They stopped at a spot on the road, and Shirley said, "I want you to collect some rocks, write the names of those people on them, and throw them into the lake." They did just that, not as a symbol that she was throwing away those people but that she was giving them over to the Lord, releasing once again her feelings of anger and bitterness.

That simple act had a powerful effect on my wife. Since then she has had the opportunity to walk with other women through a similar ritual.

Recently I preached a sermon on the Mark 11 text, in which I tried to unravel how we should deal with people who will not or cannot say "I'm sorry." At the end of the message, I asked people to write on a card any names the Holy Spirit had brought to their minds—what could be called "Mark 11:25 people." Some might be guilty of terrible sins against you—but they will not own their sin. Others might have died, but the effects of their sin linger. What do we do with such people? I then said, "If you feel so moved by God's Spirit, bring the cards bearing those names to the front as we sing a worship song together, as a symbol that you are giving that person and that issue to the Lord." It was moving to watch hundreds of people come forward, some with deep emotion. I knew only a few of the stories, but I also knew that for many it was a profound moment of worship before their forgiving God.

Now I am not so naïve as to believe that writing a person's name on a card is all that it takes to let go of the deep wounds of a person's soul. But I do know that the Lord longs for His people to develop a disposition to forgive rather than to retaliate, to release rather than to hold onto wrongs done to us. It is only a place to begin, but that first step is often the most important. So I want to challenge you to consider who the Lord has brought to your mind as you have been reading these pages. What is the most God-honoring way to proceed from here? How will you release that wrong, no matter how deep, to your Lord?

Chapter 9

RESCUED FROM REVENGE

How quickly we adjust! I have come to take for granted the massive amount of information the Internet puts at my fingertips. But I have had to learn that the Internet can be a danger zone. Human nature has a way of twisting even the best of things, using them for the least-worthy purposes. The same Internet that brings me information and services also makes available degrading pornography that can undermine my family. Thieves can use it to steal my identity and my wealth. I can use it to engage other services that are less than noble. For example, one Web site offers "revenge at its best" and advertises its services as follows (the print style reflects the original):

> ThePayback.com is your home for all of your revenge needs. So you never had a chance to get revenge on your ex-boyfriend or ex-girlfriend? Your current spouse lied to you when he said that he would never cheat on you? Well, you know the saying "**Don't get mad, get even.**" **Get Revenge** On People Who Have Done You Wrong!
>
> We stand ready to help you get revenge and let these individuals know exactly what you think of them!
>
> Join the **thousands** who have used our services to get revenge![1]

I'm certainly not encouraging you to make use of their services, although the actions of some people make it very tempting! Some forms of revenge seem relatively harmless and even humorous (in a distorted kind of way). On the other hand, every day's newspaper is filled with terrible stories that have the theme of revenge. They come in all forms: headline-grabbing, horrific acts of terrorism that shred bodies and devastate nations; personal vendettas and gang battles that pursue escalating spirals of animosity and violence; ugly divorces fueled by a passion to pay back for wrongs received; and petty acts designed to get even. One cynic has claimed that there are more lawyers than doctors in the United States, because Americans are much more interested in getting even than they are in getting better!

However, we never really do get even, and we probably don't really want to. I want my tormentor to hurt at least a little more than I have, to pay him back with interest. We concoct elaborate fantasies in our mind in which the perpetrators receive the humiliation they richly deserve, so that all can see our vindication and their shame. Thankfully, we rarely act out those fantasies, choosing to employ more discreet and socially acceptable ways of getting even and paying back. An old cliché tells us that revenge is sweet. Perhaps. But it turns sour very quickly. Worse, it often sets in motion an uncontrollable chain reaction, with significant unintended consequences and considerable collateral damage. No wonder James 1:20 says so clearly, "man's anger does not bring about the righteous life that God desires."

[Revenge] often sets in motion an uncontrollable chain reaction, with significant unintended consequences and considerable collateral damage.

It is easy to condemn revenge in the abstract. It is quite another matter to resist it when a business competitor is undercutting my reputation with my customers, or when a supervisor is mistreating me; when a person I went out of my way to help slanders me, or when my marriage partner makes a mockery of our wedding vows; when a supposed friend betrays me, or an influential person seriously misrepresents me. At such times, the impulse to get even is overwhelmingly strong, usually cloaking itself as a desire for justice. But, tempting as revenge is, our Savior calls His people to a lifestyle of forgiveness. Clearly, revenge and forgiveness cannot coexist. Besides, God's Word is clear: "Do not repay anyone evil for evil. . . . Do not take revenge, my friends, but leave room for God's wrath, for it is written: 'It is mine to avenge; I will repay,' says the Lord" (Romans 12:17, 19).

One of the most significant events in the life of David, the great king of Israel, came before he ascended to the throne. He found himself dancing on the very edge of the cliffs of harsh revenge and came perilously close to falling over. Thanks to the intervention of a remarkable woman, he did not yield. It was, however, a very close call. If he had succumbed, his life story would have unfolded very differently. David was a remarkable man. He fought many enemies in his life: Goliath, the Philistines, King Saul, and foreign kings. But, like all of us, his greatest battles were always with himself. David was the one with the greatest potential to derail God's purposes for his life. So his self-battles become not merely incidents in his personal biography, but mirrors in which we can see our own faces.

Insulted by a Fool:
The Encounter of David and Nabal

Our story is found in 1 Samuel 25, located between two chapters that create a fascinating contrast. Chapters 24 and 26 record two different, but remarkably similar, events. David was innocent of any treachery to his former sponsor, Israel's first king, Saul. Even so, Saul relentlessly pursued him with the intent of taking his life; Saul was obsessed with the idea that David was the major threat to his throne. His obsession had far more to do with Saul's personal insecurity and spiritual emptiness than with David's actions. Saul's intense jealousy led him first to drive David away from the palace and then to turn him into a fugitive. In fact, Saul devoted a major part of his personal energy and military resources to the hunt for David. But on two distinct occasions, Saul blundered into a position where, unknowingly, he was completely at David's mercy. A simple sword thrust would have ended Saul's life and David's problems. Remarkably, on both occasions, David refused to take the opportunity for revenge. He was convinced that Saul had been appointed by God as king, and that God would fulfill David's own destiny, without David having to resort to violence against "God's anointed."

The chapter between those two events, however, shows another side of David. On this occasion, he was fully prepared to take revenge, to respond violently against a man guilty of a much lesser offense than Saul. Only the intervention of a wise and courageous woman spared David from a great evil. David's victory over revenge against King Saul didn't mean that he was immune from the temptation to exact revenge against a man with a well-deserved reputation as a fool. Why is it that some people and some acts push our buttons in a way that others don't? I am not sure our story reveals the answer to that question. It does, however, give insight into how quickly our emotions can spiral out of control and take us where we don't really want to go.

Now Samuel died, and all Israel assembled and mourned for him; and they buried him at his home in Ramah. Then David moved down into the Desert of Maon. A certain man in Maon, who had property there at Carmel, was very wealthy. He had a thousand goats and three thousand sheep, which he was shearing in Carmel. His name was Nabal and his wife's name was Abigail. She was an intelligent and beautiful woman, but her husband, a Calebite, was surly and mean in his dealings.

While David was in the desert, he heard that Nabal was shearing sheep. So he sent ten young men and said to them, "Go up to Nabal at Carmel and greet him in my name. Say to him: 'Long life to you! Good health to you and your household! And good health to all that is yours!

" 'Now I hear that it is sheep-shearing time. When your shepherds were with us, we did not mistreat them, and the whole time they were at Carmel nothing of theirs was missing. Ask your own servants and they will

tell you. Therefore be favorable toward my young men, since we come at a festive time. Please give your servants and your son David whatever you can find for them.'"

When David's men arrived, they gave Nabal this message in David's name. Then they waited.

Nabal answered David's servants, "Who is this David? Who is this son of Jesse? Many servants are breaking away from their masters these days. Why should I take my bread and water, and the meat I have slaughtered for my shearers, and give it to men coming from who knows where?"

David's men turned around and went back. When they arrived, they reported every word. David said to his men, "Put on your swords!" So they put on their swords, and David put on his. About four hundred men went up with David, while two hundred stayed with the supplies (1 Samuel 25:1–13).

The story as written takes the form of a brief drama, and we are first introduced to the cast of characters. Samuel the prophet appears, only to move quickly offstage. The Lord had used Samuel to bring the nation back to Him in the early stages of renewal and revival and had also directed him to anoint the nation's first two kings, Saul and then David. While alive, Samuel probably acted as a restraint on Saul's animosity toward David, but when he died, Saul felt free to pursue his vendetta. For the rest of Saul's life, David would be on the run from the king. David was a natural leader, and he wielded an effective fighting force, organizing a group of men, who came to him "in distress or in debt or discontented" (1 Samuel 22:2). Seeking a safe retreat, he and his men had retreated to a part of the countryside David knew well, the Judean wilderness. Their sojourn brought them to the desert of Maon, an area about eight miles south of Hebron.

Nearby, in a place fertile enough to be called Garden-land (that is the meaning of Carmel, although it should be noted that this is not Mount Carmel, made famous later by the prophet Elijah), there lived a man of great wealth. The writer draws attention to his wealth, "a thousand goats and three thousand sheep" (v. 2), before he tells us his name, Nabal. A Hebrew, hearing someone tell or read the story, would immediately laugh. Nabal means "Fool." It is hard to believe that any parents would give such a name to any child. Perhaps they gave him a name that sounded similar, and others turned it into this name of disrespect, because of his difficult character. Whatever the origin of the name, it suited him. Nabal he was called and fool he was! Even those closest to him made no effort to hide the fact. One of his major servants said of him, to his own wife, "He is such a wicked man that no one can talk to him" (v. 17). Servants can be cruel and unfair behind their master's back. But even his own wife said of him, "He is just like his name—his name is Fool and folly goes with him" (v. 25). His wealth may have given power and influence, but it could not disguise the hard truth about the man: He was "surly and mean in his dealings" (v. 3).

The final member of the cast is Nabal's wife, Abigail. Since marriages were arranged rather than the result of personal romantic choices, we should not hold her responsible for her choice of a husband. Perhaps she had been the victim of her father's ambition for a financially lucrative marriage arrangement. The text provides no clues about how long they had been married, and we can only surmise that this was not the happiest of marriages. But we quickly become aware that Abigail was the exact opposite of her husband, a woman of excellence, "an intelligent and beautiful woman" (v. 3). Her special qualities shine brightly as the story unfolds.

The story takes place in sheep-shearing time, an observation that doesn't say very much to those of us who live in cities or suburbs. Sheep-shearing time, which usually occurred in late summer, was a time of community celebration, a time when owners realized their profits and workers received their share of the proceeds. Although there was a great deal of work to do, it took place in a festive atmosphere of gift-giving and banqueting. So, when David heard that Nabal was shearing sheep, he sent a delegation of ten men to him. The Judean wilderness was wild country, home to animals that would prey on flocks and to bandits and desert peoples who would use it as a launching pad for frequent raids. But the presence of David's men had changed the dynamics. They had served as an unofficial police force, protecting the herders of the region from rustlers and controlling predatory animals. They had, in fact, enriched Nabal.

But the arrangement was informal not contractual. David sent his men to request financial or practical consideration for the services he and his men had provided. This was not a kind of primitive protection racket. Nabal's servants recognized very well the value of the work of David's men and the validity of their claims. As one of them told Abigail, "These men were very good to us. They did not mistreat us, and the whole time we were out in the fields near them nothing was missing. Night and day they were a wall around us all the time we were herding our sheep near them" (vv. 15–16). Such services had undoubtedly increased Nabal's profits, and some kind of recompense was appropriate.

David's instructions to his men were very precise. They were to meet Nabal unarmed (v. 13), avoiding any suggestion of coercion and intimidation. They were to be respectful: "Long life to you! Good health to you and your household! And good health to all that is yours!" (v. 6). They were also to be moderate and reasonable in their requests, making no veiled threats or exorbitant financial demands. Rather, they would take whatever Nabal deemed appropriate. In return for our protection, they said, "Please give your servants and your son David whatever you can find for them" (v. 8).

Predictably, Nabal's response was mean and surly. His attitude to David was contemptuous: "Who is this David?" (v. 10). Anyone in Israel could have answered that question, whether they sided with David or Saul. After all, David was the great hero who had killed Goliath. He was the military leader who had led the Israelites into victory over the Philistines. He was the crowd favorite, whose popularity had driven Saul mad with envy when the women danced and sang,

Saul has slain his thousands,
  and David his tens of thousands (1 Samuel 18:7).

In fact, it could be argued that, if not for David, Nabal would likely have been serving the Philistines, not enjoying his freedom! We would expect a person like Nabal to side with King Saul against David. Fool that he was, he chose not only to reject the proposal, but also to demean David, kicking him while he was down. He contemptuously dismissed him as nothing but a "runaway slave." And he didn't stop there. Although he was dealing with military veterans, he chose to insult them as well, deriding them as "men coming from who knows where" (v. 11). There was not even a modicum of gratitude. His response reeks of arrogance and self-importance, as he used the personal pronouns I or my eight times in the Hebrew text of verse 11. Nabal's refusal was total, and his disdain was unbounded.

Nabal was playing with fire, but he was too much of a fool to know it. David's men were battle-hardened veterans, intensely loyal to their leader. Only enormous self-control kept them from immediately wiping the sneer from Nabal's face! Instead, they controlled their tempers, returned to David, and delivered their report. David's response was immediate and determined fury: "Put on your swords!" (v. 13). He then ordered four hundred men to mount up on a mission of revenge against Nabal and everything belonging to him. David was intent on massive bloodshed, as he later made clear to Abigail: "He has paid me back evil for good. May God deal with David, be it ever so severely, if by morning I leave alive one male of all who belong to him!" (vv. 21–22). There was no suggestion merely of teaching Nabal a lesson. David had a vow of blood revenge on his heart, if not on his lips.

What accounts for this response? Nabal's insult was real, but David's response was a massive overreaction. David had managed to resist retaliation against the much greater evil Saul had done to him. Why did Nabal get under his skin so badly? We cannot be sure. But we do know that David was a person with a long history of mistreatment. His father had minimized and marginalized him; his brothers had taunted and ridiculed him; his king had stripped him of almost everything valuable to him—his wife, closest friend, reputation, and physical safety. So perhaps the contempt of Nabal hit an exposed nerve or probed a wound deep in his soul. Perhaps this was the straw that broke the proverbial camel's back. Or perhaps Nabal became the lightning rod that attracted David's gathering storm. After all, he had not only been insulted, he had been shamed in the presence of his men. Not only had his services gone unrecognized, his personal worth had been attacked. To be dismissed as human scum was deeply painful.

I can still remember vividly the time a man told me, with deep disdain evident in his voice and manner, that he didn't consider me a person worth getting to know. Rejection like that is painful. Although I have sought to forgive, I can still feel the pain of his contempt.

"There was never an angry man who thought his anger unjustified."

AUGUSTINE

For whatever reasons, David, at this moment, was way out of control. Some anger may have been justified, but his was out of all proportion to the offense. He was in danger of acting the fool, imitating his nemesis, Nabal. As Proverbs warns,

Do not answer a fool according to his folly,
  or you will be like him yourself (26:4).

A fool shows his annoyance at once,
  but a prudent man overlooks an insult (12:16).

David was being anything but prudent. His intentions were evil. The response was out of all proportion to the offense. Revenge and self-vindication are like that. As Augustine observed, "There was never an angry man who thought his anger unjustified." Sadly, David had lost contact with his Lord. Nowhere is there the slightest suggestion that he had prayed or sought the Lord's guidance. His desire to strike back was instinctual not spiritual. In the process, he was in danger of becoming an even worse fool than the one he was dealing with.

Forgiveness challenges our natural instincts; revenge feeds on them. It is very seductive and powerful. A desire for justice and fair treatment is entirely appropriate, as is the desire to see evil punished. But toying with revenge is like playing with dynamite. As Schimmel observed,

> Revenge is one of the most powerful of human emotions. Acts of revenge range from the trivial to the horrific. A waiter annoyed by a boorish customer might spit in the bowl of soup before delivering it with a feigned smile. The waiter takes pleasure in knowing what he has done even though the customer is unaware of the added ingredient. At the other extreme, men have committed bloody massacres to avenge their impugned honor. . . . One retaliatory act of revenge by a victim spurs a reciprocal response by the initial perpetrator, with the cycle of vengeance and retaliation spiraling out of control until it is no longer possible to distinguish between perpetrator and victim. Eventually all who are involved in the vendetta become both victims and perpetrators of evil.[2]

The instinct to strike back is accompanied by a desire to see the offender suffer for what we believe he has done. The danger is that the greater the suffering, the greater our enjoyment. A pattern of escalation is almost inevitable. That is why the Old Testament was so careful to put strict limits on acts of judicial retribution: "an eye for an eye and a tooth for a tooth" (Exodus 21:24; Leviticus 24:17–22; Deuteronomy 19:21; see Matthew 5:38). God's Word is not promoting revenge. Its purpose is to do exactly the opposite, to define justice, to prohibit disproportionate retaliation, and to prevent escalating violence. But our hearts are sinful. So popular interpretation changed the command from a prohibition to a requirement. When injured, you needed to extract "eye for eye, tooth for tooth." It was that misreading the Lord Jesus challenged when He called His followers to turn the other cheek (Matthew 5:39). In Christ we are called to the higher law of the kingdom, the way of loving nonretaliation (Matthew 5:39–42).

Fortunately, as David set off on his course of revenge, other forces were at work. Nabal didn't know it, but his life was now in the hands of two people who knew him for the fool he was, one of his servants and his wife. And David would be restrained from evil only because a wise and courageous woman decisively intervened.

Intercepted by Wisdom: Abigail and David

Let's continue the story, found in 1 Samuel 25:14–31.

One of the servants told Nabal's wife Abigail: "David sent messengers from the desert to give our master his greetings, but he hurled insults at them. Yet these men were very good to us. They did not mistreat us, and the whole time we were out in the fields near them nothing was missing. Night and day they were a wall around us all the time we were herding our sheep near them. Now think it over and see what you can do, because disaster is hanging over our master and his whole household. He is such a wicked man that no one can talk to him."

Abigail lost no time. She took two hundred loaves of bread, two skins of wine, five dressed sheep, five seahs of roasted grain, a hundred cakes of raisins and two hundred cakes of pressed figs, and loaded them on donkeys. Then she told her servants, "Go on ahead; I'll follow you." But she did not tell her husband Nabal.

As she came riding her donkey into a mountain ravine, there were David and his men descending toward her, and she met them. David had just said, "It's been useless—all my watching over this fellow's property in the desert so that nothing of his was missing. He has paid me back evil for good. May God deal with David, be it ever so severely, if by morning I leave alive one male of all who belong to him!"

When Abigail saw David, she quickly got off her donkey and bowed down before David with her face to the ground. She fell at his feet and said: "My lord, let the blame be on me alone. Please let your servant speak to you;

hear what your servant has to say. May my lord pay no attention to that wicked man Nabal. He is just like his name—his name is Fool, and folly goes with him. But as for me, your servant, I did not see the men my master sent.

"Now since the Lord has kept you, my master, from bloodshed and from avenging yourself with your own hands, as surely as the Lord lives and as you live, may your enemies and all who intend to harm my master be like Nabal. And let this gift, which your servant has brought to my master, be given to the men who follow you. Please forgive your servant's offense, for the Lord will certainly make a lasting dynasty for my master, because he fights the Lord's battles. Let no wrongdoing be found in you as long as you live. Even though someone is pursuing you to take your life, the life of my master will be bound securely in the bundle of the living by the Lord your God. But the lives of your enemies he will hurl away as from the pocket of a sling. When the Lord has done for my master every good thing he promised concerning him and has appointed him leader over Israel, my master will not have on his conscience the staggering burden of needless bloodshed or of having avenged himself. And when the Lord has brought my master success, remember your servant."

Although Nabal was utterly blind to the stupidity of his actions, one of his servants immediately realized the likely consequences of his master's insulting behavior. Alarmed, he hurried to the only person he believed had the ability to forestall disaster: Nabal's wife Abigail. He didn't dare or even bother to approach Nabal. That, he knew, would be futile. He may also have worried about approaching his master's wife. After all, speaking hard truths about a man to his wife is always dangerous business. I have a friend who tells of the time a woman notorious for her critical spirit approached her. She wanted to give her some criticisms that she could pass on to her preacher husband. Would my friend mind? My friend's reply was classic: "Not at all, as long as you don't mind my scratching your eyes out afterwards!" But, despite the evident danger, the unnamed servant knew he had to take the risk. Abigail must be told, even at the cost of his being brutally honest about her husband. Nabal's words had been deliberately inflammatory, and the "code of a warrior" meant that David would surely respond. Failure to act would cause him to lose face before his men.

Abigail immediately realized the seriousness of the situation. She also knew that arguing with her husband or trying to involve him was useless. As Proverbs 27:22 observes,

> *Though you grind a fool in a mortar,*
> *grinding him like grain with a pestle,*
> *you will not remove his folly from him.*

One gets the sense that this was not the first time she had had to rescue Nabal from the consequences of his behavior! Shrewdly she prepared a large gift, containing the very kind of things for which David's men had asked: bread, wine, sheep, roasted grain, raisins, and figs. She then had it loaded on a caravan of donkeys, sending the caravan ahead with her servants, while she followed behind, riding her donkey. The gift would meet a real need, help David save face before his men, and perhaps mollify David's anger. By sending it ahead, she hoped to buy time, keeping David from acting before she arrived. Traveling alone also gave her time to rehearse both what she would say and how she would say it. She had no margin for error; innocent lives lay in the balance. Someone needed to keep a clear head! As she rode to save both Nabal and David from themselves, she was a picture of wisdom in action.

Meanwhile, David had been "psyching himself" into an act of unrestrained violence. "He has paid me back evil for good. May God deal with David, be it ever so severely, if by morning I leave alive one male of all who belong to him!" (vv. 21–22). For a woman, in the culture of that time, to impose herself into the middle of such a situation took great courage. She had become the Lord's flashing red light to bring the emotionally overcharged David to a screeching halt.

Her encounter with David is a model of womanly wisdom. One great preacher calls her "a cool hand on a hot head." Throwing herself at David's feet in humility and appeal, she poured out her carefully considered words. There were at least three things she wanted David to hear.

First, David needed to consider the source of the problem: Nabal was a fool. She spoke very directly to David about her husband. Despite her hard words about Nabal, she was, in fact, being completely loyal to him, acting decisively in his best interests even as she put her own life at risk. There was no guarantee that David would not take out his anger on her. She was completely honest about the man with whom she shared her life: "May my lord pay no attention to that wicked man Nabal. . . . his name is Fool, and folly goes with him" (v. 25). Hard words for a woman to speak about her husband, but undeniably true! He was indeed "wicked," an expression used often to describe someone or something that was "worthless" or good-for-nothing. She was not trying to denigrate her husband, but to save him. The situation required bold honesty, not careful subtlety!

However, she did not dwell on Nabal's character. Instead, she took the responsibility on herself, saying that she should have been present to prevent the disaster: "I did not see the men my master sent" away (v. 25). This made no sense; Nabal and Nabal alone was responsible for his own behavior. She was not the first wife (or the last!) to try to dig a foolish husband out of the hole he had dug for himself. David was in grave danger of letting a fool determine his behavior, and thus becoming like the very man he despised. An old saying, based on the observation that bears often allow skunks to cohabitate in their vicinity, comments: "Any bear can beat a skunk. But he knows that it's just not worth it." You may beat Nabal, but you still end up smelling as he does!

Second, David needed to count the cost: His God-given destiny was at stake. She spoke to David as if he had already turned back from his course of action, apparently to make it clear that turning back was the only reasonable course of action. But what she went on to say was truly remarkable. She asked him to forgive her husband "for the Lord will certainly make a lasting dynasty for my master, because he fights the Lord's battles" (v. 28). This was, in fact, what the Lord would do for David. But how could Abigail have known? The Lord would not reveal this to his prophet Nathan for many years, in what has come to be called the Davidic Covenant, recorded in 2 Samuel 7! The prophet Samuel had announced that David would rule as the next king, when he secretly anointed him for that role in the event recorded in 1 Samuel 16. Perhaps that prophetic anointing had become public knowledge. But there was no indication that God would give David a lasting dynasty. Where had Abigail come by such an idea? Was this just a good guess? Was she merely expressing her opinion or seeking to flatter David? Those do not seem to be adequate explanations. Abigail's words have the character of a God-given prophecy of David's divinely ordained destiny. Her statement here is the reason Jewish rabbis later included Abigail among the seven prophetesses of the Old Testament!

Abigail was convinced not only of David's destiny, but also that his destiny must determine his present conduct. If he could not rule himself, how could he properly rule others? Carrying out his intended act of revenge might give him short-term pleasure, but he would do devastating damage to his future rule: "Let no wrongdoing be found in you as long as you live" (v. 28). Furthermore, he would inflict significant harm on his conscience: "When the Lord has done for my master every good thing he promised concerning him and has appointed him leader over Israel, my master will not have on his conscience the staggering burden of needless bloodshed or of having avenged himself" (vv. 30–31). Abigail's confidence in David's destiny is remarkable, and it must have been a deeply encouraging reminder to David of God's calling on his life. She could see in this fugitive, guerrilla leader the future, God-appointed king of the nation! She also knew that, while revenge on Nabal might please him for a time, it would leave behind an overwhelming burden that David would carry for the rest of his life. Her wisdom was relevant: Revenge is a seductive short-term solution that leaves ugly long-term consequences.

Abigail's third piece of counsel is equally significant. *David needed to consider his options: He could leave revenge to the Lord.* She reminded David of a truth he himself celebrated repeatedly in the Psalms. God is a God who cares for and watches over His people. He will vindicate those who put their trust in Him. In fact, one of the most consistent cries in David's psalms is for God to "rise up" and deal with his enemies. But in this context, there had been no such turning to the Lord. So Abigail pointed him back to the Lord he had been neglecting, in the heat of his passion for revenge. In her speech she used the name of Yahweh seven times to remind David that he was in Yahweh's hands, not Nabal's or Saul's. The Lord is the avenger of His people, not David. This is Abigail's version of the words of Moses in Deuteronomy 32:35: "It is mine to avenge; I will repay." David had an option to revenge that he had forgotten: He could trust Yahweh to deal with Nabal and take the matter out of his own hands. After all, that must have been the way Abigail had had to live with Nabal the fool! It could not have been easy, but she had chosen not to seek her own revenge or retaliate in kind.

Miroslav Volf writes about this subject not only as a theologian, but also as a Croatian who has witnessed the terrible cost of the spiraling revenge and ethnic cleansing that ripped apart the former Yugoslavia. His warning is worth our attention: "Though victims may not be able to prevent hate from springing to life, for their own sake they can and must refuse to give it nourishment and strive to weed it out. If victims do not repent today they will become perpetrators tomorrow who, in their self-deceit, will seek to exculpate their misdeeds on account of their own victimization."[3]

Whether I take matters in my own hands or put them in the Lord's will determine whether I get His results or mine.

There is a significant lesson here. How I respond to a person who has wronged me will determine whether or not I become like the fool he has proven himself to be. And whether I take matters in my own hands or put them in the Lord's will determine whether I get His results or mine.

Protected by God: David and His Lord

There's more to the 1 Samuel 25 story . . .

David said to Abigail, "Praise be to the Lord, the God of Israel, who has sent you today to meet me. May you be blessed for your good judgment and for keeping me from bloodshed this day and from avenging myself with my own hands. Otherwise, as surely as the Lord, the God of Israel, lives, who has kept me from harming you, if you had not come quickly to meet me, not one male belonging to Nabal would have been left alive by daybreak."

Then David accepted from her hand what she had brought him and said, "Go home in peace. I have heard your words and granted your request."

When Abigail went to Nabal, he was in the house holding a banquet like that of a king. He was in high spirits and very drunk. So she told him nothing until daybreak. Then in the morning, when Nabal was sober, his wife told him all these things, and his heart failed him and he became like a stone. About ten days later, the Lord struck Nabal and he died.

When David heard that Nabal was dead, he said, "Praise be to the Lord, who has upheld my cause against Nabal for treating me with contempt. He has kept his servant from doing wrong and has brought Nabal's wrongdoing down on his own head."

Then David sent word to Abigail, asking her to become his wife. His servants went to Carmel and said to Abigail, "David has sent us to you to take you to become his wife." She bowed down with her face to the ground and said, "Here is your maidservant, ready to serve you and wash the feet of my master's servants." Abigail quickly got on a donkey and, attended by her five maids, went with David's messengers and became his wife (vv. 32–42).

One of David's most consistent and attractive qualities was his response to rebuke or correction. He did not respond to Abigail with male defensiveness, even though he had been firmly (but graciously) challenged in the presence of his men by this woman. He was not suspicious of her, even though she was his tormentor's wife. And even though he had given a rousing battle speech to four hundred men mounted and armed for action, he was not too proud to change his plans and publicly admit his mistake. In the strongest possible language, he praised her wisdom and admitted his own error of judgment. His response is a beautiful illustration of Proverbs 15:31:

> *He who listens to a life-giving rebuke*
> *will be at home among the wise.*

Even more significantly, he recognized the hand of God in the intervention of Abigail. She was God's messenger. With God now in focus, David changed his direction. "If you had not come quickly to meet me, not one male belonging to Nabal would have been left alive by daybreak. . . . Go home in peace. I have heard your words and granted your request" (vv. 34–35). He would leave Nabal in his Lord's hands and trust the outcome and his vindication to Him.

In this case the Lord intervened quickly and clearly. When Abigail returned home, she found Nabal drunk. While she had been making every possible effort to rescue him from imminent danger, he had been indulging himself and ignoring his danger, completely unprepared for the attack his wife had so narrowly averted. Had David arrived, the massacre would have been quick and total. She recognized that intelligent conversation was impossible while he was in his drunken stupor; Nabal was hard enough to talk to under the best of circumstances! So Abigail held her tongue. But the next morning, while Nabal nursed his hangover, she reported the previous day's events. The effect was dramatic: "his heart failed him and he became like a stone" (v. 37). It is not clear whether this was primarily a medical or a psychological effect. Most likely it was a combination of the judicial hand of God and psychological trauma, as he realized just how close he had come to disaster. He was not to recover.

The Lord's hand is not usually quite so clear or so quick! Within ten days Nabal had been dealt with. David could not help but see the providential hand of God, both in restraining him from evil and in dealing with his nemesis. And, as David reflected on the story, he felt himself powerfully drawn to the woman of beauty and wisdom who had been God's agent of grace in his life. He sent word to her that he desired her to be his wife. As a woman of wealth, the heir of her husband's estate, she was now in the culturally unusual position of being able to choose her own future and perhaps her own husband. Why would she choose to align herself with a fugitive bandit leader? Almost certainly because, whatever she felt about him romantically, she was convinced that the hand of God was on the life of David. So she went to David and become his wife.

Modeled by David: Leaving Vengeance to God

This is a remarkable story in its own right, but, in our context of forgiveness, it reminds us that we live in a fallen world where sinful people do great harm to others and have no intention of repenting. There is within us a deep desire for justice, for wrong to be punished, and for our cause to be vindicated. The most obvious and instinctive course of action is to strike back, to take matters into our own hands, and to handle it ourselves. As we have seen, the pursuit of justice and the punishment of evildoers is a divinely appointed governmental responsibility. But, if we pursue revenge on our own, we not only violate the Lord's commands, we may reap a bitter harvest. At first, revenge may seem successful and feel satisfying. But nearly always we set in motion an escalating spiral of retaliation and revenge. The desire for justice is not wrong. Even the saints in heaven are portrayed as praying, "How long, Sovereign Lord, holy and true, until you judge the inhabitants of the earth and

If we pursue revenge on our own, we not only violate the Lord's commands, we may reap a bitter harvest.

avenge our blood?" (Revelation 6:10). At the same time, the command of Scripture is clear: "Do not take revenge, my friends, but leave room for God's wrath, for it is written: 'It is mine to avenge; I will repay,' says the Lord" (Romans 12:19). God's Spirit calls us to imitate the Lord's costly love for His enemies, not to pursue getting even and paying back. Rather, we are to entrust ourselves to the Father, who has promised that He will take up our cause.

Intriguingly, the pattern we are called to follow was a response modeled by David himself in his conflict with Saul. On the first occasion when David refused to take the easy opportunity to kill Saul, David said, "May the Lord judge between you and me. And may the Lord avenge the wrongs you have done to me, but my hand will not touch you. . . . May he consider my cause and uphold it; may he vindicate me by delivering me from your hand" (1 Samuel 24:12, 15). In the second case, David rejected his men's plea that they be allowed on his behalf to kill the sleeping Saul. " 'As surely as the Lord lives,' [David] said, 'the Lord himself will strike him; either his time will come and he will die, or he will go into battle and perish. But the Lord forbid that I should lay a hand on the Lord's anointed" (1 Samuel 26:10–11).

David did not deny that he was being severely wronged. But three things kept him from revenge: the conviction that God was sovereign; the certainty that God was wise; and the confidence that God was just. He could therefore leave Saul in God's hands. And those same truths are crucial for us as we fight against the pull of revenge: God is sovereign. God is wise. God is just. He can be trusted to do what is right, both for our wrongdoer and for us.

Years after the Civil War, Robert E. Lee was visiting the home of a Southern woman, who poured out her bitterness at the Union soldiers who had come through her property. She took him to see the remains of a grand old tree that had been severely damaged by Union artillery fire. She cried bitterly, with tears that showed that her grief was mixed with grief over the fate of the Confederacy. She waited for Lee to join in her lament. But Lee, who knew the horrors of war all too personally, simply looked at her and declared, "Cut it down, Madam, and then forget it." Good advice both for her and for us. Even better: having cut it down, to plant a new tree, in anticipation of a new harvest, in the grace of God.

Chapter 10

BRIDGE UNDER REPAIR

*L*et me introduce myself. My name is Zaphenath-paneah. It's a bit of a tongue twister, I know, and that was my reaction when Pharaoh gave it to me. It is an Egyptian name, and I felt better when he told me what it means: "God speaks and lives." That has been the story of my life. It isn't the name I was born with. You know me better by my Hebrew name, Joseph, given to me at birth by my mother, Rachel. She had waited a long time for me. Being childless had been the great shame and heartbreak of her life, one that caused her and everyone around her great pain. But when I was born, the son she had longed for for so many years, she instinctively poured out her heart's desire in prayer: "May the Lord add to me another son" (Genesis 30:24). So I became known as Joseph, which means "May God Add." He answered her prayer, allowing her once again to become pregnant, but she died giving birth to my brother Benjamin.

Perhaps you know at least part of my story; I lived it and then told it to my children so they could learn from it. Others repeated it, and then the Lord led Moses to write it in the first book He gave to His people, the book of Genesis. So down through the centuries, people have heard the story of Joseph and learned something of the mysterious goodness of God. I won't take the time to recount my entire life story. But I thought you might be helped by what I have learned about forgiveness, as well as about rebuilding relationships that seemed hopelessly broken. In fact, my story isn't really about me at all, but about Yahweh, my God, the One who has been my Keeper and Protector through all that has happened.

My father, Jacob, had himself learned about forgiveness the hard way. He could be a hard man; his name, Deceiver, suited him! He spent a lot of his life deceiving or trying to deceive almost everyone who had anything to do with him, especially his father, his brother, and his uncle. But there came a time when he experienced God's forgiveness in a powerful way. He loved to gather his boys around him and tell us about the strange night when he was attacked and had to protect himself, by wrestling with a mysterious stranger. This unknown attacker turned out to be the angel of God Himself. Our father delighted to recall how the stranger suddenly touched him and dislocated his hip. Father recognized this was no ordinary person, and he wouldn't let go until the stranger blessed him and forgave him. He knew he had met with God Himself, and so he called that place Peniel, which means "the face of God." He said that God had given him two things that morning that he always retained: a new name and a bad limp. The name was Israel, a name that meant he had struggled with God and prevailed. That was a great change, from Deceiver to Prevailer! The limp, he told us, reminded him that he needed to depend on God and not try to do things on his own. He was amazed that he had seen God and lived to talk about it; from then on, he wanted to be a different kind of man.

But he then had to face his brother, Esau, an encounter he had dreaded for years. More than twenty years earlier, he had deceived his father, cheated his brother, and fled for his life, far away from home. Though he thought it would be only a matter of weeks, two decades passed. But you can't just keep running forever. There comes a time when you have to face what you have done and put it right with the people you have hurt. Now that my dad had met God, he was ready to confront what he feared the most. He wouldn't have been surprised if Esau had tried to kill him, but he discovered that God had gone ahead of him and made Esau open to reconciliation. He loved to tell me how he had learned that true repentance is the key to deep forgiveness, and how good it felt finally to be able to let go of the chains of the past he had been dragging around for years.

Even though our father was a changed man, I guess so many things had happened in our family that it wasn't easy for us boys to really hear what he said. With all those boys and four different mothers, we always seemed to be fighting about something. So my story is also about forgiveness. The part I want to emphasize took place when I was about forty, but you'll understand it better if I tell you what led up to one of the greatest days in my life.

Forgiveness: A Choice About the Past

Anyone looking at me realistically would say I was a prime candidate for bitterness. They didn't use the term *dysfunctional* back then, but if they had, my family would have topped the list. Let's just say my father ended up with twelve boys mothered by four different women, an arrangement that led to all kinds of jealousies and rivalries. I was number eleven, the long-awaited first son of Rachel, my father's favorite wife.

When my mother died giving birth to my brother Benjamin, my father was heartbroken. I was already my father's favorite child, and now he seemed to transfer all the things he'd felt for my mother to me, favoring me in all kinds of ways. He couldn't do enough to show everyone how much he loved me. My older brothers had already been taught by their mothers that I was their biggest threat. They were a pretty tough bunch; some of them had earned a reputation for violence and rape. So now I became the prime target for their envy and anger and for their bitterness about the way my father had treated their mothers and them. I was young and immature, and I guess I said and did some things that only made matters worse.

One day my father sent me on an errand to my brothers, tending our flocks out in the countryside. After a long search, I found them out in the middle of nowhere. I hadn't been worried about finding them, but suddenly I realized I was completely vulnerable. They could do whatever they wanted to me. I heard them talk about killing me, about getting rid of me once and for all. I could hardly believe my ears! Then when some Bedouin traders happened by, headed for Egypt, my brothers decided they could get rid of me and make some money in the process. They could sell me to these traders, as a slave. I pleaded with them not to do it. (How could they even think such a thing?) But they wouldn't listen, and I was hauled off like a piece of merchandise.

In Egypt I didn't know anybody and couldn't speak the language. I can't find words to tell you how terrified I was. And confused. The Lord had given me a dream of His plans for me. I had trusted what He had shown me. This didn't make any sense. Had He totally forgotten me?

In Egypt I was sold to Pharaoh's chief executioner. As you can imagine, he was a hard man. But I was a good worker. In fact, working hard was the best way to avoid thinking about all that had happened to me and how unfair it was. So I did my best, and he increased my responsibilities. Soon I was in charge of all his affairs. But that only led to another problem. His wife began showing me the kind of attention I did not want. Despite everything that had happened, I wanted to live the way Yahweh wanted. I remembered the stories I'd heard from my father and grandfather Isaac, about who our God was and what He had promised. I didn't want to do something that would be as offensive to Him as committing adultery, even if my master never found out about it. I tried to avoid her, but she kept after me. Finally I had to say no in a way that infuriated her. She turned it all around and claimed I had tried to rape her! I don't think my master really believed her. After all, I'd seen him execute slaves for much less serious things, with no proof at all. He spared my life, but I ended up in prison.

By now I was thirty years old. Every relationship I had ever known, every person I had given my best to, every situation I had been responsible for—everything always turned sour. As far as I could tell, I was going to be inside prison walls for the rest of my life.

Then, in one day, everything changed. Pharaoh had a dream that he sensed had special meaning. He was relentless in his search for an interpreter, though no one could make any sense of it. Finally his chief cupbearer, who had spent some time in prison with me, got up the courage to tell Pharaoh that I had prophetically interpreted one of his dreams. So I was dragged before the king, to hear the dream and try to interpret it. As he recounted his dream, Yahweh immediately made it perfectly clear to me! I told Pharaoh what the Lord had revealed to me, and he immediately sensed the truth of my words, which had come from God—predicting years of good harvest followed by years of famine. The Lord also helped me set out a plan to deal with the famine. Instantly everything changed. Pharaoh not only released me from prison; he made me the number-one person in his entire kingdom!

From prison to the palace in one fell swoop! Suddenly I was in a position of almost absolute power. I could do almost anything to anyone, and no one could or would stop me. At times I was tempted to use that power to get even. I would find myself thinking, *Never again. No one is ever going to treat me the way I've been treated. No one can hurt me now!* I would think about the things I could do to people who had done me so much wrong. But that was not the kind of person I wanted to be. I remembered what Pharaoh had said, just after I'd told him what his dream meant and laid out the plan I believed God had given me. He looked all around the room, at everyone standing there. "Can we find anyone like this man, one in whom the spirit of the gods lives?" It was amazing to me. Despite everything that had happened to me, he could see my God in my life, even though he didn't have a clear idea of who Yahweh was.

People have asked me, "How did you survive all those terrible things that were done to you? How did you keep from getting bitter? Why didn't you get hardened?" I tried to give the answer when I named my boys. Pharaoh had changed my name by now to an Egyptian one: Zaphenath-paneah, as I told you. But I was very careful to give my first son a Hebrew name. I wanted him to know who he

really was, one of the covenant people to whom the Lord had given
great promises. His name, Manasseh, means "Forgotten." I know
that's an unusual thing to call a child, but I had a reason. When I
named him, I said, "God has made me forget all my trouble and all
my father's household."[1] I wanted his name to be a continual reminder
to me, as well as a statement to others, that I had made a choice not
to live in the past. People, especially my brothers, had done so many
evil things. I knew I had a choice: I could let them and what they had
done control my life, or I could let God control me. I could hold onto
those sinful things and let them hold onto me, or I could give them
over to God. That was why I

Forgetfulness is the key to fruit-
fulness; if you spend all your life
looking back over your shoulder
at the things others have done to
you, you will never be fruitful
where the Lord has placed you.

named my son Manasseh. It
was my declaration that the
past was past. It was forgotten,
given to God. Don't misunderstand me. That did not mean
that I never thought of my
father and my brothers. In fact,
I thought of them every day. I
hadn't forgotten what they had
done to me. But I refused to brood over them, turning them over and
over in my mind. I had given them to the Lord. Every time I call my
son, his name reminds me that I've let it all go.

Then I had my second son. By now we were living in a palace,
not a slave's quarters or a prison. So I called him Ephraim or "Fruitful." I wanted people to know why. "It is because God has made me
fruitful in the land of my suffering."[2] There is a connection between
those two names. I think that forgetfulness is the key to fruitfulness;
if you spend all your life looking back over your shoulder at the
things others have done to you, you will never be fruitful where the
Lord has placed you. Forgetfulness is a spiritual matter. It's all about
what you really believe about God, about His sovereignty and His
goodness.

Rebuilding Trust: A Work in the Present

The funny thing about the past is that it can suddenly become very present. I was going about my job as prime minister of Egypt, a position I'd held for nine years. There had been seven years of bumper crops and abundance, just as the Lord had revealed. My plan to lay in store for the seven hard years had been a great success. Now we were in those hard years. We were two years into the cycle of famine the dream had foretold, and I was busily involved in the supervision of a storehouse area. Hearing there was food available in Egypt, people from bordering countries began to arrive. We were worried that our provisions would make us the target of military raids, and we suspected that spies were already coming to evaluate our readiness. So I had given orders that foreign visitors were to go through a special screening process.

I happened to be onsite when a group of foreigners was conducted into my presence. There was nothing unusual about this; they were just another batch of outsiders, until their speech caught my ear. They were using the language of my youth, one I hadn't heard for years. When I looked more closely, those weren't strangers; they were my brothers, ten of them! My brothers, my very own brothers! I looked anxiously for the youngest, Benjamin. He wasn't there. What did that mean? Was he still alive? What about my father? Was he alive? Was he well? A million questions filled my heart.

They had no idea who I was. After all, it had been more than twenty years since they had gotten rid of me. They had no way of knowing whether I was dead or alive, and they could never have imagined that I had become the governor of Egypt. Here I was, standing before them in all my regal finery, surrounded by my officials and all the trappings of my power! Besides, they were desperate. They needed food for their families and would do anything not to offend an official who could decide whether they received it or not. They were almost afraid to lift up their heads and to look me in the eye. They didn't know who I was, but I knew who they were, and I had a decision to make. I could have done anything I wanted to them. It would have been easy just to walk away, to turn them down flat. Let them die! After all, that's what they had been willing to do with me. I didn't owe them anything. Or I could have inflicted whatever punishment I desired. No one would have dared to object or even to ask any questions. They were completely at my mercy.

But it wasn't that simple. I wanted to know about my father. Was he still alive? What about Benjamin? But there was even more than that. God had a purpose for my family. He had declared it to my great-grandfather Abraham and then to Grandpa Isaac and my father. If I rejected them, what would become of God's purpose for us all?

I had another option. I could have told them who I was, embraced them, and taken it from there. I could plaster over our differences and pretend they didn't matter. But if I chose that way, we would never really be united, just a group of strangers putting up with one another. Had my brothers changed? Could I trust them? Or were they still the same as always?

I suppose it is easy to misunderstand. But I wanted my family to be a family. I wanted us to realize the vision that God had given Abraham when He said we would be a blessing to the nations. That's sure not what we'd been up until now! The only way that could happen was if they had had a heart change, if there had been true repentance, if they were different men through what had happened. What they had done had certainly changed my life. Had it changed theirs? Had it even bothered them? If I ignored those questions— just accepted them and ignored the past—that would probably only guarantee that something like it would happen all over again. If they had had a change of heart, I needed to know whether it was superficial or significant, whether they viewed life differently.

So I developed a plan that no one knew but me. It involved a couple of tests. I must admit that I played it up a bit. I accused them of being spies, of being there to probe Egypt's vulnerabilities. They were alarmed, because they knew that this was a serious accusation.

Immediately they protested their innocence. "We're just brothers," they said. "Ten of us are here, and the youngest is back home with our father." That was good news; Dad and Benjamin were still alive! But I didn't let on.

"Listen, I don't buy your story," I said. "The only way you'll convince me is to bring back your youngest brother. One of you can go back and get him; the rest stay here." Then I threw them in jail for three days.

When I brought them back in, I changed the rules. I would keep only one of them; the rest could go home. The brother I kept would be released only if they all returned with their youngest brother. Perhaps you can sense what I was trying to discover. I wanted to see whether they would care about a brother who was in danger or in need. After all, they had been willing to ignore my calls for mercy and throw me away. Had anything changed, or was it still every man for himself? It was hard not to show my emotions when they began to talk back and forth to one another. They didn't have any idea that I could understand them. I was *A sensitive conscience* stunned that they were talking about me! *is a sign of hope.* "This is because of what we did to Joseph. We didn't listen to him when he pleaded with us. This is payback." And my brother Reuben talked about how he'd tried to stop them: "Now we must give an accounting for his blood."[3] So they hadn't forgotten, even after twenty-two years! In fact, it sounded as if they were haunted by what they had done to me. That gave me hope that something had changed in my brothers. Their consciences were heavy with their sin against me. A sensitive conscience is a sign of hope.

But I needed to learn more. Was their attitude just regret, or was it real repentance? I turned my back to regain my composure. Then I ordered guards to seize and bind Simeon. After he was led away, I had my men fill my brothers' sacks with food—and put their money back in their sacks without their knowledge. Then I sent them on their way. All I could do was wait. What would happen next?

My brothers told me later what did happen. When they stopped for the first night and undid their feed sacks, they found the money. They were terrified. They were sure that the absence of the money would be discovered, suspicion would fall on them, and they would be accused as thieves as well as spies. Return to Egypt now seemed very dangerous indeed. They would be risking their lives. Their earlier discomfort gave way to a conviction that this was God's judgment upon their old sin against me, that they were getting what they deserved: "What is this that God has done to us?"[4] Their chickens were coming home to roost! The whole situation was made worse when they returned home to Dad without Simeon. When they told my father all that had happened, and the requirement that Benjamin must accompany them on any return trip, all he could say was, "Everything is against me. I've lost Joseph and Simeon is as good as dead. You can't expect me to risk Benjamin! It isn't going to happen. He isn't going to Egypt."

But that's when it became clear that something had happened in the hearts of my brothers. My brother Reuben stepped forward to say that he would let his father hold Reuben's two sons as hostages. If Benjamin didn't come back, Jacob could kill his two boys. It was actually a pretty foolish suggestion. What good would it do for my father to kill two of his grandsons? But it showed the depth of Reuben's concern for his father and his brother. My father didn't pay any attention to him; he refused to think about the situation as long as there was food. But the famine grew worse, and the family's situation became desperate. The brothers pleaded with my father to let Benjamin go with them. They were rapidly reaching the point of no return: if they didn't get more food, the whole family might die, and Simeon would be abandoned. There was no point in returning without Benjamin. This time it was my brother Judah who stepped forward. He had been one of the leaders when my brothers had attacked me. But now he told our father that he personally would guarantee Benjamin's safety, that he would put his life on the line and bear the blame for what happened. It was a new thought—one of the brothers being willing to die to protect Jacob's favorite son, in this case Benjamin, not me. So, very reluctantly, Jacob sent them back, accompanied by Benjamin and extra money to pay for the money returned the first time.

I'll never forget the moment they stood before me the second time. When they entered the country, my agents met them and carried out my instructions. They were brought directly to my house, an action that worried them greatly. There was Benjamin! I had waited so long to see him! But I kept my distance and had my servants look after them. They tried to return the money, but the servant reassured them and told them it wasn't necessary. Then Simeon was released and reunited with the brothers. Finally my chief steward led them into a special room arranged for a special banquet. When I arrived, I still didn't reveal my identity. They presented their gifts. I asked about the health of their father, trying to learn as much as I could, and then had them present Benjamin to me. At that point, I had to leave the room to regain my composure. When I returned, I ordered them to sit. Seating arrangements are always important at such formal meals, and I had arranged theirs carefully. They were startled to discover that they were seated in their birth order. *Surely it had to be coincidence, because how could anyone in Egypt know such details?* I also made sure that Benjamin received special honor, receiving five times as much as anyone else. I wanted to find out how they felt when the favored son was favored.

Finally it was time to send them on their way. Again, I told my servants to return their money to their sacks, secretly, but this time to put my special silver cup in Benjamin's sack. After they had gone, I ordered my men to set out after them and accuse them of theft of state property, my special cup. This was my ultimate test. My plan made it appear, even to his brothers, that Benjamin was guilty of an egregious theft. How would the other brothers respond? Would they point fingers at Benjamin and abandon him in his guilt? Would they stand by their father's favorite, even if it put them in jeopardy? Would they care about the effect on their father and honor their promise to him?

They passed with flying colors. Before the sacks were opened, the brothers protested their innocence and told my men that they would take the consequences. If one of them had taken the cup, he should be executed and the rest would become slaves. But when it was found in Benjamin's sack, they changed their tune, to protect their youngest brother. They all returned without hesitation. When they stood before me, Judah stepped forward to say that they would all be my slaves, attempting to spare Benjamin. When I insisted that only the thief would be punished, Judah again stepped forward to tell me about his father. With great passion he spoke about how much Benjamin meant to his father, how the old man would die if Benjamin didn't return, and how he had already lost his special son. Then he pleaded, from his very heart, with words I can still hear, "Now, then, please let me remain here as your slave in place of the boy, and let the boy return with my brothers. How can I go back to my father if the boy is not with me? No! Do not let me see the misery that would come upon my father."[5] As he talked, I looked at the other brothers and realized that he was speaking for them all.

It was obvious that these weren't the same men who had heard me crying and pleading and had hard-heartedly sold me anyway. These weren't the sons who had been willing to break the heart of their father, just to satisfy their jealousy toward me. These weren't the same people who had treated me with cold indifference and calculated evil. Each had experienced a genuine change of heart. A brother who had been willing to sell me as a slave just to get rid of me was now willing to become a slave to save my brother, Rachel's younger son. My brothers had repented! They cared about their brother and their father, even more than they cared about themselves.

Reconciliation: A Door to the Future

That was all I needed to hear and all I was able to bear. I was about to break down, so I ordered everyone but my brothers out of the room. This was too sacred a moment for anyone else to share. Others didn't need to know our family secrets and our sins. I didn't want others to know about issues that we could deal with and keep just between us. I didn't want others to see my brothers and think of the terrible way they had treated me. But, when my servants had gone, my control cracked. Years of suppressed pain, sadness, and grief erupted from inside me. I began to weep and wasn't sure I could ever stop. And my brothers just stood there stunned. Finally I blurted it out in Hebrew: "I am Joseph! Is my father still living?"[6]

If they were worried before, they were stunned and terrified now. With my words, they could now recognize that I really was Joseph. What was I going to do to them? This looked to them like a turn for the worst, beyond their most terrible imaginings! But I wanted them to know that the past was past. I could trust them now, and entrust myself to them. I tried to find words to tell them it was over, that God had been in the midst of it all. I called them closer and told them: "I am your brother Joseph, the one you sold into Egypt! And now, do not be distressed and do not be angry with yourselves for selling me here, because it was to save lives that God sent me ahead of you. For two years now there has been famine in the land, and for the next five years there will not be plowing and reaping. But God sent me ahead of you to preserve for you a remnant on earth and to save your lives by a great deliverance.

"So then, it was not you who sent me here, but God. He made me father to Pharaoh, lord of his entire household and ruler of all Egypt."[7]

Then I talked about the future, about how the Lord had put me in a position that could be the salvation of our family. We could use Egypt to save our family from the famine and to rebuild it in on an entirely

If you are really going to forgive somebody, you need to face what has happened, deal with the facts. You can't pretend.

new basis. Most of all, I wanted them to see God's hand in all of this. I tried to say it as clearly as I could: "God sent me ahead of you. . . . It was not you who sent me here but God."

I've thought a lot about that whole process, and I think I learned some things about forgiveness and about rebuilding a relationship that seems hopelessly broken. Let me share them with you. I think if you are really going to forgive somebody, you need to *face what has happened*, deal with the facts. You can't pretend. That's why I said it to them: "You sold me into Egypt." Later on, I had to say it even more directly: "You meant it for evil." And they had. Their behavior and their motives had been unspeakably evil. I knew it, and so did they. You've got to face what has really happened.

I also learned that you need to *feel it*. That's why I wept the way I did. There were so many layers of emotion: the pain of what had happened, the wasted years of separation, the joy of seeing the change in them. I needed to feel the hurt; even more, I needed to feel the forgiveness.

But if you asked me what was even more important, I would tell you that you need to *faith it*. I know that sounds strange, but that was why I kept saying, "God sent me." I needed to cultivate a divine perspective in all that happened. They meant it for evil, that was true, but God had meant it for good. So much had happened that reminded me that I wasn't a victim of circumstances but a child of God. Despite the depth of sin that had flowed around me, God's grace had been deeper and richer. Seeing Him and trusting Him was the only way I made it through. God is sovereign, and He hadn't ignored what had happened or wasted what happened. That's why I named my son Manasseh. It wasn't just that I forgot. God *made* me forget.

And then I needed to *forgive it*, to declare it was over and finished. I may not have used the word, but when I told them not to be distressed, I was telling them that it was over. I simply refused to go back into the past, to pick the scabs of all their failures and endlessly rehearse the ugliness of what had happened. I had already let it go to the Lord. Again, that's why I had called my son Manasseh. But now I could declare it to them. It was over. I was concerned about living for the future, not the past.

But I eventually learned something else, long after my brothers returned to Canaan, told my father the amazing news, and brought the entire family, seventy of them, back to Egypt. What a wonderful reunion with my father! The whole family remained with me in Egypt, and we were not only able to survive the famine, we were also able to begin rebuilding our family. My boys were able to meet and enjoy their grandfather, and I was able to make up a little for those lost years. Then, after seventeen special years, my father died. It was hard to say good-bye. But what grieved me most was that, after his death, my brothers came to me, asking forgiveness for what they had done so long ago. They even offered to be my slaves. We had buried my father, but they hadn't buried the past. This made me weep. They had been keeping their sins alive in their hearts all these years in Egypt. I'd let go of it, but they had kept holding on to it. I'd buried it, but they had kept digging it up. I didn't want them to be my slaves; I needed them to be my brothers. They thought I had forgiven them for the sake of my father. I hadn't. I had forgiven them for their sakes and for my own sake. But most of all, I had forgiven them for the sake of the Lord.

Now I needed to *refresh it*. So I did: "Don't be afraid. Am I in the place of God? You intended to harm me, but God intended it for good to accomplish what is now being done, the saving of many lives. So then, don't be afraid. I will provide for you and your children."[8] Forgiveness is not just a one-time event. You need to refresh it in your own heart, and sometimes for the sake of those who are having trouble letting go of their past.

I guess if there's one truth, more than any other, that I would like you to take from my life story, it's found in those words: "You

intended to harm me, but God intended it for good." Forgiving my
brothers, exposing their forgiveness, and starting to rebuild our relationship was hard work that drained all my emotional resources. But
what I learned most of all about those hard things in life is that people
may mean them for evil. People are capable
Forgiveness is not of doing terrible things to one another. But
just a one-time event. the God whom we serve means it for good,
not perhaps as we immediately see good,
but for a good that accomplishes His purposes in astonishing ways.
When we really trust Him, we are safe in His hands.

So that's my story. Perhaps there's something in it you can find
for your life. May God give you a Manasseh, a "making you forget."
And may He grant you the privilege of an Ephraim, of fruitfulness
in the land of suffering, perhaps in a glorious moment when authentic repentance is met by heartfelt forgiveness. May you have the
privilege, as I did, of seeing the Lord restore and rebuild relationships
that seem hopelessly broken, as He works to bring about authentic
repentance, true forgiveness, and careful reconciliation. Most of all,
may you rest in the God who always means whatever happens for
your good and for His glory.

Chapter 11

GOOD GRIEF

On September 11, 1998, President Bill Clinton spoke at a prayer breakfast in the White House. In January of that year, he had ended a televised speech to the nation by wagging his finger and declaring, "I did not have sexual relations with that woman, Ms. Lewinsky." He also had solemnly assured his cabinet, his staff, and his wife that he had been telling the truth. But he hadn't. After months of legal maneuverings, he was required to appear before a grand jury on August 17 to answer questions under oath. Because of that testimony, he had gone on national television that evening to make a carefully guarded admission: "While my answers were legally accurate, I did not volunteer information. Indeed, I did have a relationship with Miss Lewinsky that was inappropriate. In fact, it was wrong."

The public remained unconvinced. In the opinion of many, his four-minute speech had raised far more questions than it answered. So at the September prayer breakfast, Mr. Clinton was determined to speak more clearly:

> I was not contrite enough. I don't think there is a fancy way to say that I have sinned. It is important to me that everybody who has been hurt know that the sorrow I feel is genuine. . . . I have asked for their forgiveness. But I believe that to be forgiven, more than sorrow is required—at least two more things. First, genuine repentance—a determination to change and to repair breaches of my own making. I have repented. Second, what my Bible calls a "broken spirit"; an

understanding that I must have God's help to be the person
that I want to be.[1]

Those were remarkable words to come from any public figure, never mind the president of the most powerful nation on earth.
Predictably, there were all kinds of responses, most concerned more
about politics than morality. Some were satisfied, wanting to accept
his apology and get on with it: "He did it. He said he's sorry. That's
enough for me. Let's put it behind us and move on." On the other
end of the spectrum were people who wouldn't believe anything Bill
Clinton said about anything. Nothing short of his resignation would
have satisfied them. Their attitude was clear: "The man's just a liar.
He lied before, and he's lying now. He's not capable of repenting.
He's just sorry he got caught."

I am not interested in renewing the debate about the character
or the conduct of Bill Clinton. That will be the subject of studies and
debates for generations to come. But the sad story that played out
across the national media does raise some very important questions
about failure, repentance, and restoration. What are the marks of
genuine repentance? What do we do when someone truly repents?
If I repent and others forgive me, does that cancel all consequences?
Does repentance immediately produce reconciliation or restoration?
Those questions become urgent when I face the issue of my own or
someone else's failure. Perhaps I have failed deeply and need to find
some way back. Is that possible? On the other hand, I may be on the
receiving end, because someone has violated me greatly. Now she is
telling me she is "oh, so very sorry." How am I supposed to respond
to that? Do I just take her at her word, or should I look for something
more?

We have been discussing forgiveness, about being forgiven and
becoming forgivers. Our central passage has been the Lord's challenging words in Luke 17:3–4: "If your brother sins, rebuke him, and
if he repents, forgive him. If he sins against you seven times in a
day, and seven times comes back to you and says, 'I repent,' forgive

him." Up to this point, we have focused on the forgiving side of the equation. Now we need to probe the nature of repentance and struggle with what it really involves. What are the characteristics of true repentance? Is it the same thing as an apology, or is it something more? Does restitution have any part? The biblical passage that addresses some of those questions most directly is found in 2 Corinthians 7:8–13. It contains an intensely personal interaction of the apostle Paul with his friends in the church with which his relationship had proven to be the most difficult. He is discussing a letter he had written, which had addressed some of his concerns very directly:

> *Even if I caused you sorrow by my letter, I do not regret it. Though I did regret it—I see that my letter hurt you, but only for a little while—yet now I am happy, not because you were made sorry, but because your sorrow led you to repentance. For you became sorrowful as God intended and so were not harmed in any way by us. Godly sorrow brings repentance that leads to salvation and leaves no regret, but worldly sorrow brings death. See what this godly sorrow has produced in you: what earnestness, what eagerness to clear yourselves, what indignation, what alarm, what longing, what concern, what readiness to see justice done. At every point you have proved yourselves to be innocent in this matter. So even though I wrote to you, it was not on account of the one who did the wrong or of the injured party, but rather that before God you could see for yourselves how devoted to us you are. By all this we are encouraged.*

Second Corinthians is the most personal of the letters Paul penned to the young churches he had planted across the Mediterranean. The church in Corinth was dear to his heart, but, more than any other, it was the one that caused him deep pain. The particular reasons for the tensions are not always clear to us, because we possess only one side of the correspondence between Paul and the church. But by piecing together information we are given in chapters 2 and 7, we are able to reconstruct some important aspects of the particular issue that led Paul to write as he did here.

The apostle had been forced to make a special visit to Corinth to deal with a serious problem in the church. This he described as a "painful visit" (2:1), probably because of the strong positions some were taking and the strong emotions that were aroused. Those who have been part of a divided church can attest to how difficult such experiences can be. Apparently, at some point in that conflict, an unnamed individual vehemently attacked Paul, publicly defaming and slandering him. We are not told the man's motives; he was probably trying to advance his own agenda, whether personal or theological. Attacking Paul, who represented his major obstacle, was a way to advance his own cause. The public attack was painful in itself. But what particularly distressed Paul was the tepid response of the Corinthian church in rising to his defense. He had every reason to expect them to defend his integrity, to protect his reputation, and to set the record straight. They had failed him miserably.

Paul left Corinth to return to his previous area of ministry, but that "painful visit" nagged at his soul. It wasn't only that they had failed to rally to his defense. The central concern on such occasions is not the presence of conflict, but the absence of appropriate ways of dealing with it. Their tolerance of the man's sinful behavior had failed the cause of God's truth and threatened the health of the church. Healthy systems have an immune system that immediately rallies to drive out what is dangerous and destabilizing. Their tolerance of the intolerable showed that the congregation was seriously ill and needed strong medicine. Paul decided against "another painful visit" (2:1) and instead wrote them a letter of rebuke. It was not an easy letter to write. As he observes in 2:4, "I wrote you out of great distress and anguish of heart and with many tears." He also knew it would not be an easy letter to receive; it would cause them sorrow (7:8) and distress (2:3). There was a real danger of a permanent rupture in their relationship. However, the issue was simply too important for him to ignore. The future well-being of the church demanded a radical change of behavior.

A problem with letters, especially in the ancient world, was the long delay between the time the letter was written and a reply was received. Waiting, when the letter was intensely personal, could be difficult. So, as Paul waited, he worried. He had sent the letter with his trusted friend Titus, who had not only carried the letter, but would also be able, as a close and trusted coworker, to speak as Paul's representative. But Titus took longer to return than Paul had hoped. Paul shortened the distance by relocating to Troas, the port city near Ephesus, where Titus would land. Amazingly God opened great evangelistic opportunities in that town. But Paul could not enjoy them, because, as he said, "I still had no peace of mind, because I did not find my brother Titus there. So I said good-by to them and went on to Macedonia" (2:13). Even there, he observed, "this body of ours had no rest, but we were harassed at every turn—conflicts on the outside, fears within" (7:5). A great number of those fears were related to the response of the Corinthians to Paul's letter. Paul's turmoil showed just how much this relationship mattered to him. Finally Titus arrived. Second Corinthians is his response, full of the joy he felt both in meeting up with Titus and in hearing his good news. The Corinthians had received Paul's letter of rebuke in an entirely appropriate way. He can hardly contain himself as he wrote back to them:

> *I have great confidence in you; I take great pride in you. I am greatly encouraged; in all our troubles my joy knows no bounds. . . . God, who comforts the downcast, comforted us by the coming of Titus, and not only by his coming but also by the comfort you had given him. He told us about your longing for me, your deep sorrow, your ardent concern for me, so that my joy was greater than ever* (2 Corinthians 7:4, 6–7).

The entire episode gives us a vivid insight into the process of godly confrontation. I hate confrontations, especially with people I deeply value. I lose sleep and worry about the outcome. But sometimes there is too much at stake to avoid an issue or to pretend that the problem really isn't all that serious. Some things require surgery, not therapy. When we received the diagnosis that my wife had breast cancer and that significant surgery was required, I agonized. But I knew that there was no real choice. She had to submit to the surgeon's knife. The issue in Corinth was a cancer not a passing fever. It required serious attention. Paul had to address the issue, but, even as he did, he was very careful to make it clear how deeply he loved these people he had felt constrained to "hurt": "Make room for us in your hearts. We have wronged no one, we have corrupted no one, we have exploited no one. I do not say this to condemn you; I have said before that you have such a place in our hearts that we would live or die with you. I have great confidence in you; I take great pride in you. I am greatly encouraged; in all our troubles my joy knows no bounds" (7:2–4).

Some things require surgery, not therapy.

Those are the events that bring us to the statement in verse 8 that begins our centerpiece paragraph for this chapter: "Even if I caused you sorrow by my letter, I do not regret it. Though I did regret it—I see that my letter hurt you, but only for a little while." The pain of confrontation had been an unavoidable pain.

True Repentance Is the Evidence of a Changed Heart

When we are confronted with sin in our life, we can respond in one of four different ways.

Rejection

The first is that of *rejection*. This may be a blatant denial that any wrongdoing has occurred or a rationalization that redefines the action or scapegoats the victim. Stephen Sandage led a research study of college students that attempted to discover any predictors of who would and wouldn't seek forgiveness, when they had wronged another. The conclusion is significant: "The strongest predictor of unwillingness to seek forgiveness was inability or unwillingness to empathize with others. Unforgiving people often failed to see how much they hurt others. They could not imagine others' suffering so they could not imagine that they might need to apologize or make things right through making restitution."[2] People with that kind of heart condition have almost no capacity to come to godly repentance. They are blinded by pride and self-deception.

Evasion

A second response is that of *evasion*. This may occur in the form of excuses, which pay lip service to the wrong done but deny that any intention was involved. Both parties were victims of circumstances. There are more subtle forms. We can parse verbs and play word games, as President Clinton became notorious for doing, during the Monica Lewinsky scandal. "It all depends on what the meaning of the word 'is' is."

Or we can subtly play hurt and shift the blame. I was disturbed by a recent

> *Unforgiving people often failed to see how much they hurt others.*
>
> STEPHEN SANDAGE

example of a pastor, accused of significant sexual misconduct and other wrong behavior, for which there was abundant evidence. His response was worded carefully, to avoid the truth and deflect the blame: "I never did what they say. . . . It's not what it looks like. . . . I got so beat up by people who claimed to be friends." Perhaps it could be debated whether those who had confronted him about his behavior had done it perfectly. Debatable statements and unfortunate responses may have been made, but the core issues were beyond question. His denial was full of both self-pity ("I'm the victim here") and evasion. As one person, himself guilty of massive moral failure as a Christian leader, observed about his own behavior, "Running from the darkness does not mean running into light. . . . The easiest way for me to escape my ugliness has been to focus on the ugliness of others."[3] I have seen married couples who, when dealing with a serious moral failure on the part of one partner, choose to divert their anger onto others. One mistreated wife I observed at close hand chose not to direct her anger at her husband, who had clearly violated appropriate marital boundaries. Instead, she directed her rage at those who had been forced to deal with the consequences of his misbehavior. Their response was not perfect. It almost never is. But by choosing to vent her anger at them for their shortcomings or perceived mistakes, she was shielding herself from dealing with the pain of the betrayal and allowing her husband to avoid fully owning his responsibility. Her less-than-righteous anger was only an evasion that kept both partners from dealing with the pain of the betrayal involved and from fully owning their own responsibility.

Another kind of evasion is content with a simple admission of wrongdoing that avoids grappling with the true nature of the offense or wrestling morally with the issues involved. Pharaoh was willing to say, "I have sinned" to Moses and Aaron (Exodus 9:27), but subsequent events showed that he was merely stalling for time, not pondering real change. King Saul was a man who could become very emotional as he admitted wrongdoing: "I have sinned," first said to Samuel (1 Samuel 15:24), and then to David (1 Samuel 26:21). But neither Samuel nor David took him at his word. They heard in his words an empty repentance; a ploy, rather than a heartfelt change. Repentance goes far deeper than mere apology or admission.

Regret

A third response is that of *regret*, or, as Paul also calls it in this passage, *worldly sorrow*. I will never forget sitting with a man, quite a good friend, as he revealed his involvement in an affair that threatened his marriage. As I pressed him for an explanation, he began to cry: "I'm sorry I'm hurting you, and Debbie and the kids. I feel terrible. I'm so, so sorry."

"I'm glad to hear it," I responded. "Now there's the phone. I want you to call X right now, tell her it's over, and that you have no intention of ever seeing her again."

"I'm not ready to do that yet."

He never was. But he was ready, months later, to go into court to rewrite the history of his marriage and accuse his wife of terrible failings, which contradicted everything he had told me about their relationship and his wife's fine qualities. It is a cheap regret that says, *I'm sorry, but not sorry enough to quit.*

Another kind of regret focuses on the consequences. This is a man who comes to see me, caught in some misbehavior and terrified about the potential consequences of his actions, consequences now beyond his control. He is in danger of losing his job or his family and perhaps his freedom, by time in jail. Almost all of his conversation is about himself, about his fears and feelings, not the deep wrong he has done to others and the pain he has inflicted on them. Then time passes, the worst fails to happen, and the consequences seem far more manageable. Suddenly all the fine words about life-change and new direction vanish like fog in the midday sun. His is a case of worldly sorrow and hollow regret.

> *Confession is good for the soul, but false confession causes relational chaos.*
>
> LES PARROT

There is a less obvious variation of regret: emotional despair, which leads someone to wallow in self-pity. Too often the entire response is about personal anguish, perhaps a ravaged sense of self-worth, but not a God-centered, heart-deep repentance. I have vivid memories of someone in my life who was an almost professional "regretter." Les Parrot describes one client who suffered from a similar pattern:

> Confession is good for the soul, but false confession causes relational chaos. I know a woman who could win a blue-ribbon for the originality and frequency of her confessions. She takes full responsibility for any and every unfortunate situation. She sees herself as responsible for bad weather ("I'm sorry about this rain; I should have known better than to schedule a picnic in late spring."), unexpected road construction ("Why didn't I call AAA before we left home?"), or anyone's disappointment about anything ("I'm so sorry; I would do anything to make you

feel better."). Her guilt is boundless. Like Atlas, she carries the whole world on her shoulders. She has caused such strife in her home due to her compulsion for repeated confessions that in a counseling session her daughter said, "If Mom says 'I'm sorry' one more time, I'm going to explode!"[4]

The supreme example of worldly sorrow in Scripture is Esau. He wept aloud when he did not receive the blessing he desired from his father Isaac (Genesis 27:38). But those were tears of regret not repentance. As the writer of Hebrews observes, "See that no one is sexually immoral, or is godless like Esau, who for a single meal sold his inheritance rights as the oldest son. Afterward, as you know, when he wanted to inherit this blessing, he was rejected. He could bring about no change of mind [literally: repentance], though he sought the blessing with tears" (12:16–17). As Doug Schmidt notes:

> True repentance is not always a deeply emotional experience. Depending on the personality type, the full acknowledgment of specific sins—and the resulting damage they have caused—can be an intensely cognitive experience. But while it may not always produce tears and the beating of one's chest, it is, nonetheless, often one of the most gut-wrenching things a person can do. So consequently, many people often avoid taking this painful step.[5]

Repentance

The fourth kind of response, the only appropriate one and the one Paul delights to find in his Corinthian friends, is *repentance*. Repentance is different from regret. On the one hand, my friend regretted the pain he was causing his family, but he would not repent of it, for he had enshrined his personal pleasure as the supreme god in his life. On the other, there are things I may regret but do not need to repent of.

On one occasion, playing rugby against a friend, I tackled him hard and he was injured. I felt terrible, but I had no doubt that the hit had been completely within the rules. There was no need to repent. However, I did regret what had happened to him. Paul regretted that he caused the Corinthians sorrow by his letter; it had hurt them, and he did not enjoy seeing their pain. But he could not and did not repent of writing and sending the letter, because it had been a necessary step in their healing.

Biblical repentance involves deep-seated heart change. The New Testament word is *metanoia*, which describes a fundamental change of mind or perspective. It is, in fact, a return to reality about oneself. The Old Testament equivalent is *teshuvah*, a word that describes a turning or reversal of direction. Three things characterize true repentance.

> *Biblical repentance involves deep-seated heart change.*

First, *true repentance centers on God, not just other people.* It is called "godly sorrow," because it drives us to God, causes us to see our behavior as He does, and forces us to do business with Him. The epitome of such repentance is found in David's great outpouring of heart in Psalm 51:2–4:

> *Wash away all my iniquity*
> *and cleanse me from my sin.*
> *For I know my transgressions,*
> *and my sin is always before me.*
> *Against you, you only, have I sinned*
> *and done what is evil in your sight,*
> *so that you are proved right when you speak*
> *and justified when you judge.*

Second, *true repentance centers on sin, not just consequences.* Judas, the betrayer, immediately recognized the enormity of the consequences of his betrayal of Jesus, strongly enough that he took his own life (Matthew 27:5). But there was no hating of or turning from his action as a sin, hateful to God, that drove him to his God in repentance. As Miroslav Volf observed, "To repent means to make a turnabout of a profound moral and religious import. Repentance implies not merely a recognition that one has made a bad mistake, but that one has sinned."[6]

Third, *true repentance commits to change, not just shame.* Regret wallows in disabling shame and even despair. Repentance brings a profound energy that seeks core change, not merely of behavior, but especially of character.

True Repentance: A Process

Understand that repentance, when it is authentic, is more than a crisis experience. Rather, it becomes a lifestyle. Most often there is a precipitating crisis, a time of breakthrough. But, if it is to be more than just a passing emotional outpouring, repentance must produce a new pattern of life. Christ-followers don't just repent; they are repenters, constantly dealing with sin as it enters their lives. I am rather concerned about trying to analyze repentance too carefully, chopping it into a set of precise steps. Life is always more complex than neat little formulae. Yet there are components that will always be present when true repentance is taking place. I want to suggest at least five.

> *Repentance always involves a return to reality, a seeing of things as they really are, not as we imagine or wish them to be.*

Remorse

The first is *remorse, the owning of wrong.* I must own the sin that I have committed, without any rationalization or excuse. This is the response of the Prodigal Son, who, in the pigpen, "came to his senses" (Luke 15:17). Repentance always involves a return to reality, a seeing of things as they really are, not as we imagine or wish them to be.

This first requires *insight,* a change of mind, so that we see what we have done clearly and differently. We all possess a high capacity for self-deception and self-centeredness, which often makes it difficult to see ourselves honestly. One of the primary ministries of the Holy Spirit, especially as He uses the Scriptures, is to "undeceive" us. That is why we need constant exposure to God's Word, in whatever ways we can, so that we can see things as they truly are.

Insight must lead to *ownership*, a change of heart involving a holy shame before a holy God. It is the response of an Isaiah, seeing God in His glory, instinctively and immediately responding, " 'Woe to me!' I cried. 'I am ruined! For I am a man of unclean lips, and I live among a people of unclean lips, and my eyes have seen the King, the Lord Almighty' " (Isaiah 6:5). Such an experience is both painful and purifying, because it sets us free from our moral blindness.

> "Repentance is always difficult, and the difficulty grows still greater by delay."
>
> SAMUEL JOHNSON

Ownership, in turn, leads to *brokenness*, a change of emotions that disrupts the core of our personal complacency. But there is a wonderful truth that David learned in his own life-shattering experience of authentic repentance:

> *The sacrifices of God are a broken spirit;*
> *a broken and contrite heart,*
> *O God, you will not despise (Psalm 51:17).*

These three ingredients of remorse—a change of mind, a change of heart, and a change of emotions—form the foundation of authentic repentance. The absence of any of them threatens the validity of anything that follows. No wonder Samuel Johnson wrote, "Repentance is always difficult, and the difficulty grows still greater by delay."

Reversal

The second component is *reversal of behavior, the renouncing of sin.* The essence of repentance is not feeling but "turning." If we are on the road, headed the wrong way, as our remorse has shown, the only solution is a U-turn. We must admit that we are lost, that we are headed the wrong way, and that the best time to turn around is right now. That sounds deceptively simple, but, as my wife can attest, there are times when I am driving when I will stubbornly insist on heading the direction we are going, even though all the evidence suggests that I am heading the wrong way.

On a recent trip to France, we rented a car to tour Normandy. My knowledge of French is less than rudimentary, and I had carefully plotted our journey on a map. But it was a holiday, and a massive beach festival led to an unexpected detour that threw us off our plotted course. I asked for directions from well-meaning locals. But they couldn't understand me, and I couldn't understand them. I tried my best to interpret their enthusiastic gestures, and on we went. My unerring sense of guidance had left me completely convinced that the English Channel was on my left, and so, with great sincerity, I continued on my course. My wife wasn't quite as convinced, and she gently suggested that the map and the signs contradicted my intuitions. Not only did I not listen to her, I drove faster. But driving faster in the wrong direction never gets you to your destination. It wasn't until several landmarks were not where I was convinced they should be that I repented by reversing course. Ultimately we reached Omaha Beach. That reversal of course is the essence of repentance.

Repentance involves visible change. John the Baptist challenged those who came to him with the exhortation: "Produce fruit in keeping with repentance" (Matthew 3:8). In a very similar way, the apostle Paul described his message as follows: "I preached that they should repent and turn to God and prove their repentance by their deeds" (Acts 26:20). This is very significant. Repentance is more than verbal affirmation; it is made visible by tangible deeds. Saying "sorry" is far from enough.

Request

A third ingredient is *requesting forgiveness, the confession of guilt.* I miss the old *Calvin and Hobbes* comic strip. In one of them, Calvin expresses regret for having "called Susie names." Hobbes suggests that Calvin "apologize to her." Calvin ponders this for a time, and then answers, "I keep hoping there's a less obvious solution." We all do. It is humbling to go to another and frankly and freely admit our wrongdoing. But that is what repentance calls for. True confession rejects evasions and excuses. It faces both the wrong and the wronged. Honest confession means that I go to the person and name the offense. I reject the kind of vagueness that says, "If I've done anything to hurt you. . . ."

I remember a young couple who came from another city to see me. She had become pregnant prior to marriage. Their goal was to have the baby out of town, so that none of their friends or family would discover their behavior. Thankfully, abortion wasn't on their radar screen. We had a long talk about Proverbs 28:13:

> *He who conceals his sins does not prosper,*
> *but whoever confesses and renounces them finds mercy.*

In response, they returned home, faced the consequences, received the loving embrace of their family and church, and entered into a marriage that they both truly wanted. What a joy it was to meet their daughter years later and to hear their gratitude for my directing them to God's Word and the path of true repentance.

The language of confession is direct and specific. A repentant person does not say, "If I have done anything to hurt you. . . ." He names his sin. There is no "maybe" or "perhaps." There is no subtle shading of responsibility. On the other hand, repentant confession does not involve a groveling that takes more responsibility than is appropriate. Confession should be as public as the commission of the sin, and it should be done to heal, not to hurt or to embarrass. David Augsburger wisely observed that it "should not be so intimate, revealing, or painful that it will wound or scar the person to whom it is confessed."[7] It is self-indulgence, not biblical confession, to go to someone who is completely unaware of any problem and say, "Please forgive me for the terrible things I have been thinking about you." That just shifts to the other person a problem that you should be taking to the Lord. What is she supposed to do with the information now that she has it?

Restitution

A fourth step is too often ignored: *restitution, the repayment of loss.* There are many things for which no restitution is vaguely possible. How can you make restitution for murder or adultery or even malicious gossip? But God's Word commands restitution where it is possible. The Old Testament, as is indicated in the following passages, requires repayment plus a penalty.

> *The Lord said to Moses: "If anyone sins and is unfaithful to the Lord by deceiving his neighbor about something entrusted to him or left in his care or stolen, or if he cheats him, or if he finds lost property and lies about it, or if he swears falsely, or if he commits any such sin that people may do—when he thus sins and becomes guilty, he must return what he has stolen or taken by extortion, or what was entrusted to him, or the lost property he found, or whatever it was he swore falsely about.* He must make restitution in full, add a fifth of the value to it and give it all to the owner on the day he presents his guilt offering. *And as a penalty he must bring to the priest, that is, to the Lord, his guilt offering, a ram from the flock, one without defect and of the proper value. In this way the priest will make atonement for him before the Lord, and he will be forgiven for any of these things he did that made him guilty"* (Leviticus 6:1–7, emphasis mine).

> *The Lord said to Moses, "Say to the Israelites: 'When a man or woman wrongs another in any way and so is unfaithful to the Lord, that person is guilty and must confess the sin he has committed.* He must make full restitution for his wrong, add one fifth to it and give it all to the person he has wronged. *But if that person has no close relative to whom restitution can be made for the wrong, the restitution belongs to the Lord and must be given to the priest, along with the ram with which atonement is made for him. All the sacred contributions the Israelites bring to a priest*

will belong to him. Each man's sacred gifts are his own, but what he gives to the priest will belong to the priest' " (Numbers 5:5–10, emphasis mine).

A great New Testament illustration of restitution occurs in the story of Jesus' meeting the tax collector Zacchaeus, who responded by saying, "Look, Lord! Here and now I give half of my possessions to the poor, and if I have cheated anybody out of anything, I will pay back four times the amount." The Lord's delighted response? "Today salvation has come to this house" (Luke 19:8–9). The point is that true repentance very often requires specific acts of restitution. It may be as obvious as financial repayment or as demanding as public confession of the wrongdoing.

Rehabilitation

A fifth ingredient of authentic repentance is *rehabilitation, the rebuilding of character.* Sadly I have seen many cases where, once the crisis passes, life returns quickly to its old routines. But true repentance is concerned with fundamental character change. This may require counseling, an accountability or support group, or wise personal mentoring. True repentance is a process that reaches to the core of one's being. Soren Kierkegaard wisely observed, "Sudden, quick repentance wants only to down the bitterness of sorrow in a single [gulp] and then hurry on. It wants to get away from guilt, away from every reminder of it. . . . What a delusion!"[8]

True Repentance Opens the Door for Renewed Relationships

Repentance Doesn't Necessarily Cancel Consequences

Powerful as repentance is, it doesn't, by itself, cancel consequences. Common sense tells us this. We know that a person who has lost an eye in a drunken brawl will not regain his sight, just because he repents. A woman who has had an abortion will not have her pregnancy restored, no matter how deeply she grieves her mistaken choice. David fathered a child in his adultery with Bathsheba, but his infant son died, even though David had come to repentance (2 Samuel 12:13–18). Repentance doesn't automatically restore the status quo, and that is true of relationships as well. I may genuinely repent, but that does not mean that irreparable damage has not been inflicted on a friendship or a marriage. Repentance does, however, mean that God's grace will enable us to live with the consequences.

There is a striking illustration of this in the Old Testament. The Lord had promised the children of Israel that He would lead them into the Promised Land. Before they invaded, twelve spies were sent out to do reconnaissance. But when they returned, ten of them reported that an invasion would be disastrous. This was a blatant rejection of God's promises, but their unbelief caused the people to rebel against the Lord and His appointed leaders. The Lord threatened to destroy them and to begin again with Moses. But Moses interceded for his rebellious people: "In accordance with your great love, forgive the sin of these people, just as you have pardoned them from the time they left Egypt until now" (Numbers 14:19). The Lord's reply deserves careful consideration:

> *The Lord replied,* "I have forgiven them, *as you asked. Nevertheless, as surely as I live and as surely as the glory of the Lord fills the whole earth, not one of the men who saw my glory and the miraculous signs I performed in Egypt and in the desert but who disobeyed me and tested me ten times*—not one of them will ever see the land I promised on oath to their forefathers. *No one who has treated me with contempt will ever see it*" *(Numbers 14:20–23, emphasis mine).*

This is a solemn reminder that repentance and forgiveness do not necessarily remove all negative consequences. Sins leave scars, and we reap what we sow. The damage done by marital abuse or unfaithfulness, by financial irresponsibility or wrongdoing, or by some other breach of trust may make it impossible or unwise for a former relationship or responsibility to be resumed. Forgiveness and repentance do not necessarily mean a return to what used to be. A child abuser may be repentant and forgiven; he ought never to be allowed to work with children again. Repentance does not cancel the crop, but it does bring the grace of God to deal with the harvest. That is why, every single day of Israel's almost-forty-year journey through the wilderness, they received food from heaven, followed the supernatural guidance God provided, and experienced His miraculous intervention against their enemies.

Repentance Should Change Attitude

On the other hand, repentance should change our attitudes toward an offender. In 2 Corinthians 2 Paul expressed his concern about how the Corinthians were treating the man who had been responsible for the painful letter Paul had written. Initially, they had been slow to respond to his sin and had failed to discipline him. But when they disciplined him, he had come to a place of sincere repentance. Ironically, they were now reluctant to restore him. Paul made it clear that the purpose of discipline is restoration; we are not to keep repentant people perpetually in a penalty box, for their sins. In fact, it is as wrong to exclude a repentant brother as it is to include a sinning, unrepentant one. The process is set forth in 2 Corinthians 2:6–8: "The punishment inflicted on him by the majority is sufficient for him. Now instead, you ought to forgive and comfort him, so that he will not be overwhelmed by excessive sorrow. I urge you, therefore, to reaffirm your love for him." There are three key words: *forgive, comfort* (or encourage), and *reaffirm.*

In our own congregation one Sunday a man who had been publicly caught in sin and responded appropriately to the discipline of the leadership of the church gave public testimony to the working of God's grace in his life, despite his sin. It was a courageous act, and in each of the three services, the congregation responded with a spontaneous standing ovation, which celebrated his restoration and affirmed our love and acceptance of our valued brother.

There is such a thing as good grief, the "godly sorrow . . . that leads to salvation and leaves no regret" (2 Corinthians 7:10). God's reclaiming, restoring grace is seen in the life of many of the great heroes of faith in the Bible, none of whom was exempt from the failures of sin. Whether it be Abraham, Moses, David, Peter, or Paul, the grace of God shines in a repentant heart. As our God declares,

"This is the one I esteem:
he who is humble and contrite in spirit,
and trembles at my word" (Isaiah 66:2)

Chapter 12

THE GIFT OF FORGIVENESS

Everett Worthington is a committed follower of Christ who, as a professor of psychology, has made a careful study of forgiveness a central part of his professional career. He has also served as the executive director of the Templeton Foundation's Campaign for Forgiveness Research. So there was every reason to believe, when he and two colleagues published the results of their research in 1997 in a book titled *To Forgive Is Human*,[1] that he was as thoroughly informed about the dynamics of forgiveness as was humanly possible.

Then, on New Year's Eve of that year, two young thugs invaded his elderly mother's home and brutally beat her to death with a crowbar. The perpetrators were never identified, never mind arrested. Worthington's brother, who lived nearby, tried to contact his mother to wish her a happy New Year. When he could not reach her, he went to her home, concerned. There he discovered a horrific crime scene. After contacting the police, he phoned his brother, who immediately set out by car for the agonizing trip to his mother's home in Knoxville.

At his brother's home, Everett heard details: blood everywhere, a trashed house, indications of ugly brutality. As his brother related his horrendous account, Worthington felt an intense rage welling up within him. All he could think to say was "I'd like to have him alone in a room with a baseball bat for thirty minutes. I'd beat his brains out."

Everett was a world-class expert on forgiveness, a leader in the emerging forgiveness research movement. But as he tossed and turned on his bed and walked the floor . . . "I confess that during that night, forgiveness never entered my mind." Instead he found himself asking a multitude of questions:

> I was a Christian. Was it wrong for me to indulge my rage? Was it wrong to want both the law and God to punish those youths? . . . I was a consulting psychologist. I had seen people deny experiences, stuff their worst feelings inside. Was it wrong to consider forgiveness while I was so angry and sad? . . . I was a researcher who, ironically, studied forgiveness. I had read philosophical, religious, devotional, and literary accounts of forgiveness. I had pored over psychological studies of forgiveness. Yet all day, I had not thought the word *forgiveness*.[2]

In a later edition of his book, he writes,

> I began to ask myself questions. Can I ever forgive this? Is it good to forgive? What if the police catch the youths? Will I want them to get the death penalty? I was eyeball to eyeball with my convictions—carefully thought out in times unclouded by emotion. But the impact of this death and the horror of my images of what my mother must have experienced were an in-your-face confrontation.[3]

Worthington was able to come to a place of forgiveness, but it wasn't easy. It also wasn't instantaneous, despite all the insight learned and received through his deep faith and his research. His experience causes us to recall C. S. Lewis's observation: "Everyone says forgiveness is a lovely word, until they have something to forgive."[4] Or as Lewis Smedes said, "We talk a good forgiving line as long as somebody else needs to do it, but few of us have the heart for it while we are dangling from one end of a bond broken by somebody else's cruelty."[5]

Throughout this book we have celebrated one of the great truths of the Christian gospel: *Our God is a forgiving God, who freely forgives those who trust in His Son.* His forgiveness is a costly forgiveness, grounded in the death, burial, and resurrection of His Son. But we have also seen that there is a closely allied second truth: *As followers of Christ, forgiven people must be forgiving people*. As Ephesians 4:32–5:2 exhorts:

> *Be kind and compassionate to one another, forgiving each other, just as in Christ God forgave you.*
>
> *Be imitators of God, therefore, as dearly loved children and live a life of love, just as Christ loved us and gave himself up for us as a fragrant offering and sacrifice to God.*

As we come to the end of our study of forgiveness, our goal is to review that central idea: that forgiven people must be forgiving people.

The story is told of a Persian king who was furious to learn that the citizens of a far-off city-state named Athens had rebelled against him. Caught up in the middle of other affairs, he worried that he would become distracted and forget the depth of his anger against the Athenians. To prevent that, he ordered a servant to whisper in his ear at every mealtime, "Sir, don't forget the Athenians." The result, I suspect, was not only fresh indignation, but also recurring indigestion. We don't usually need someone to remind us of the wrongs done to us. Most of us have highly developed memories of other people's failures and wrongdoings. But our personal mental computers have much-used "delete" buttons for our own failures.

Because of the Lord Jesus, Christ-Followers Are Forgiven People

> *You see, at just the right time, when we were still powerless, Christ died for the ungodly. Very rarely will anyone die for a righteous man, though for a good man someone might possibly dare to die. But God demonstrates his own love for us in this: While we were still sinners, Christ died for us (Romans 5:6–8).*

This wonderful passage confronts us with four great truths.

The Need for Forgiveness Is Universal

All of us need forgiveness, because sin and guilt are universal realities. A famed actor, at the apex of his career, won an Oscar for best supporting actor. He was already enjoying immense financial, professional, and personal success. An interviewer posed the question: "Would you describe yourself as 'happy' right now?"

The actor was silent for a time, and then he quietly replied: "Well, I guess I'm happy, except that I have this gnawing sense of guilt inside that somehow I'm doing something wrong." I suspect that at least some of that feeling was not true guilt. Other people and an overactive conscience can play games with us and make us feel guilty, when we shouldn't. But even when we have stripped away all the barnacles of false guilt, we find ourselves with a guilt we cannot deny or dismiss. The actor, like all of us, was right to feel that "gnawing sense of guilt." Sinfulness is the background condition of our lives. We all stand truly and deeply guilty in the presence of a holy God and in the court of our innermost being.

We all stand truly and deeply guilty in the presence of a holy God and in the court of our innermost being.

These three short verses from Romans use three terms to describe all humans. We are *powerless*, that is, spiritually weak and sick. Furthermore, we are *ungodly*. It is important to see the implications of this word. We often refer to something as "un-American." Americans were scandalized by the sadistic and humiliating abuse some Iraqi prisoners of war received at the hands of Americans in a military prison in Baghdad. The president publicly denounced such abuse, not only as illegal and shameful, but also as "profoundly un-American." He obviously did not mean that Americans could not do such things; sadly, they clearly had. What he meant was that such actions violate deeply cherished American values, American laws, and American standards. They are not just an aberration; they are a violation: "They do not represent what America stands for." In fact, they represent a kind of attack on America itself. In a similar way, to be ungodly is not merely to be "nongodly." It is to stand in direct opposition to God's character and purposes. That is why, in the following verses, Paul describes us as "God's enemies," not just indifferent but actually hostile to Him. We are also "sinners," people who have missed God's mark and violated His standards. These all combine to make it clear that we stand in deep need before God, and only His radical forgiveness can solve our problem.

The Cost of Our Forgiveness Is the Cross

A British newspaper once held a contest for the most sensational headline that used no more than four words. Among many amusing and arresting entries, one stood out as the obvious winner: "Pope elopes." Very clever. Were such a thing to occur, you can hardly imagine the media frenzy! But there is an even better candidate, one that has the advantage of being true. Unfortunately familiarity has drained it of its drama and shock value: "Christ crucified." Think of what it says—that God's anointed, promised Savior was executed in the cruelest of ways, as a dangerous criminal. How could a crucified criminal be God's anointed Messiah? How could one truly sent by God suffer capital punishment? Yet that is exactly what happened, and the reason is given in this wonderfully compact passage.

Forgiveness came at the ultimate price. Paul underlines that cost by stating it twice: "Christ died for the ungodly"; "Christ died for us" (vv. 6, 8). His death was not only on our behalf; it was also in our place. He was the Substitute who took our sins upon Himself, and endured the penalty of a holy God against our sins. Another paid our debt in full, and, in turn, we receive the gift of His righteousness through faith. Our forgiveness is full and final, declared by a holy God. As Paul writes later in Romans: "Who will bring any charge against those whom God has chosen? It is God who justifies. Who is he that condemns? Christ Jesus, who died—more than that, who was raised to life—is at the right hand of God and is also interceding for us" (8:33–34). The death of the Lord Jesus on our behalf turned us from enemies into friends of God and cleanses our consciences before Him (Hebrews 9:14).

A strange theft recently occurred. Caretakers in a church in New York City discovered that someone had removed a two-hundred-pound plaster statue of the crucified Jesus from a wooden cross near the church's entrance. It was no small task; the statue, with a steel core, was bolted to the cross in four places. A church caretaker was puzzled: "We don't know why they just took him. We figure that if you want the whole crucifix, you take the whole crucifix."[6] Someone observed that the whole episode was very revealing. After all, many modern people want Jesus, but don't want anything to do with His cross! But that separation is not possible. There is no authentic Jesus who is not the crucified Christ. One virtue of Mel Gibson's *The Passion of the Christ* is that it riveted our attention on the cross. That alone made many critics uncomfortable. Why not focus on the Lord's life and teaching instead? But to desire a Jesus apart from His cross is not only to attempt to separate the inseparable, it is to miss or dismiss the central purpose of His life. Yet we must remember that the essence of the crucifixion is found not merely by considering His physical sufferings, intense as they were. The wonder of the cross is that Jesus died as our Sin-bearer. "He himself bore our sins in his body on the tree" (1 Peter 2:24).

Many modern people want Jesus, but don't want anything to do with His cross! But that separation is not possible.

The Source of Our Forgiveness Is Grace

Forgiveness is given, not earned. It is for the ungodly, not the worthy and self-improved. It was while we were *still* sinners, *still* weak and powerless, that Christ died for us. In the larger context of Romans 5:6–8, Paul makes it very clear that we receive the benefits of the cross through faith and through faith alone. But, important as faith is, it is not the basis of our forgiveness. Faith is the divinely ordained means by which we lay hold of Christ's work on our behalf. Our salvation rests entirely upon the finished work of Christ and the lavish grace of God. Forgiveness is costly to give, and it is humbling to receive. We must admit that we do not deserve it and cannot, in any way, qualify to receive it. We are utterly dependent on God's grace.

As a boy, one of my heroes was Mickey Mantle. I remember very well, in the summer of 1961, listening to the radio every morning at breakfast with my father, wanting to hear whether he had hit any home runs the previous night, as he and Roger Maris chased Babe Ruth's record. He was my hero, as he was for thousands of boys. I would have loved to be what he was—the world's greatest baseball player (although some of my friends insisted Willie Mays deserved this title). Unfortunately, childhood idols often prove to have feet of clay. Later years revealed that, off the field, Mickey Mantle was anything but a hero. He squandered his talent with a self-destructive lifestyle, mainly alcohol and womanizing, and seriously failed as a husband and father. His biography, released not long before his death, was full of his expressions of guilt, regret, and shame for the bad choices he had made and opportunities he had wasted. When news came, in 1995, that he needed a liver transplant, Mantle held a news conference, not only to break the story, but also to warn others against his destructive choices. He pleaded with his young admirers, "Don't become like me. I'm not a role model."

Early one morning Mantle phoned one of his old Yankee team-mates, Bobby Richardson. Richardson is a committed Christ-follower, who had received more than his share of abuse from his teammates for his spiritual commitment. Now he heard Mantle saying, "Bobby, I want you to pray for me. I'm really hurting." Bobby immediately prayed and shared the gospel over the phone. A few weeks later, he flew to Dallas to be with Mantle, when his condition turned for the worse. When Richardson walked into the hospital room, Mickey had a great big smile on his face. "Bobby! I can't wait to tell you—I've accepted Christ as my Savior." Richardson was thrilled, but his wife was skeptical. After all, Mantle had resisted Bobby's witnessing for forty years. When she got a chance, not long before he died, she knelt by Mantle's bed and asked, "Mickey, how do you know you're saved?" Mantle whispered, "For God so loved the world that he gave his one and only Son. . . ." That is the same gracious promise the Lord makes to all who believe.[7]

The Power of Forgiveness Is Transforming

Forgiveness causes us to respond to our God gratefully, a truth powerfully illustrated in the story from Luke 7 that we considered in chapter 3 of this book. Forgiveness teaches us to see ourselves clearly, with a humble recognition of our complete dependence on God's grace. It also enables us to relate to others graciously, because forgiveness received propels us to forgiveness extended.

Recently I received a letter from a missionary friend, telling of the experience of his son, a student at a Christian college. On spring break they had gone on a missions trip to a state penitentiary, the largest maximum-security prison in the United States, holding five thousand inmates. The Lord has been at work in this penitentiary in a remarkable way, and these college students were going to be involved in a weeklong discipling ministry that took them a long way out of their comfort zone. Many of the prisoners had been convicted of violent crimes, including rape and murder. Here is a part of what he shared:

> We were all a little nervous and fidgety because we had no idea what to expect. . . . Well, it only took a few minutes of experiencing and participating in the inmates' worship (which was led by a full and very talented prison band) for us to realize that we had stepped into the most passionate, alive and real Church that we had ever been to! The whole place was burning with a joy and passion that I have never felt or seen anywhere else! These were not manufactured emotions, but emotions overflowing from a heart full of thanksgiving for what Christ has done for us. You see, I don't think I had ever realized the power and depth of Christ's forgiveness. . . . These inmates had truly grasped how sinful they were, had "come clean" with

God, and had accepted the incredible vastness of God's grace and forgiveness of our sins through the blood of Christ.

Throughout the week, Christ was the focus of every service and on the tip of all the believers' tongues in every conversation. They were utterly focused on the fact that God had forgiven them despite all the terrible things they had done and they were THANKFUL, truly thankful. . . . Those men were the most joyful, contented people I had ever met in my life. . . . The lesson I learned from this week is that God is capable of working in any situation with anyone, and that Christ is truly capable of transforming people's lives, no matter what they may have done.

Following Christ:
Forgiven People Must Be Forgiving People

Everything about the Christian life centers on the Lord Jesus. We are saved, not by following His example, but by trusting in His unique work for us upon the cross. Having trusted Him, He becomes our great pattern of life.

On a Personal Level

Supremely, *the Lord Jesus is our model of forgiveness.* As Peter declares, He left us an example so that we "should follow in his steps" (v. 21). It is important to recognize that Jesus experienced the full range of human sinfulness against Him, especially in the events surrounding His execution. Think of them: betrayal (Judas); insensitivity to His needs and concerns (the disciples arguing about who was greatest or falling asleep in Gethsemane); abandonment (they all fled at the time of His arrest); denial and disloyalty (the threefold denial by His most assertive follower, Peter); misrepresentation (the false witnesses at His trial); injustice (the maneuverings of the Jewish leaders); brutality, abuse, and cruelty (the attack by the Roman soldiers); humiliation (being stripped naked and crucified); mockery and verbal abuse (the taunts of the onlookers); and the deep brutality of the crucifixion itself. All of this was inflicted on an entirely innocent and righteous victim.

In the midst of all this, Jesus left a model of forgiveness and submission to the Father's will, rather than one of retaliation and revenge. Peter, borrowing language from Isaiah 53, puts it in words that reach our souls:

> *"He committed no sin,*
> *and no deceit was found in his mouth."*
>
> *When they hurled their insults at him, he did not retaliate; when he suffered, he made no threats. Instead, he entrusted himself to him who judges justly. He himself bore our sins in his body on the tree so that all might die to sins and live for righteousness; by his wounds you have been healed (1 Peter 2:22–24).*

His submission to the cross is not only the great saving event; it is also the model I am to pursue, trusting in His enabling grace.

However, we have more than a model of forgiveness: *We live under a mandate of forgiveness.* We are to forgive others, because the Lord commands it as well as demonstrates it. In fact, His clear message is that an unforgiving heart is a symptom of an unforgiven heart. We need to see unforgiveness for what it is—a dangerous spiritual condition. John MacArthur expresses it well:

> Unforgivingness is a toxin. It poisons the heart and mind with bitterness, distorting one's whole perspective on life. Anger, resentment, and sorrow begin to overshadow and overwhelm the unforgiving person—a kind of soul-pollution that enflames evil appetites and evil emotions. Such bitterness can even spread from person to person, ultimately defiling many (Hebrews 12:15). Forgiveness is the only antidote. Forgiveness is a healthy, wholesome, virtuous, liberating act. Forgiveness unleashes joy. It brings peace. It washes the slate clean. It sets all the highest virtues of love in motion.[8]

Anne Lamott, in her intriguing account of her encounter with the grace of the Lord Jesus, describes her struggle with forgiveness with typical honesty, and with a vivid metaphor:

> I went around saying for a long time that I am not one of the Christians who is heavily into forgiveness—that I am one of the other kind. But even though it was funny, and actually true, it started to be too painful to stay this way. . . .
>
> In fact, not forgiving is like drinking rat poison, and waiting for the rat to die.[9]

Her last line is worth pondering. We often imagine that by withholding forgiveness, we hurt the other person. Perhaps we sometimes do. More often, I think, the other person is blissfully unaware of the acid that is eating away at our inner being and does not particularly care that we are withholding our forgiveness. We, however, care, very much, and unforgiveness begins to take hold of our hearts in a toxic way. Corrie ten Boom, speaking from her perspective as a survivor of the Nazi death camps, observed, "People able to forgive their former enemies were able to return to the outside world and rebuild their lives, no matter what the physical scars. Those who nursed their bitterness remained invalids. It was as simple and as horrible as that."[10] I suspect that she has overstated the case, but not to forgive is to live contrary

We often imagine that by withholding forgiveness, we hurt the other person.

to the way the Lord has called us to live. We are to forgive *because* the Lord has forgiven us, *as* the Lord has forgiven us, and *because* He has commanded us.

On a Community Level

Biblical forgiveness is not merely a personal activity. Followers of Christ are to become a community of forgiveness. This does not mean that we do not take sin seriously. In fact, quite the opposite is true. One of the downsides of living in Southern California is the inordinate attention paid to the entertainment industry, perhaps the most self-absorbed and self-congratulatory segment of our society. When a successful actress was charged with shoplifting, great attention was paid to the trial. Afterward, her publicist described the support the actress had received during the entire process. "Hollywood is such a forgiving community," she declared, "that unless it's a heinous crime, the industry is incredibly supportive."

Her analysis was entirely wrong. Hollywood isn't a forgiving community but a condoning one. There is a huge difference. A condoning community can ignore misdeeds, because it does not really take sin seriously (unless, of course, the offense violates current standards of political correctness). In contrast, a truly forgiving community cannot simply condone sin. It knows only too well how ugly and how costly sin is, because it cost the Lord Jesus death upon a cross.

It is because we take sin seriously that we can live forgiveness deeply. Paul described the church in Corinth in memorable terms:

> Do you not know that the wicked will not inherit the kingdom of God? Do not be deceived: Neither the sexually immoral nor idolaters nor adulterers nor male prostitutes nor homosexual offenders nor thieves nor the greedy nor drunkards nor slanderers nor swindlers will inherit the kingdom of God. And that is what some of you were. But you were washed, you were sanctified, you were justified in the name of the Lord Jesus Christ and by the Spirit of our God (1 Corinthians 6:9–11).

It wasn't what they had been, but what they had become in Christ, that mattered. The cross makes everything different for the family of God, and that ought to be true of every group of believers. Unfortunately, all too often, it isn't.

In the 1960s Jerry Cook planted a church in Gresham, Oregon. It grew rapidly, becoming well-known and influential in the community. One morning Cook received an angry phone call from a local pastor. Some of his members had left his congregation to attend Cook's church, and he was not at all happy about that. After registering his complaints, he snidely commented that most of the people coming over to Cook had huge personal problems and sinful habits: "You'll never build a church around those kinds of people." Finally he said, "You know what you are out there? You're nothing but a bunch of garbage collectors!"

After Cook shared that story in church one Sunday, a man came up to him with a big smile on his face. As it happened, he owned a garbage collection company. "Jerry," he said, "let me tell you something about garbage. We don't just dump it; we recycle it. There is a landfill near here. For ten years, we used it as a place to dump trash and garbage. Do you know what it is now? A beautiful park!"[11] And that's what the Lord does with human garbage. He takes us in our brokenness and failure and builds something beautiful from what others see only as worthy of being discarded. The Lord intends our churches to be places of human transformation, where God's grace involves us in the recycling of lives to the glory of God and the good of others.

Grace is the basic operating principle of the kingdom of God. We enter by grace, we live by grace, and we live with grace toward others. When the United States invaded Iraq, it was dealing with a society held together by fear and terror. Saddam Hussein's regime was built by force and was united only by hard boundaries. But when the power of the regime was broken, chaos ensued. Nation-building proved to be far more difficult than regime destruction, because there was nothing at the center to hold the various forces together. The church of Jesus Christ is a centered institution, held together by loyalty to the Lord Jesus. He is the magnet who holds us all in place.

Grace is the basic operating principle of the kingdom of God.

A Story of Forgiveness

On March 18, 1982, Mark Farnum headed across the border from Wyoming to Colorado and robbed a bank. He then headed back home. Not long after he crossed the state line, a highway patrolman named Stephen Watt signaled him to pull over, not realizing that he was a robbery suspect. Farnum jumped out of his car, firing. One of his bullets went through Watt's windshield and sunglasses, destroying his left eye. Farnum then walked to the police cruiser, opened the door, and shot Watt four more times. He then returned to his own car and sped away, only to be stopped at a roadblock a few miles down the highway. He was captured, tried, and given a life sentence for his various crimes.

Stephen Watt survived, although he was now blind in one eye, and three bullets that doctors were unable to remove caused constant pain. But the greatest damage wasn't physical. His failure to make the arrest filled him with shame, and he was full of hate and anger at his assailant. He quit his job as a state patrolman, drifting from one meaningless job to another and spiraling into depression and drunkenness. Then, almost a year after the shooting, he gave his life to Christ. He said he felt as if a load had been lifted from his shoulders. He knew himself to be a forgiven man.

But even that forgiveness didn't bring an instant end to his problems. He was still miserable. Finally his wife, Marian, challenged him to forgive his assailant. He claimed he had, but he sensed he hadn't. A long, hard, inward struggle began, and eventually he broke down and wrote Farnum a letter. That began an exchange of letters that led Farnum to ask for Watt's forgiveness and freed Watt to declare his forgiveness. He not only did that; he made a series of trips to the prison to meet with his assailant. In fact, their relationship developed into a strange but significant friendship. Watt today says, "I would trust him with the things I value most—my wife, my children, and my life."

Forgiving Farnum marked a turning point in his life. Watt was able to pull his life together and go back into police work. He became a deputy sheriff, then ran for and won a seat in the state legislature. In 2002 he ran in the Republican primary as a candidate for governor. That led to a perhaps unprecedented campaign plank. Farnum's only possibility of release from prison before 2037 is by a governor's pardon. Watt announced that, if elected, he would review Farnum's file, and "based on what I know, I'd probably release him." This—the very man who had left him for dead and sentenced him to a life of constant pain and partial blindness!

There was to be no fairy-tale ending. Stephen Watt polled only 6 percent of the vote and had to bid farewell to his gubernatorial aspirations. But, he says, "Being shot was the best thing that has ever happened to me. If I could change anything that happened on March 18, 1982, I wouldn't."[12] It is a remarkable story of God's grace in the lives of two men. It reminds us that although the record of the past cannot be erased, it can be forgiven, and in that there is great hope. Forgiveness rewrites the future!

Forgiveness rewrites the future!

Personal Challenge

Forgiveness is powerful. It can break the chains of the past, turn apparent defeat into genuine victory, and open a door to God's new thing. That is true both of the vertical forgiveness that we receive from our gracious God and the horizontal forgiveness we extend to others in His name.

- Are you willing to trade in your sense of righteousness and self-dependence for God's forgiveness that comes through faith in the Lord Jesus Christ?
- Are you willing to trade your resentment over the wrongs done to you for the freedom of forgiveness? This will mean putting into God's hands the judgment of those who have wronged you and resigning any right to be involved in the process.
- Are you willing to allow God alone, not your adversary, to be the one who controls and directs your life? Forgiveness

is a declaration of your confidence in your Lord's ability to accomplish what is good and just on your behalf.

- Are you willing to "live a life of love, just as Christ loved us and gave himself up for us as a fragrant offering and sacrifice to God" (Ephesians 5:2)? One hopes the offender will repent, and there will be significant restoration and reconciliation. But even if he does not, we are called to love our enemies and to pray for those who mistreat us (Matthew 5:44). The way of the cross is our path, whatever the offender's response.
- Are you willing to embrace the future rather than clinging to the past, ruminating over the wrongs that have been done?

These are easy questions to ask, but they become much harder when the wrongdoer's face fills our minds.

———

Be kind and compassionate to one another, forgiving each other, just as in Christ God forgave you (Ephesians 4:32).

BIBLIOGRAPHY

Adams, Jay. *From Forgiven to Forgiving*. Amityville, N.Y.: Calvary, 1994.

Arnold, Johann Christoph. *Seventy Times Seven: The Power of Forgiveness*. Farmington, Pa.: Plough, 1997.

Arthur, Kay. *Our Covenant God*. Colorado Springs: WaterBrook, 1999.

Augsburger, David. *Caring Enough to Confront*. Ventura, Calif.: Regal Books, 1981.

————. *Caring Enough to Forgive; Caring Enough to Not Forgive*. Ventura, Calif.: Regal Books, 1981.

————. *The Freedom of Forgiveness: 70 x 7*. Chicago: Moody Press, 1970.

————. *The New Freedom of Forgiveness*. 3rd. ed. Chicago: Moody Press, 2000.

Carson, Donald. *Love in Hard Places*. Wheaton, Ill.: Crossway, 2002.

Davis, Ron Lee. *A Forgiving God in an Unforgiving World*. Eugene, Ore.: Harvest House, 1984.

Dunn, Ron. *Surviving Friendly Fire*. Nashville: Thomas Nelson, 2001.

Enright, Robert. *Forgiveness Is a Choice: A Step-by-Step Process for Resolving Anger and Restoring Hope*. Washington, D.C.: American Psychological Association, 2001.

————, and Joanna North, eds. *Exploring Forgiveness*. Madison: University of Wisconsin Press, 1998.

Ensor, John. *Experiencing God's Forgiveness: The Journey from Guilt to Gladness*. Colorado Springs: NavPress, 1997.

Farrel, Bill, and Pat Farrel. *Love, Honor, and Forgive: A Guide for Married Couples*. Downers Grove, Ill.: InterVarsity Press, 2000.

Flanigan, Beverly. *Forgiving the Unforgivable: Overcoming the Bitter Legacy of Intimate Wounds*. New York: Macmillan, 1992.

Hallowell, Edward M. *Dare to Forgive.* Deerfield Beach, Fla.: Health Communications, 2004.

Harvey, Robert W., and David G. Benner, *Understanding and Facilitating Forgiveness.* Grand Rapids: Baker, 1996.

Henderson, Michael. *Forgiveness: Breaking the Chains of Hate.* Wilsonville, Ore.: BookPartners, 1999.

Jeffress, Robert. *When Forgiveness Doesn't Make Sense.* Colorado Springs: WaterBrook, 2000.

Jones, L. Gregory. *Embodying Forgiveness: A Theological Analysis.* Grand Rapids: Eerdmans, 1995.

Kendall, R. T. *Total Forgiveness.* Lake Mary, Fla.: Charisma House, 2002.

Ketterman, Grace, and David Hazard. *When You Can't Say "I Forgive You."* Colorado Springs: NavPress, 2000.

Kober, Ted. *Confession and Forgiveness: Professing Faith as Ambassadors of Reconciliation.* St. Louis, Mo.: Concordia, 2002.

Kroll, Una. *Forgive and Live.* London: Mowry, 2000.

Kushner, Harold. *How Good Do We Have to Be? A New Understanding of Guilt and Forgiveness.* Boston: Little, Brown, 1997.

Lampman, Lisa Barnes, ed. *God and the Victim: Theological Reflections on Evil, Victimization, Justice, and Forgiveness.* Grand Rapids: Eerdmans, 1999.

Lockerbie, Jeanette. *Forgive, Forget, and Be Free.* Chappaqua, N.Y.: Christian Herald Books, 1981.

Lutzer, Erwin. *Putting Your Past Behind You.* Nashville: Here's Life, 1990.

Lynch, Chuck. *I Should Forgive, But. . . .* Nashville: Word, 1998.

MacArthur, John F. *The Freedom and Power of Forgiveness.* Westchester, Ill.: Crossway, 1998.

McCullough, Donald. *The Wisdom of Pelicans: A Search for Healing at the Water's Edge.* New York: Viking Compass, 2002.

McCullough, Michael E., Kenneth I. Permagent, and Carl E. Thomas, eds. *Forgiveness: Theory, Research, and Practice.* New York: Guildford, 2000.

McCullough, Michael C., Steven Sandage, and Everett L. Worthington, Jr. *To Forgive Is Human: Putting Your Past in the Past*. Downers Grove, Ill.: InterVarsity Press, 1997.

McKnight, Scot. *The Jesus Creed*. Brewster, Mass.: Paraclete, 2004.

McMinn, Mark C. *Why Sin Matters*. Wheaton, Ill.: Tyndale, 2004.

Narramore, Bruce, and Bill Counts. *Freedom from Guilt*. Santa Ana, Calif.: Vision House, 1974.

Nieder, John, and Thomas M. Thompson. *Forgive and Love Again: Healing Wounded Relationships*. Eugene, Ore.: Harvest House, 1991.

Parrott, Les. *Shoulda Coulda Woulda: Live in the Present, Find Your Future*. Grand Rapids: Zondervan, 2003.

Plantinga, Cornelius, Jr. *Not the Way It's Supposed to Be: A Breviary of Sin*. Grand Rapids: Eerdmans, 1995.

Sande, Ken. *The Peacemaker*. Rev. ed. Grand Rapids: Baker, 2004.

Schimmel, Solomon. *Wounds Not Healed by Time*. New York: Oxford University Press, 2002.

Schmidt, Doug. *The Prayer of Revenge*. Colorado Springs: Nexgen, 2003.

Shults, F. Leron, and Steven J. Sandage. *The Faces of Forgiveness: Searching for Wholeness and Salvation*. Grand Rapids: Baker, 2003.

Sittser, Jerry. *When God Doesn't Answer Your Prayer*. Grand Rapids: Zondervan, 2003.

Smedes, Lewis. *Forgive and Forget: Healing the Hurts We Don't Deserve*. San Francisco: HarperCollins, 1984.

———. *The Art of Forgiving*. New York: Ballantine, 1996.

Spring, Janis Abrahms. *How Can I Forgive You? The Courage to Forgive, the Freedom Not To*. New York: HarperCollins, 2004.

Stoop, David. *Real Solutions for Forgiving the Unforgiveable*. Ann Arbor, Mich.: Servant-Vine, 2001.

Tutu, Desmond. *No Future Without Forgiveness*. New York: Doubleday, 2000.

Volf, Miroslav. *Exclusion and Embrace: A Theological Exploration of Identity, Otherness, and Reconciliation*. Nashville: Abingdon, 1996.

Wiesenthal, Simon. *The Sunflower.* With a Symposium. New York: Schocken, 1976.

———.*The Sunflower: On the Possibilities and Limits of Forgiveness.* Rev. ed. New York: Schocken, 1997.

Worthington, Everett L., Jr., ed. *Dimensions of Forgiveness: Psychological Research and Theological Perspectives.* Philadelphia: Templeton Foundation Press, 1998.

———. *Five Steps to Forgiveness: The Art and Science of Forgiving.* New York: Crown, 2001.

———. *Forgiving and Reconciling: Bridges to Wholeness and Hope.* Downers Grove, Ill.: InterVarsity Press, 2003.

NOTES

Introduction

[1] Dennis Prager, "The Sin of Forgiveness," *Wall Street Journal* (December 15, 1997). Retrieved September 30, 2004, from www.murdervictims.com/ *Forgiveness*.htm.

[2] I owe this idea to John Ensor, who uses it in a slightly different way in his helpful book, *Experiencing God's Forgiveness* (Colorado Springs: NavPress, 1997), 80.

[3] "How the Link Between Forgiveness and Health Changes with Age," The University of Michigan News and Information Services, December 11, 2001. Retrieved April 9, 2004, from www.umich.edu/~newsinfo/ Releases/2001/Dec01/r121101a.html.

[4] Edward M. Hallowell, *Dare to Forgive* (Deerfield Beach, Fla.: Health Communications, 2004), 37–38.

Chapter 1: Wiping the Slate Clean

[1] Cornelius Plantinga, Jr., *Not the Way It's Supposed to Be* (Grand Rapids: Eerdmans, 1996), xii.

[2] "The Roots of Evil," *Newsweek* (May 21, 2001), 32.

[3] See Numbers 14:18; 2 Chronicles 30:9; Nehemiah 9:17; Psalm 86:15; 103:8; 111:4; 112:4; 116:5; 145:8; Jeremiah 32:18; Joel 2:13; Jonah 4:2; Nahum 1:3.

[4] Charles H. Spurgeon, "Abundant Pardon," *The Metropolitan Tabernacle Pulpit 1874* (London: Passmore and Alabaster, 1875), 548.

[5] John Bunyan, *The Pilgrim's Progress* (New York: Washington Square Press, 1957), 36–37.

[6] This is referred to as a theophany, or more specifically a Christophany, an appearance of God or Christ in human form, prior to the Incarnation. Examples can be found in Genesis 18:1–33; 32:28–30; Judges 13:21–22.

[7] Plantinga, *Not the Way It's Supposed to Be*, 12.

[8] Plantinga, *Not the Way It's Supposed to Be*, 5.

[9] Aleksandr I. Solzhenitsyn, *The Gulag Archipelago 1918–1956,* trans. Thomas P. Whitney and Harry Willetts, abridg. Edward E. Ericson, Jr. (New York: Perennial Classics, 2002), 75.

[10] Pete Rose with Rick Hill, "Pete Rose's Confession," *Sports Illustrated* (January 12, 2004), 82.

[11] Miroslav Volf, *Exclusion and Embrace* (Nashville: Abingdon, 1996), 25.

Chapter 2: A Costly Forgiveness

[1] James Carroll, "An Obscene Portrayal of Christ's Passion," *The Boston Globe* (February 24, 2004). Retrieved April 2, 2004, from www.boston.com/news/globe/editorial_opinion/oped/articles/2004/02/24/an_obscene_portrayal_of_Christs_p.

[2] Susan Hogan Albach, "The Purpose of the Passion," *Dallas Morning News* (February 21, 2004). Retrieved April 2, 2004, from www.dallasnews.com/sharedcontent/dws/dn/religion/stories/022104dnrrelatonement.2796.html.

[3] Barry Webb, *The Message of Isaiah: The Bible Speaks Today,* ed. J. A. Motyer (Downers Grove, Ill.: InterVarsity Press, 1996), 209.

[4] Leon Morris, *The Cross in the New Testament* (Grand Rapids: Eerdmans, 1965), 371–372.

[5] Martin Hengel, *Crucifixion* (Philadelphia: Fortress, 1977), 22, 37, 62.

[6] Alex F. Metherell, "The Passion of the Christ: The Most Amazing Love Story of All Time: A Review from a Biomedical Engineering Perspective." Retrieved from www.layman.org/layman/news/2004-news/metherell-passion-review.pdf.

[7] John Shelby Spong, *Why Christianity Must Change or Die* (San Francisco: HarperSanFrancisco, 1998), 95. Spong goes on to claim that the idea of "a supernatural redeemer who enters our world to restore creation" is "pre-Darwinian superstition and post-Darwinian nonsense . . . a theistic myth" (99). In part, this is because "we human beings do not live in sin" (98).

[8] "Letters," *Time* (May 3, 2004), 9.

[9] John N. Oswalt, *The Book of Isaiah: Chapters 40–66. The New International Commentary on the Old Testament* (Grand Rapids: Eerdmans, 1998), 388.

Chapter 3: From Guilt to Gratitude

[1] Kay Arthur's story is told in a variety of places. I have pieced this together from several of her books. One accessible source is her book *Our Covenant God* (Colorado Springs: WaterBrook, 1999).

[2] John 12:1–8 gives the account of the anointing of Jesus by Mary of Bethany, just prior to the crucifixion events. Although there are similarities between the two events, the differences are clear. Luke's occurred in Galilee, in the early stage of the Lord's ministry; John's, near Jerusalem in the last days of His ministry. Luke's woman is a Galilean and a notorious sinner; Mary, a Jerusalemite and, as the sister of Lazarus, a longtime follower and friend of Jesus. The similarities of the two events should not cause us to confuse them. They are two distinct events.

[3] The original text of verse 47 raises some questions of translation and interpretation. The first phrase reads, "Her sins, which are many, are forgiven her because she loved much." Although this could be taken to mean that she has been forgiven because she loved Jesus (as seen in the anointing), this interpretation seems very unlikely. What caused her to display such emotion if she had not already been declared forgiven? That is surely the message of the parable. It is therefore best to understand her love as the evidence, not the basis, of forgiveness. Salvation is by faith, not love.

[4] The same point is made by the enemies of Jesus in Mark 2:7, when the Lord forgave a paralyzed man: "He's blaspheming. Who can forgive sins but God alone?" Their problem was not their conviction that only God could forgive sins, but their ignorance of Jesus as the God-man. He then demonstrated His authority and His identity by healing the paralyzed man.

[5] Ramona Cramer Tucker, "Enough Is Enough: Donna Rice Hughes," *Today's Christian Woman* (September–October 1996). Retrieved February 16, 2004, from www.christianitytoday.com/tcw/6w6/6w5042.html.

[6] James Denney, *The Christian Doctrine of Reconciliation* (London: James Clark, 1959), 13–14.

[7] © John and Tonya Mace, *Awesome God*. Used with permission.

Chapter 4: Living in Forgiveness

[1] "Beliefs: Spiritual Blend Appeals to People of Many Faiths," *Los Angeles Times* (December 27, 2003), B2.

[2] Dan Mihalopoulos, "Rampage Killer All but Asks for Death," *Chicago Tribune* (November 20, 2001), 1.

[3] Mark R. McMinn, *Why Sin Matters* (Wheaton, Ill.: Tyndale, 2004), 48–49.

Chapter 5: From Forgiven to Forgiving

[1] C. S. Lewis, *Mere Christianity* (New York: Scribners, 1952), 89.

[2] Everett L. Worthington, Jr., *Forgiving and Reconciling* (Downers Grove, Ill.: InterVarsity Press, 2003), 31.

[3] These teaching blocks are found in chapters 5–7 (the Sermon on the Mount), 10 (the commissioning of the Twelve), 13 (the parables of the kingdom), 18 (kingdom relationships), and 24–25 (the Olivet Discourse).

[4] Talmud *Toma* 86b–87.

[5] Solomon Schimmel, *Wounds Not Healed by Time* (New York: Oxford University Press, 2002), 42.

[6] G. K. Chesterton, *Orthodoxy* (New York: Doubleday, 1990), 95.

[7] Translations are divided. For example, the *New American Standard Bible* and the *English Standard Version* read "seventy times seven," while the *New International Version* and the *New Revised Standard Version* read "seventy-seven times." Scholarly opinion leans toward "seventy-seven times."

[8] The only difference is that the evil servant added the word *everything*.

[9] Ken Sande, *The Peacemaker*, rev. ed. (Grand Rapids: Baker, 2004), 207–208.

[10] Jerry Sittser, *When God Doesn't Answer Your Prayer* (Grand Rapids: Zondervan, 2003), 93.

[11] Worthington, *Forgiving and Reconciling*, 157.

Chapter 6: Learning to Forgive

[1] Simon Wiesenthal, *The Sunflower*, rev. ed. (New York: Schocken, 1997), 53–54.

[2] Wiesenthal, *The Sunflower*, rev. ed., 198.

[3] John Ensor, *Experiencing God's Forgiveness* (Colorado Springs: NavPress, 1997), 66.

[4] C. S. Lewis, *The Business of Heaven* (San Diego, Calif.: Harcourt, 1984), 62.

[5] Mark R. McMinn, *Why Sin Matters* (Wheaton, Ill.: Tyndale, 2004), 161.

[6] L. Gregory Jones, *Embodying Forgiveness* (Grand Rapids: Eerdmans, 1995), 147.

[7] Lewis Smedes, *Forgive and Forget* (San Francisco: HarperCollins, 1984), 39.

[8] Smedes, *Forgive and Forget*, 12–13.

[9] Frederic Luskin, "Nine Steps to Forgiveness." Retrieved November 12, 2002, from www.learningtoforgive.com/nine_steps_to_forgiveness.htm.

[10] Walter Bauer and Frederick Danker, *The Greek-English Lexicon of the New Testament and Other Early Christian Literature*. 3rd ed. [electronic version]. (Chicago: University of Chicago Press, 2000), loc. cit.

[11] R. T. Kendall, *Total Forgiveness* (Lake Mary, Fla.: Charisma House, 2002), 54. His comment is based on Joseph's words to his brothers in Genesis 50, but his use of the verse is misleading. This episode occurs decades after Joseph declared his forgiveness to them. But in that process he had, very intentionally, inflicted pain upon them. See chapter 10 of this book.

[12] Desmond Tutu, *No Future Without Forgiveness* (New York: Doubleday, 2000), 270.

[13] C. S. Lewis, *Letters to Malcolm, Chiefly on Prayer* (San Diego, Calif.: Harcourt, 1991), 27.

[14] Cited in Una Kroll, *Forgive and Live* (London: Mowry, 2000), 111.

[15] Corrie ten Boom with Jamie Buckingham, *Tramp for the Lord* (Fort Washington, Pa.: Christian Literature Crusade, 1974), 57.

Chapter 7: Forgiving or Forbearing?

[1] Dwight D. Eisenhower, *At Ease: Stories I Tell to Friends* (New York: Doubleday, 1967), 52.

[2] Miroslav Volf, *Exclusion and Embrace* (Nashville: Abingdon, 1996), 125.

[3] I am unable to trace the source of this quotation.

[4] C. S. Lewis, *Letters to an American Lady* (Grand Rapids: Eerdmans, 1971), 95.

[5] W. McKane, *Proverbs: Old Testament Library* (Philadelphia: Westminster, 1970), 530.

[6] Lewis Smedes, *Forgive and Forget* (San Francisco: HarperCollins, 1984), 64.

[7] Ken Sande, *The Peacemaker*, rev. ed. (Grand Rapids: Baker, 2004), 83.

[8] Will Durant, "We Have a Right to Be Happy Today," Will Durant Foundation. Retrieved October 7, 2004, from www.willdurant.com/ youth.htm.

[9] Gordon MacDonald, *Rebuilding Your Broken World* (Nashville: Oliver Nelson, 1988), 192.

Chapter 8: When There's No "I'm Sorry"

[1] "God of Forgiveness, Do Not Forgive." Retrieved March 3, 2003, from www.wujs.org.il/activist/programmes/tekasim/shoah/elie_wiesel.shtml.

[2] *Mishnah Yoma* 8:9.

[3] Cited in John Stott, *The Contemporary Christian* (Downers Grove, Ill.: InterVarsity Press, 1992), 48.

[4] Cited in Ken Sande, *The Peacemaker*, rev. ed. (Grand Rapids: Baker, 2004), 195. Sande's book is a very helpful guidebook to dealing with conflict on both personal and congregational levels.

[5] L. Gregory Jones, *Embodying Forgiveness* (Grand Rapids: Eerdmans, 1995), 186.

[6] David Augsburger, *The New Freedom of Forgiveness*, 3rd. ed. (Chicago: Moody Press, 2000), 25.

[7] John MacArthur, Jr. *The Freedom and Power of Forgiveness* (Westchester, Ill.: Crossway, 1998), 152.

[8] Don Carson, *Love in Hard Places* (Wheaton, Ill.: Crossway, 2002), 72.

[9] Solomon Schimmel, *Wounds Not Healed by Time* (New York: Oxford University Press, 2002), 61.

[10] Wayne Grudem, *Systematic Theology* (Grand Rapids: Zondervan, 1994), 369.

[11] Although nearly all translations of the New Testament contain this verse, it should be noted that it is missing from a number of early and reliable manuscripts. But strong internal evidence and the parallel to Acts 7:60 support its inclusion.

[12] Jeff VanVonderen, *Families Where Grace Is in Place* (Minneapolis: Bethany House, 1992), 28.

Chapter 9: Rescued from Revenge

[1] Retrieved March 10, 2003, from www.thepayback.com.

[2] Solomon Schimmel, *Wounds Not Healed by Time* (New York: Oxford University Press, 2002), 11.

[3] Miroslav Volf, *Exclusion and Embrace* (Nashville: Abingdon, 1996), 117.

Chapter 10: Bridge Under Repair

[1] Genesis 41:51.
[2] Genesis 41:52.
[3] Genesis 42:22.
[4] Genesis 42:28.
[5] Genesis 44:54.
[6] Genesis 45:3.
[7] Genesis 45:4–8.
[8] Genesis 50:19–21.

Chapter 11: Good Grief

[1] Mr. Clinton's speech was retrieved March 31, 2003, from www.pbs .org/greatspeeches/timeline/clinton_prayer_s.html.

[2] Cited in Everett Worthington, Jr., *Forgiving and Reconciling* (Downers Grove, Ill.: InterVarsity Press, 2003), 192–193.

[3] Donald McCullough, *The Wisdom of Pelicans* (New York: Viking Compass, 2002), 20.

[4] Les Parrott, *Shoulda Coulda Woulda* (Grand Rapids: Zondervan, 2003), 100.

[5] Doug Schmidt, *The Prayer of Revenge* (Colorado Springs: Nexgen, 2003), 42–43.

[6] Miroslav Volf, *Exclusion and Embrace* (Nashville: Abingdon, 1996), 113.

[7] David Augsburger, *The New Freedom of Forgiveness*, 3rd. ed. (Chicago: Moody Press, 2000), 74.

[8] Soren Kierkegaard, "Emissaries from Eternity: Repentance and Remorse." Retrieved October 7, 2004, from www.bruderhof.com.au/articles/Emissaries.htm.

Chapter 12: The Gift of Forgiveness

[1] Michael E. McCullough, Steve J. Sandage, and Everett L. Worthington, Jr., *To Forgive Is Human* (Downers Grove, Ill.: InterVarsity Press, 1997).

[2] Everett Worthington, *Five Steps to Forgiveness* (New York: Crown, 2001), 4–5. The story is also told in the revised edition of that book, *Forgiving and Reconciling* (Downers Grove, Ill.: InterVarsity Press, 2003), 17–20.

[3] Worthington, *Forgiving and Reconciling*, 19.

[4] C. S. Lewis, *Mere Christianity* (New York: Scribners, 1952), 89.

[5] Cited in Worthington, *Five Steps to Forgiveness*, 23.

[6] "Thieves Take Figure of Jesus, but Not the Cross," *New York Times* [electronic version] (August 25, 2003). Retrieved from www.nytimes.com/2003/08/nyregion/25STAT.html.

[7] The story of Mantle's last days was widely reported in the media at the time, and Bobby Richardson shared much of the story at Mantle's funeral. One source is a tract by the American Bible Society, "The Mickey Mantle Story." Retrieved on October 2, 2004, from www.garywalterbaseballcards.com/mantle/.

[8] John MacArthur, Jr., *The Freedom and Power of Forgiveness* (Westchester, Ill.: Crossway, 1998), 160.

[9] Anne Lamott, *Traveling Mercies* (New York: Anchor Books, 1999), 128, 134.

[10] Corrie ten Boom, *Tramp for the Lord* (New York: Berkley, 1978), 56–57.

[11] Jerry Cook with Stanley C. Baldwin, *Love, Acceptance, and Forgiveness* (Ventura, Calif.: Regal, 1979), 21–22.

¹² The account is compiled from various Internet sources. See "Death of a Dream, Birth of a Nightmare." Retrieved January 31, 2003, from www.wyomingcops.com/features/stevew.asp. Angus M. Thuemer, Jr., "The Cop and the Robber," *Jackson Hole News and Guide*. Retrieved January 31, 2003, from www.jhguide.com/Archives/FeatureArchive/2002/020320-feature. html ."Candidate Forgives Man Who Shot Him." Retrieved October 3, 2002, from www.kansascity.com/mld/kansascity/news/politics/3893239.htm.

NOTE TO THE READER

The publisher invites you to share your response to the message of this book by writing Discovery House, P.O. Box 3566, Grand Rapids, MI 49501, USA. For information about other Discovery House books, music, or DVDs, contact us at the same address or call 1–800–653–8333. Find us online at dhp.org or send e-mail to books@dhp.org.